DINNER AT MINE

6 PEOPLE, 3 COURSES, 1 HOUR

ANNIE NICHOLS

from the author of the blog **HOT MEALS NOW**

This book is dedicated to Winnie Nichols, for a lifetime of food made with love. You are simply the best. X

Acknowledgements
No, no, I insist, thank YOU!

Here is my chance to say a few massive thankyous to some very special people who have been involved in creating and supporting me and this book. It would, as they say, have not been possible without them.

Team Kyle
To everyone at Kyle Books. To Kyle Cathie herself, who swept me up with her enthusiasm and excitement about making my column into a book in the first place. To my editor Sophie Allen, for her painstaking direction in managing this mammoth project (never underestimate the importance of a great editor). And thanks too, to Laura Foster and Steve Lam.

Team PFD
To my agent Robert Caskie at PFD, (Peters Fraser & Dunlop) for his constant encouragement and support. With more thanks for Lucy Dundas as Robert's brilliant back-up.

Team Stella
To Anna Murphy and Elfreda Pownall at *Stella* magazine whose never-ending belief in me and my column was so very much appreciated. So too for Amy Bryant's constant enthusiasm and more-than-meticulous editing by Katie Drummond.

Team Sion
To Sion Phillips's designing that took my ideas to another level. Thanks too goes to Joe Hole.

Team Annie
To Lady P (Petra Hall), for being a constant ray of sunshine and a passionate and brilliant assistant!

To Laura Fyfe, for her gorgeous food and thoughtful shopping.

To Gina G (Gina Lundy), for her photographic assistance and whose encouragement from the beginning led me on my journey with her mutual love of street light!

To GJ (Guillermo Becerra), for his sound digital work and advice and unending patience.

To Ola O. Smit, for her photographic assistance, the joy of her company and stories of love.

To Helen Osgerby, for helping me decide who I am!

To Francis Shotonwa, for keeping me sane with our walks and talks of politics and *EastEnders*!

To John Bentham, who told me to just do it!

To John, Duncan, Lisa and Jason at Panzer's fruit and veg, for many years of brilliant service and laughs in the early mornings.

To Chris and Jerry at Frank Godfrey butchers, for a lifetime of top meat, and of course Kitty!

To Tasting Places and the Ravida family, for a world of experience in Sicily I will never forget.

To my friends, whom I adore very much and who I hope understand that I will always be around in sprit, even if I'm not always around as physically as I'd like to be!

Finally, sending out huge love to all my family, Sarah, Jane, Dave and Andy, and all their lovers, Dave Ding Dong, Jem, Sand and Angie, and their girls and boys, Lucy, Katy, Sophie, Dan, Jess, Alex, Rory, Matt, Abi and Bella.

First published in Great Britain in 2011 by Kyle Books

23 Howland Street
London W1T 4AY
www.kylebooks.com

ISBN: 978 0 85783 028 9
10 9 8 7 6 5 4 3 2 1

Annie Nichols is hereby identified as the author of this work in accordance with section 77 of Copyright, Designs and Patents Act 1988.

* All images by Annie Nichols except page 12 © Jacob Love, page 165 second right © Kate Whitaker, page 201 © Yuki Sugiura, page 249 © Lauren Bradley.

Design copyright © 2011 by Kyle Books

DESIGN: Sion Phillips
PHOTOGRAPHY: Annie Nichols
FOOD STYLISTS: Annie Nichols and Laura Fyfe
PROJECT EDITOR: Sophie Allen
PROOFREADER: Ruth Baldwin
INDEXER: Lisa Footit
PRODUCTION: Nic Jones and David Hearn

A CIP record for this title is available from the British Library.

Colour reproduction by Scanhouse, Malaysia

Printed and bound in China by Toppan Leefung Printing Ltd

CONTENTS

INTRODUCTION AND HOW TO USE THIS BOOK

'It's the combination of who's cooking, the food and the people you're with.'

I was bought up in Somerset, in the West Country. It wasn't always idyllic, but my Mum was always in the kitchen cooking up simple, basic meals for us five kids, making use of the fruit and veg my Dad grew in the back garden. She says now that she was an unconfident cook and I wish she had known then just how good she was. After I left school, I wanted to go to art college, but after my parents had a discussion with a well-meaning neighbour, I was discouraged from going. My next option was going into catering, and I threw myself into it completely and trained and worked as a chef for ten years.

I was lucky enough to then become a food stylist, preparing and cooking food for photography for magazines and cookbooks (I didn't even know this unusual job existed before then), and it appealed to my artistic side and used all of my chef skills. Although my classical training as a chef had taken me around the world, it was when I became a food stylist, constantly working for different celebrity chefs and authors, that I was opened up to a much wider range of world cuisines, cultures, flavours and ingredients.

While working as a food stylist I also became a cookery writer, writing four of my own cookbooks and recipes for numerous magazines, drawing on my training and experiences from across the globe. My recipes were once described by my friend, wonderful food writer Rosie Stark, as having a 'get me to the kitchen – right now' appeal.

Another of my great friends, the brilliant cookery writer and teacher Maxine Clark, was teaching cookery in Sicily and asked me to go out and give her a hand. It was teaching for cookery holiday organisers Tasting Places. I ended up helping her out, twice a year, for about a decade. It was an amazing experience, and it was there, and with her, that I began to learn the true significance of using good seasonal ingredients. Sicily imported very little, so the cooking relied on what was available locally and in season, and my time spent there has really influenced my cookery style.

It was around this time I realised my dream of going to art college, and took myself off to study for a full-time fine art degree at Central St Martins (now part of the London Institute). I relished the conceptual thinking and experimental freedom of art and I gained a new perspective in my use of colour, space and dimension, and was able to bring that back into my working life. I have since been inspired to host parties where I would transform my studio, where some sort of performance would take place, and it's been a lost property office, Silicone Valley, and a 1920s speakeasy. I'm now renowned for hosting large parties, loosely based around the theme of a 'tea party', with moonshine being served from teapots into tea-cups, and going on for about two days.

Another of my greatest pleasures is cooking up lunches and dinners for a bunch of friends, anything from 4 to 24 people. I always encourage friends to help prepare the food with me, and I find, on the whole, they love to be involved in the preparation, and it's also a big help! It's a great icebreaker for guests who don't know each other and I really love seeing my mates bond over peeling spuds or podding peas in the kitchen. It's the combination of who's cooking, the food and the people you're with.

I had been writing a column 'Cheat's Dinner Party' for about four years, when I decided I wanted to expand on it, and create a beautiful, fun and inspirational cookbook. I realised from talking to friends that what they felt was needed most in a good cookbook was not only inspiration, and easy, good, uncomplicated recipes (without long lists of hard-to-get ingredients), but that it was instructive and practical, explaining some basic cookery techniques simply and clearly. So I've included some key, basic skills and methods to help broaden your cookery knowledge, with extra tips, to help you to produce really delicious food on a budget, easily and quickly.

Dinner At Mine is a collection of 52 of the 'Cheat's Dinner Party' menus. Each menu is a three-course meal for six people, to be cooked in around an hour, sometimes a little more, sometimes a little less. It can be a busy hour, but it is broken down into the easy-to-follow format of ten-minute chunks, and combines the preparation and cooking of the three recipes to use your time most efficiently. Cooking can be a bit of a balancing act, but these menus teach you to use your time cleverly – for example, by getting something roasting or baking in oven, while you cook other things on the hob, while something else is marinating, soaking, etc. I also give the three recipes separately if you fancy cooking them individually or mixing and matching your own menu combinations. Feel free to be creative with the recipes yourself and add or change accompaniments if you want.

Mise en Place

To make your cooking life easier, it takes a bit of organising. *Mise en place* ('put in place') is a French cheffy term, used in professional kitchens, that means to have everything ready and prepared as much as possible before restaurant service. This is a really good system to use in your own kitchen.

So one really important point is to make sure you always **read the menu or individual recipes all the way through first,** before you start cooking.

Next preheat your oven or grill to the required temperature as soon as you can, as most take about ten minutes to get up to temperature.

Get out all the ingredients you need. Ingredients in the menus and recipes are placed in order of how they are used in the method (except salt and pepper, which sit underneath). So the first ingredient listed is what you'll need to reach for first. When using eggs, size does matter. The **egg size I use in the recipes is medium.**

Clean, scrub, peel and prepare. I assume all ingredients are trimmed where necessary and your vegetables are scrubbed, washed, ready to go and peeled (for example onions) unless I state otherwise, as peeling vegetables is not always necessary. You can eat the peel of most, so although aesthetically they may look grubby, the flavour, texture and nutrients will be intact. Sometimes I suggest peeling something after it has been cooked.

Read the recipe again…

So you've got everything you need in front of you, and you're ready to go. **Don't worry when cooking**, and remember that everything you do teaches you something, even mistakes and disasters. It's all about practice and taking risks: the more you do it, the easier it becomes as you grow more proficient.

Use a timer, especially when cooking things like nuts that take only a short time to toast and can easily be forgotten.

Always **check the things you are cooking** a little before the end of the cooking time stated in the recipe. Oven temperatures vary, so an oven thermometer would be an investment if you're unsure how accurate yours is. Don't worry if things take a bit longer than the stated time.

I'm becoming increasingly aware of the environmental impact of food, and I have started to make more informed decisions on what I buy. What I do know, and what I experienced in Sicily, is that it seems to make sense to use seasonal and locally made or grown produce where you can. And enviromentally that makes sense too. It's important to understand that when ingredients are in season they are at their best, and bursting with flavour. They are also in abundance, so in turn should be cheaper.

I feel spoilt by the choice I have in the supermarket all year round, as so many things are now imported, and it can be difficult to know what is actually in season. Be aware that even though we have things like avocados, citrus fruits and bananas for 12 months of the year, they are going to be in season and taste their best only at certain times. Do some research if you want – www.eattheseasons.com (UK/Ireland and US/Canada) is a good, informative website – otherwise use this book to help you make your own informed choices, as all the menus have been written using seasonal ingredients and run seasonally through the book.

Buy organic or free-range where possible, do what you can, but don't feel guilty about what you don't do. Don't deny yourself; just be aware of what you are eating and when you are eating it. Buy what you can afford, and treat yourself to something lovely once in a while.

IN THE CUPBOARD

I don't expect you to run out and buy all the following ingredients, but these are a few of my favourites that I turn to again and again and like to keep close at hand.

FLAVOUR & SPICE

Cayenne
A pungent mix of ground hot chillies. A tiny pinch will give a good kick to your food.

Dried Chilli Flakes
Just a pinch of chilli flakes can lift a dish.

Chilli Powder
This varies in flavour and strength from sweet and mild to fiery hot.

Paprika
Varying in strength from mildy pungent to fiery. Spanish paprika is different from that produced in central Europe, some of which has a smoky aroma and flavour and ranges from sweet 'dulce' to hot 'picante'. Don't overdo the smoked version and remember that it may not be interchangeable with a non-smoked paprika.

Cumin
Available as whole seeds and ground to a powder that imparts a very distinctive flavour.

Fennel Seeds
As you will notice from the recipes this is one of my very favourite spices. My fondness for it developed while I was working in Sicily, where this aniseed-flavoured, pungent seed is used widely used in stews, salads and sausages.

Dried Oregano
Pretty powerful in its dried form this is the only dried herb I really use in cooking.

Juniper Berries
Primarily used in making gin (my favourite tipple!), juniper has a very distinctive bitter-sweet flavour with a hint of pine needles.

Saffron
A luxurious spice, that gives a wonderful mustiness and a shocking yellow colour.

Green Cardamom Pods
Beneath their dry, green husks lies a cluster of tiny, black, aromatic seeds. Used in both sweet and savoury dishes. Used whole, but crushed lightly or the seeds are removed and ground to make a powder. Add a tiny pinch to fresh coffee for a perfumed aroma.

Cinnamon
A warm, sweet, woody spice used in both sweet and savoury dishes. Again, use sparingly as it can overpower.

Vanilla – Pods/Paste/Extract
Beautiful, sweet vanilla is one of my favourite food flavourings.

Split the whole vanilla pods open (see page 28) revealing the thousands of miniscule, black, almost caviar-like, aromatic seeds inside. Scrape these seeds out and use in sweet dishes. Once you have cooked with the scraped-out pod, wash and dry it well, then sink into a jar of sugar, which will infuse pretty quickly to give vanilla sugar to use in or sprinkled on desserts.

If buying in liquid form, try to get 'pure' vanilla extract as opposed to the often synthetic-tasting essence. Vanilla paste is now available too: this is a sweetened paste made from the seeds.

Nutmeg – Ground & Whole
Grating whole nutmeg will give you a fresher, cleaner flavour, but you can of course use ready-ground.

Mace
This is the dried outer coating of the nutmeg seed. It's similar in flavour to nutmeg but more earthy in tone.

Chinese Five-spice powder
As the name suggests, this is a blend of five spices: star anise, Schezuan peppercorns, cinnamon, fennel seeds and cloves. This slightly aniseedy mix is pretty potent, so use sparingly.

Allspice
Whole berries or ground, allspice resembles a mix of spice flavours: cinnamon, cloves and nutmeg.

Stock Cubes and Liquid Bouillon
The reality is that we don't always have fresh stock to hand, and although fresh stocks are far superior, I always have stock cubes or bouillon as a stand-by. Remember that the cubes and bouillon can be very salty.

Salt
I always keep a fine sea salt for cooking (which is more easily dissolved and combined into food), and to season food I also like to use sea salt flakes which imparts a sweeter note.

Pepper
I always make sure I've got extra black peppercorns waiting in the cupboard to fill the peppermill, as there's nothing worse than running out in the middle of cooking.

SAUCY SAUCES & CONDIMENTS

Soy Sauce – Dark & Light
By turning a bottle each of dark and light soy sauce upside down and upright again you'll understand the difference. Dark soy is much thicker and gloopier and will cling to the side of the bottle for dear life, whereas the thinner light soy will wash back and forth with very little trace. Use both sauces carefully, because if overused they can (especially dark soy) be too overpowering, strong and salty.

Dijon Mustard
A smooth, gentle mustard, good for dressings.

Wholegrain Mustard
A sweet, nutty mustard, great used in dressings or marinades, or stirred into mashed potato.

Worcestershire Sauce
A classic sauce, to sprinkle as a savoury seasoning.

Horseradish Sauce
Potent and fiery, this should be used with caution. Try to get grated horseradish in a jar or a good-quality sauce (sometimes horseradish sauce or creamed horseradish can be too vinegary). Of course, if you can get hold of the fresh horseradish root (grate finely), then even better.

Hoisin Sauce
A sweet, sticky and intense aromatic Asian sauce.

Fish Sauce/Nam Pla
A fishy and salty liquid from Southeast Asia, which, when used sparingly is great as a seasoning.

Sweet Chilli Sauce
Sticky, sweet and hot, delicious as a condiment with all sorts of foods.

Wasabi
Wasabi is an extremely fiery horseradish from Japan. Sometimes sold as a readymade paste in tubes or as a powder to mix with water.

Rose Harissa
Harissa is a fiery Middle Eastern blend of chillies and spices. Rose harissa is warm and perfumed (with the addition of rose water), but not so hot. If using regular harissa proceed with caution, as it can be very, very fiery!

Miso Paste
Available in white, red and yellow forms. Be careful when cooking with miso, because if you get it too hot the flavour is destroyed.

GRAINS & PULSES

Rice/Risotto Rice
I mostly use basmati or jasmine rice as an accompaniment. For risotto you'll need Carnaroli or Arborio rice. The short, stubby rice grains of these are perfect for risotto.

Polenta
Polenta is cornmeal. It can be added to boiling water and cooked into thick, molten folds or used dry as a light, crispy coating, in the same way as breadcrumbs.

Beans – Dried & Tinned
If you have the time or inclination, soaking and cooking dried beans will give a much firmer, nuttier end result than using tinned. But tinned beans are a brilliant alternative. When cooking with dried beans you'll probably need to add more liquid to a dish as they are drier than the tinned version. If you're using dried beans, for every 400g tin of beans specified in a recipe you'll need to soak and cook about 100g dried beans.

PRESERVED & PICKLED

Anchovies
Cured anchovies are one of my favourite cupboard ingredients. I try to keep a tin or jar at hand; either little tins of anchovy fillets preserved in oil or layered whole in salt. Used subtly, they can be used as a salty flavouring. When using the salted anchovies, rinse well before use, then remove the backbones.

Olives
A vast range of olives is available. My favourite at the moment are dried black olives, which are intense and liquorice-like. Avoid imitation black olives that are in fact green olives dyed black – they have all the flavour of a car tyre.

Capers Salted/in Brine
Another favourite Sicilian influence. These are the tangy buds of a Mediterranean bush, usually pickled in brine or layered in salt. Make sure you rinse them well before use.

Dried Porcini Mushrooms
Porcini or cep mushrooms have an intense mushroom flavour which intensifies even more when they are dried. The dried ones are usually sold sliced, and although they are pretty expensive you need to use only a few to get a punchy flavour. Soak in lots of hot water to rehydrate (keep the highly flavoured liquid to use in what you're cooking too). Strain through a fine sieve, being careful to leave behind any grit that may have settled in the bottom of the container you have soaked them in.

FLOURS

Plain flour
An all-purpose flour.

Spelt Flour
This ancient grain is a relative of wheat, but spelt has a nuttier and sweeter flavour. It is naturally high in protein and fibre.

Self-raising Flour
Plain flour with bicarbonate of soda and baking powder added as raising agents.

Wholemeal Flour
The whole brown wheat grain ground to a flour.

SUGARS

At one end of the spectrum you have the highly refined, bleached white icing (powdered) sugar, through to the delicate crystals of caster sugar, then grainier granulated sugar and finally unrefined (raw and golden) sugars.

Sugar from beet needs to be highly processed (refined and bleached), so is unable to produce the range of raw textures and flavours which cane sugar can. Sugar cane can naturally produce a wide range of raw sugars from demerara, golden caster and golden granulated, to soft light brown and dark brown and on to intense fudgy-flavoured muscovado and molasses sugar.

DRIED FRUIT & NUTS

Ground Almonds
Blanched almonds ground to a coarse powder. You can make your own ground almonds by whizzing whole blanched almonds in a food processor.

Currants
These are dried small black grapes.

Sultanas
Usually dried large white grapes.

Raisins
Usually dried large black grapes.

Candied Fruit/Peel
Buy whole pieces of dried candied peel and chop it yourself. The ready-chopped stuff is usually strong and pretty unpleasant.

Walnuts & Almonds
Toasting nuts takes them to another tasty level.

SWEET THINGS

Cocoa Powder
Ground bitter chocolate for use in desserts and baking.

Stem Ginger & Crystallized Ginger
Nuggets of preserved ginger in syrup are called stem ginger. Chop and use in sweet and savoury dishes. Crystallised ginger is also preserved ginger, but candied and rolled in sugar crystals.

Orange Flower Water
A fragrant and exotic scent of the Middle East. Use carefully as brands vary in strength.

Rose Water
A distilled water made from rose petals. Beautifully perfumed, it is wonderful sprinkled into desserts or over fresh fruit. But, as with orange flower water, add sparingly – it can be pretty potent.

Honey
Wonderful natural sweetener, from amber runny to crystallised solid.

Meringue Nests
A pretty handy little standby. A purée of fruit, some softly whipped cream and a few crushed meringues and you'll have a very fine 'mess'!

IN THE LIQUEUR CUPBOARD

Cassis & Crème de Mure
Cassis is a sticky and sweet liqueur made from blackcurrants; crème de mure is made from blackberries.

Shaoshing
Chinese cooking wine.

Mirin
A Japanese rice wine.

Sake
Rice-based alcohol.

Grand Marnier & Cointreau
Both are sweet orange-based liqueurs.

Also in my liqueur cupboard...

Rum, Marsala, Amaretto, brandy, Armagnac, sherry and gin – to keep the cook happy!

IN THE FRIDGE/FREEZER

Once again, I don't expect you to have all these ingredients all of the time,
but I do try and keep some of them close to hand.

IN THE FREEZER

Breadcrumbs
Pop any excess fresh breadcrumbs you have made (see page 27) into plastic bags and freeze as a great standby.

Bread
I slice fresh crusty bread and freeze it in plastic bags for convenience.

Pastry
Have some puff or shortcrust pastry frozen ready to defrost to make a quick tart.

Stock
Homemade stock really is far superior to any cube or liquid you can buy. Make it, strain it, cool it and freeze in manageable containers.

Vanilla Ice Cream
Although the intention is to have some of this at hand to scoop for pudding, it rarely lasts longer than the day I bought it!

Ice
Well, I need some for my G&T, don't I?!

Frozen Peas
When fresh aren't in season, these are a brilliant frozen back-up to make pea purée or soup.

Lime Leaves
These intensely citrussy and fragrant South Asian leaves can now be bought frozen (they are better frozen than dried) in Southeast Asian shops and big supermarkets (though they are now being grown here too!). I always keep a stash in my freezer for dropping into Asian-flavoured soups and stocks.

IN THE FRIDGE

Bay Leaves
I'm very fond of this leaf. A few leaves in a stock give it a delicious musty pungency. Add a couple to sweet dishes too (see Baked Cherries with Bay on page 275). Bay is a classic addition to rice pudding. I try to keep a few fresh leaves at hand, but you could pop them in the freezer or dry them. Remember that dried bay leaves are stronger than fresh.

Parmesan/Percorino Cheese
Pecorino is a hard ewe's milk cheese from Italy. It has a salty, almost fruity flavour and is a really good and a more reasonably priced alternative to Parmesan.

Greek Yogurt & Crème Fraîche
Gorgeous, unctuous, thick Greek yogurt may be drizzled with honey for breakfast or spooned on top of sweet or savoury dishes. Lightly soured crème fraîche is a brilliant standby to enrich a savoury sauce or serve alongside a pudding.

Lumpfish/Herring Roe
A faux caviar or cheat's caviar substitute. I prefer the slightly lighter-flavoured herring roe, to the saltier lumpfish roe.

Chorizo Sausage
This highly spiced Spanish paprika sausage comes ready to cook, or cured and ready to eat like a salami. Once it starts to cook it gives up a wonderful amber oil.

Pancetta/Lardons
Pancetta is tasty seasoned salt-cured (smoked or unsmoked) belly of pork from Italy. You buy it as a solid piece from which to cut lardons, which are little chunky strips (or are sometimes available ready chopped) to use in cooking or cured and thinly sliced to serve as an antipasto. Streaky bacon makes a good alternative.

Gentleman's Relish/Anchovy Paste
Potent pastes that add a salty and fishy edge to savoury dishes (only the tiniest of scraping is needed).

Mayonnaise
Good to have a handy jar of good quality mayonnaise, but I do try to make my own (see page 33).

Goat's Cheese
Available from soft, fresh, almost wet to hard and easy to grate. Love it or hate it, I try to keep some in stock.

Celery, Leek, Carrot
I usually try to have this little selection of vegetables at hand as basic flavourings, so I can knock up a stock quickly and easily.

Mint
A sprig of fresh mint, submerged in boiling water, plus a little sugar to taste, makes a wonderful and fresh tea.

ON THE SIDE

These are easily accessible and the most used ingredients I have. If I've got them sitting on the side, readily available, I'm happy.

VINEGARS

I'm using more sherry vinegar (nutty and smoky) these days and I still like the stickiness of balsamic vinegar, but it's not great for everything. Use rice vinegar for Asian-inspired dishes and cider or wine (red or white) vinegar for dressings (see page 32).

OILS

Most oils are are affected adversely by direct light and heat (they easily lose their flavour), so unless you use them regularly, keep them stocked away in the cupboard.

Extra-virgin Olive Oil
When I worked in Sicily we all stayed (and cooked) in a crumbling palazzo owned by the Ravida family, who have a working farm growing grapes (for wine), lemons, and olives with which they make an award-winning (the Tuscans were non too happy!) extra-virgin olive oil. It's emerald green and citrus in its undertones and gorgeous; although it's very special, we used it by the bucketful, deep-frying aubergines for caponata, drizzling over pasta or dressing our salads.

Because of this I am inclined to use extra-virgin olive oil as my first choice when cooking, if an olive oil is called for (though sadly rarely Ravida's as it would be prohibitively expensive), even though purists would argue that the flavour is depleted once it's cooked. If you can't afford extra-virgin, buy the next best olive oil you can.

Groundnut Oil
Groundnut oil is made from peanuts and is quite flavourless, but brilliant for deep-frying as it has a high smoking point, which means you can deep-fry at a higher temperature than with most other oils. You can reuse it too. Allow it to cool completely before letting it drip through a single layer of kitchen paper, then rebottle in the bottle it came in.

Sesame Oil
Not to be used as a cooking oil, but more as a flavouring, usually drizzled at the end when cooking or used sparingly in dressings.

Walnut Oil
This is another oil to use just as a flavouring, you can add at the end of cooking or add a splash to salad dressings.

OTHER THINGS I KEEP ON THE SIDE

Eggs
I keep these on the side so they remain at room temperature — they're much better for baking this way.

Garlic, Onions, Red Onions, Shallots, Ginger, Chillies, Limes & Lemons
These are used on such a regular basis that they don't hang around for long. I never put garlic or onions in the fridge as other foods are prone to taking on their flavour. I always try to use unwaxed limes and lemons.

THINGS THAT MAKE LIFE EASIER

Equipment I really do use and the reasons why.

The equipment I own is influenced by my cheffing background: heavy baking trays that don't buckle; solid equipment that lasts. Try catering suppliers for a comprehensive selection, of good-quality and reasonably priced equipment.

Once you buy some of these things you'll never have to buy again. Also check car boot sales, jumbles and charity shops for cheaply priced, quirky retro equipment – it often has more character than anything new you could buy.

I can't stress enough how important it is to have at least one sharp knife. It will really make your cooking life easier. Lots of different knives are available: stainless steel, carbon steel, ceramic... When shopping for them, see how they feel in your hands. Do the shape and weight suit you? I have large hands and tend to use a larger, weightier knife. And proof that a good-quality knife will last is that I still have knives from my very first knife set at catering college, many moons ago; all I have to do, is keep them sharp.

I've split my selection of equipment into three ranges. For those new to cooking or unsure what equipment to buy, I've created a list of basics for you to gather which will really help to improve your cooking experience and make your life easier.

To step up a level, add the mid-range equipment list to the basic list to help you work efficiently and effortlessly in the kitchen. This is a key set of equipment which will really make your life easier.

The final advanced range of equipment consists of more specialised items, not essentials, but if you're a keen cook they will certainly help to refine your cooking ability and the resulting dishes.

HERE'S A LIST OF BASIC EQUIPMENT THAT WILL REALLY HELP TO MAKE LIFE EASIER IN THE KITCHEN. DON'T WORRY IF YOU DON'T HAVE SOME OF IT. GO TO 'WHAT IF YOU DON'T HAVE ANY OF THAT?' (PAGE 20)

01 Medium saucepan   Invest in a good pan with a heavy base if you can. Quality will last you a lifetime.

02 Medium knife   A good all-rounder. If you could have only one knife, you could actually survive with a medium-sized knife.

03 Paring knife   Even a good-quality paring knife is quite inexpensive. Handy for peeling, trimming and poking food to test it's cooked.

04 Serrated bread/carving knife   Ever tried cutting bread without a serrated knife? It's a nightmare, isn't it? It's impossible to get even slices and you end up squashing the bread to pulp. A serrated knife is also great for peeling tough, hard-to-handle fruit or vegetables like pineapples, celeriac or swede.

05 Fish slice   A very handy, broad and slotted, metal blade, perfect for turning and lifting foods.

06 Large metal spoon   This is the best spoon for folding ingredients together easily.

07 Wooden spoon   Perfect for beating and stirring.

08 Wire balloon whisk   This is brilliant for easily aerating foods such as egg white or cream. Get a good-sized one with long wires and use with a large bowl for best effect.

09 Peeler   I own two: a traditional potato peeler, which has a fixed strong blade, the sort with the spear-like tip, that is good for peeling and boring out blemishes from fruit and vegetables, and a speed/swivel peeler. The latter is great for creating cheese slivers and strips of citrus zest, and making fine vegetable ribbons – from carrots and courgettes, for example.

10 Fine-meshed sieve   A fine-meshed sieve is what you need to strain and separate different-sized foods from each other. It also helps to aereate flour when baking.

11 Baking tray   A baking tray is made of metal and usually has a turned-up edge all round, and differs from a baking sheet (see page 16). Get a good heavy one, as it really does help to prevent buckling in the oven while cooking.

12 Parchment paper/greaseproof paper
Parchment paper is very slightly waxed, so really helps when lining tins as it won't stick to food. Greaseproof paper needs to be greased well, but even then it's prone to sticking and I tend not to use it.

13 Silver foil   Always handy to have, to cover or wrap foods and also to use where a tight-fitting lid is needed.

14 Cling film   Again, good to have in the kitchen for wrapping and keeping foods sealed and fresh. But if you would rather not use plastic, use plates, bowls or food covers to protect your foods in the fridge etc.

15 Measuring scales   I'm a fan of digital scales, but choose the sort you are happy using.

16 Measuring cups   You can buy a range of these handy Americanised measuring cups, but if you use the same teacup throughout a recipe this will do the same job as the ingredient ratios will be the same.

17 Measuring jug   Always good to have a couple of plastic or glass ones when needing to measure numerous liquids in a recipe. Just make sure that the measurements on the side are clear and easy to read.

18 Chopping board   I prefer wooden boards and have a selection of sizes. First choice would be one large board as it will make chopping large bunches of herbs, handling those larger vegetables and fruit, or big pieces of meat, much easier. A really invaluable tip is to lay a tea towel or damp cloth underneath your board while chopping, as it will stop the board slipping on the work surface. Don't bother with glass boards as they will only blunt your knives.

19 Non-stick frying pan   Get yourself a good-quality, heavy-based pan if you can and make sure it has metal or other heatproof handles so you can cook on the hob, then transfer the whole pan to the oven to finish off cooking.

20 Mixing bowl   I would suggest that if you are intending to buy one, then get a large bowl (best for whisking, and beating) and make it a heatproof one (useful for melting chocolate over a pan of hot water).

21 Grater   Get a basic grater with a fine and coarse side.

22 Good tea towels   Good-quality, strong tea towels are best for use in the kitchen. Never use a damp or wet tea towel to pick up hot pans or trays as you will burn yourself instantly.

23 Scissors

24 Tin opener

25 Bottle opener/corkscrew

ADD THESE ITEMS TO THE BASIC LIST IF YOU'RE UP FOR REGULAR COOKING

01 Small saucepan   As with your medium pan, invest in a good-quality pan.

02 Peppermill   There is nothing worse than a peppermill that doesn't grind! Get yourself a basic but good-quality one if you can as the quality of the grind is really important. I still use the one that was given to me by my head chef when I was first starting out as a commis chef.

03 Colander   Bigger than a sieve, this is like a bowl with large holes that you use to strain bigger pieces of foods such as vegetables from liquid. If you buy a metal or heat-proof colander, it can double up as a steamer.

04 Lemon squeezer/juicer   I have a traditional glass lemon squeezer that collects the juice in a little moat around the edge of the saucer below the pointed dome. This type is also good to squeeze out the juice of pomegranates (though they need to be ripe). I also have a vintage wooden squeezer with a handle, that you squeeze into the fruit and twist to remove the juice.

05 Ladle   A deeply scooped bowl with a long handle for transferring liquid, most useful for soups.

06 Rolling pin   I prefer a solid wooden rolling pin.

07 Garlic crusher   Rather annoying as most of the crushed garlic gets stuck in the crusher and isn't easy to remove. But it is quite handy to crush small pieces of fresh ginger to squeeze out the juice. I tend to crush my garlic on a board with a large knife (see page 23).

08 Roasting tin   Get a really strong and sturdy roasting tin if you can. Sometimes it's good to be able to start what you're cooking in the tin on the hob first (to get colour on the food before you roast), but if the tin is made of thin metal it will buckle and is likely to flick hot liquid at you.

09 Oven-proof dish   An oven-proof dish tends to be made of thick, heavy ceramic and is good for baking foods that need to cook fairly slowly in the oven. For roasting, on the other hand, you need a metal roasting tin which can conduct a higher heat, to roast and colour the food.

10 Potato masher   Just that! A tool to crush softened food to a smooth, lump-free purée like mash potato. Make sure you invest in a really strong one as I've had mashers in the past that bent under the weight of the foods I was mashing.

11 Rubber spatula   One of these is invaluable for scraping out every last morsel of mixture from a bowl or pan.

12 Slotted spoon   This is a large metal spoon with holes in its bowl. It is perfect for lifting and draining food from liquid.

13 Baking sheet   A flat metal sheet used for baking. It's really handy as you can slide items from it easily once it's removed from the oven. It's important to have at least one turned-up edge, so it's easy to pull from the oven. (As in the case of the baking tray, page 14, it's a really good idea to get a heavy, good-quality one.)

14 Tart tin   I mostly use a fluted tart tin, which gives the tart a pretty frilly edge, with a removable base. To get your tart out of the tin easily, once it's cooked, stand the tart over a small bowl and let the tin sides drop away.

15 Measuring spoons   Handy to remember that 1 tablespoon = 3 teaspoons. As with measuring cups, if you don't own measuring spoons, as long as you use the same-sized cutlery teaspoon for a teaspoon measure and a large cutlery spoon for a tablespoon measure throughout a recipe, you'll be fine for measurements.

16 Wok   For stir-frying, but this deep, wide pan is also my pan of choice for deep-frying as it gives plenty of space for the food to cook and move around.

17 Baking beans   Used to bake blind, where you need to part cook a pastry shell, but also need to weight it down and prevent it from rising (see page 35). You can buy specially made baking beans, but I usually find that they are expensive and come only in small quantities. A cheap substitute which works perfectly well is dried beans or pulses to weight the pastry down. And they can be re-used over and over again.

18 Pastry brush   A small brush (I prefer a flat one) used for brushing food with glazes or to brush oil on baking tins. Buy a decent one as cheaper versions shed their hairs easily.

19 Pencil   Keep a pencil in the kitchen drawer, ready for when you need to draw around a baking tin to measure paper for it.

20 Kitchen string   Useful for tying up meat.

21 Ruler   To measure pastry when rolling out.

22 Wooden skewers   When using these for kebabs, etc., soak them for at least 30 minutes beforehand. You still need to watch them during cooking, however, as they can still burn.

FANCY BEING A CHEF? THEN GET THESE THESE ITEMS TO ENHANCE YOUR COOKING SKILLS

01 Steamer   Set a steamer over simmering or boiling water to steam vegetables or fish. These vary in size and type. I have a set of really useful and inexpensive bamboo steamers in different sizes.

02 Griddle pan   A ridged griddle pan is great for searing and cooking meat and vegetables over a high heat with very little fat or oil. Also brilliant for toasting bread to give the bread a slight charred flavour.

03 Wooden whisk   Similar to the wire balloon whisk on page 14, but made of wood and great for whisking sauces, it won't scratch and wreck the surface of non-stick pans.

04 Knife steel   Keep your knives good and sharp. I use a knife steel as I feel comfortable with it (but there are other sharpeners available). With the knife blade at a 45-degree angle, sweep the blade all the way along the steel from handle to tip, then repeat on the other side. Do this a few times backwards and forwards and you should then have a sharp edge. If your knife is at the point of no return, ask your butcher to sharpen it for you as they will use a sharpening stone which will give it a razor-sharp edge. (Always be extremely careful with new or newly sharpened knives as you'll forget how sharp they are after using a blunt old thing.)

05 Mandolin   This inexpensive gadget is one of my favourite tools to use and is invaluable for slicing vegetables wafer-thin. I can't emphasise enough that, although I think this is brilliant, you must remember how razor-sharp the blades are. You need to pay full attention when using a mandolin. Keep your fingertips as far away from the blade as possible at all times. Usually they come with a guard to protect your fingers, but if there isn't one, spear a fork into the vegetable you are slicing, and use it as a handle to push the vegetable up and down over the blade.

06 Large knife   A good large knife is brilliant for chopping herbs easily and attacking large, hefty vegetables.

07 Palette knife/metal spatula   Not a knife for cutting, a palette knife has a long, delicate blade with a rounded tip, that easily slips under food items, making it really handy for lifting and turning food.

08 Wooden spoons   I have a bit of a collection of these and can't resist buying different versions wherever I go, especially when travelling overseas. They're good as emergency salad servers!

09 Microplane grater   Invest in a microplane grater which produces very delicate flakes of different sizes.

10 Apple corer   A hard metal tube that you use to twist and bore into apples to remove the tough core and to create a tunnel into which you can push a stuffing.

11 Cooling rack   Usually made of wire; you'll need one of these if you like baking. It raises the cooked item above the work surface on little legs, allowing the food to cool evenly all round and protecting your surface from the heat.

12 Cake tins   A spring form tin which has removable sides is handy for getting cakes out easily.

13 Pestle and mortar   This needs to be quite heavy and solid so you can pound spices and herbs easily. I use a ceramic one.

14 Cherry pitter/olive stoner   A handy gadget to remove the stones from small fruit or olives easily. Sit the fruit on the little ring and squeeze the handles together, which in turn pushes a rod straight through the centre of the fruit, taking the stone with it.

15 Zester   Not an imperative tool but really handy for stripping tiny curls of zest from citrus fruit.

16 Oyster knife/shucker   This needs to have a solid short blade to manoeuvre the lids off oysters.

17 Mixing bowls   I have a selection of these. Little bowls are great for weighing out ingredients.

18 Large saucepan/casserole   A good, solid, heavy-based casserole with a tight-fitting lid is what you need for long, slow cooking. It should be deep, wide and flame-proof so that it can work on the hob and go into the oven. I have one, large trusty Le Creuset, which is also great for making risotto.

19 Stock pot   As stocks need to be cooked slowly over a prolonged amount of time, a stock pot needs to be tall, narrow and large with a thick, heavy base to avoid scorching the ingredients at the base of the pot and allowing just enough heat to bubble up gently from the bottom.

20 Wooden cocktail sticks   Perfect to spear meat parcels together.

OTHERS THINGS THAT COULD BE USEFUL (EXTRAS NOT SHOWN)

<u>Kettle</u> To boil water quickly.
<u>Muslin</u> Very fine fabric that is used to strain ingredients finely, such as stocks and sauces. Cooks' shops usually have it, but it tends to be overpriced, so check out a haberdashery where it will be much cheaper.
<u>Ice-cream scoop</u> Get a good, strong one; others will just bend and break.
<u>Tongs or long-pronged fork</u> Useful for turning hot foods easily and safely.
<u>Tea strainer</u> Useful for straining small amounts of liquid.

INSPECTING GADGETS

THESE ARE SLIGHTLY MORE ADVANCED/PRICIER USEFUL GADGETS, TO MAKE LIFE EVEN EASIER

01 Food processor   A food processor is invaluable for speedy cooking. Breadcrumbs can be whizzed up in seconds, pastry made quickly and fresh mayonnaise whipped up in minutes.

02 Blender   If you can, invest in a good-quality blender with a strong motor. If you want to blend hot liquids (I still make this mistake, but advice is always easier to give than folllow!), don't be impatient enough to blend the liquid too soon after cooking. Leave it to cool for at least 10 minutes, otherwise a vacuum builds up and blows the lid off the blender, spraying you with the boiling-hot contents. Blending liquids always gives a much smoother result than a food processor.

03 Mouli   If you don't have a food processor or blender, this lo-fi food mill is brilliant for making soups as it blends and strains at the same time.

04 Hand-held electric whisk   An inexpensive piece of equipment which makes life so much easier, saving a huge amount of time and energy when whisking and beating.

05 Electric spice grinder   When you need to crush or grind a small quantity of ingredients, but there is more than enough to be a chore by hand, keep a coffee grinder specifically for this purpose. Don't be tempted to use it to grind your coffee too, unless you want it to taste of the spices you've been grinding recently.

06 Free-standing mixer   My old retro mixer was bought by my Mum at a car boot sale years ago and is still going strong. Perfect for beating, whisking or kneading anything in a large quantity or that takes a long time to mix.

07 Electric Juicer   Not absolutely necessary, but this is an inexpensive item that minimises effort if you have a lot of juicing to do.

OTHERS THINGS THAT COULD BE USEFUL (EXTRAS NOT SHOWN)

Oven thermometer   Oven temperatures vary, so get yourself one of these to see how your oven checks out.

Sugar thermometer   A specialised piece of equipment which is invaluable when making caramel for checking you have the correct temperature to give you the best result. Also used for jam and preserve making.

Salad spinner   Not an essential piece of equipment, but makes light of drying freshly washed salad leaves (see page 25).

WHAT IF YOU DON'T HAVE ANY OF THAT?

CLEVER ALTERNATIVES IF YOU HAVE VERY LITTLE EQUIPMENT

A wine bottle makes a great emergency rolling pin.

Measuring jug   A washed-out empty carton or juice or water bottle gives you a good indication of liquid measurements.

Food processor   To make breadcrumbs by hand, use a grater. It's a bit of a faff and takes longer, but it is possible. Failing that, rip the bread into tiny pieces.

Rolling pin   If you don't have a rolling pin, use a wine or other large glass bottle to roll out pastry.

Muslin   If you need to strain something finely, an old but clean piece of cotton fabric will do the trick.

Measuring cups and spoons   Just use a normal teacup or normal cutlery. As long as you are constant with what you use throughout a recipe, you'll be fine.

Pestle and mortar   Use the end of a round-ended rolling pin to crush spices in the bottom of a mug or cup. Another good alternative method is to crush them on a board using the back of a wooden spoon. But I find the most effective way is under a small frying pan. Place the pan flat over the spices on a board, twist the pan and press hard with the heel of your hand in the base of the pan to grind the spices down.

Ladle   A jug, mug or cup makes a good alternative.

Ramekins   I've cooked using some of my vintage teacups as ramekins over and over with no problem. But only ever do this in a bain-marie (see page 28), which reduces the temperature of the oven so the cup and contents cook at a lower temperature for longer. But maybe I wouldn't risk using your Nan's bone china.

Cutters   Need cutters? Use an upturned glass or cup to stamp out the shape you need, or use saucers for larger shapes.

Piping bag   Just cut off a corner from a clean plastic bag and use that as a piping bag.

Mixing bowl   Use a saucepan.

Cake tin   A saucepan or deep-frying pan can work well as a cake tin if it's got heat-proof handles.

Lemon squeezer   Spike the centre of a cut lemon with a fork and twist and squeeze to get out the juice.

Colander   Use the pan lid to strain cooked vegetables. No pan lid? Use foil to create a lid or lay a baking tray or sheet over the pan to create one. It speeds up boiling.

Cooling rack   Use a rack/trivet from a grill pan .

Knife   Use scissors to snip chives or to chop other herbs or cut flatbread.

Steamer   If you have a metal or heat-proof colander, it can double up as a steamer.

Cherry stoner/olive pitter   Use a knife or pinch the stones out with your fingers.

METHODS MOST USEFUL

In this section I explain some simple methods and techniques that really help make cooking a lot easier. Once you get a grip on them, you'll be amazed how much simpler cooking becomes. Learn how to crush, chop, slice and cube (did you know there was a difference?) and you'll find your new efficiency takes any pain out of cooking swiftly.

Did you know that slicing is different from chopping and dicing? When I trained to be a chef, the very first lesson I ever had was on how to chop and slice vegetables. It has stood me in good stead ever since, and once you learn to how to chop and slice with ease, it will change your life, (well, your cooking life anyway!). Keep your fingertips tucked under and use the sides of your fingers to guide the knife.

CHOPPING AN ONION

Using a large, sharp knife, cut the top off the onion and pull off the brown outside skin. Leaving the root attached, cut the onion in half.
Taking one onion half at a time, place it cut-side down on a board. With the knife tip pointing towards the root end, cut slices down (the narrower the slices, the finer the eventual chopped onion), almost but not all the way to the root. Make 2 slices horizontally across the onion and then slice across again towards the root to create dice.

SLICING AN ONION

Using a large, sharp knife, cut the top off the onion, cut the onion in half and pull off the brown outside skin, leaving the root attached.
Taking one onion half at a time, place cut-side down on a board. Working from the opposite end from the root, cut half-moon slices down, as thinly as needed.

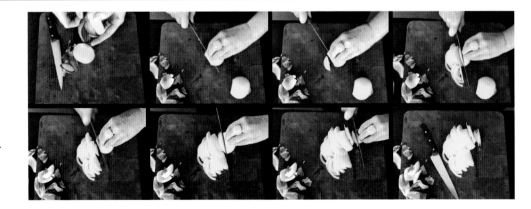

PEELING GARLIC

Using a large knife, place the blade's flat side on top of the garlic clove and, using the heel of your hand, press down to crush slightly. This will crack the skin and make it easier to peel.

DESEEDING A CHILLI

Slice the chilli in half lengthways and, using a small, sharp knife, scrape out the seeds and cut away the stalk in one motion. Discard.

FINELY CHOPPING GARLIC

Peel the garlic, then slice thinly lengthways. Create a stack of the garlic slices and cut again lengthways into little matchsticks. Cut across into tiny dice.

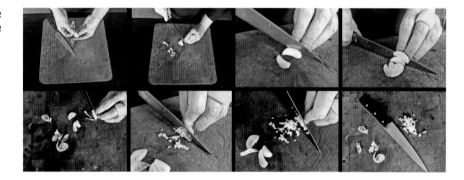

CRUSHING GARLIC

Peel the garlic and sprinkle a little salt on the board (which helps to stop it slipping). Using the flat side of a large knife blade, crush the whole clove, pressing with your fingers on the back of the knife and rotating it in a clockwise direction, pivoting the knife towards you and crushing as you go. Repeat until the garlic is crushed well.

BRUSHING MUSHROOMS

Wild mushrooms especially will need picking over to remove any bits of dirt or grit. Using a pastry brush, gently brush away any bits and pieces.

PEELING FRESH ROOT GINGER

To peel ginger, use the tip of a teaspoon to scrape away the thin peel.

FINELY CHOPPING GINGER

Peel the ginger, then cut into thin lengthways slices. Create a stack of the slices and cut again lengthways into little matchsticks. Cut across into tiny dice.

ROASTING AND PEELING PEPPERS

Place the whole pepper in a roasting tin and roast for for 20–30 minutes or until charred all over and very tender. Remove from the oven and cover with a damp cloth or place in a paper or plastic bag as this helps to steam off the skin, making it easier to peel. Leave until cool enough to handle before peeling.

BAKING BEETROOT

Freshly cooked beetroot really does have a superior flavour to those bought ready-prepared. Trim the beetroot, removing any stringy root and trimming the stalk to about 3cm. Scrub really well and place in a roasting tin or oven-proof dish. Cover with foil and place in a preheated oven at 190°C/gas mark 5 for 45 minutes–1 hour or until tender. Once the beetroot is cooked and cool enough to handle, the skin will easily scrape away. If you don't want to have magenta-stained hands, wear rubber gloves to protect your delicate fingers.

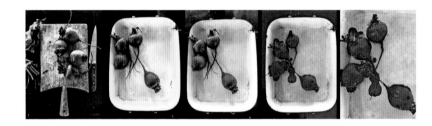

PEELING CELERIAC OR SWEDE

These boulder-like vegetables always seem completely unapproachable and a nightmare to peel. The easiest way is to use a large, sharp knife to slice off about 1–2 cm off the top and bottom, then, with a cut side flat on a board, slice off the thick skin in strips from top to bottom, working around the vegetable until it is completely peeled.

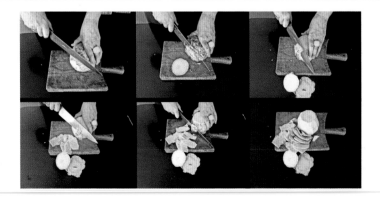

REMOVING THE CORE FROM CABBAGE/ LETTUCE/ FENNEL

To remove the tough core from any large vegetable, such as cabbage or fennel, cut into quarters and then cut away the core with the tip of a knife.

WASHING LETTUCE LEAVES

A lot of lettuce we buy is ready-washed and packed by the supermarket, but even so I like to refresh it and, if there's time, submerge it in a large bowl of water to rejuvenate it (it is a living thing, so treat as you would flowers). If it's not ready washed, make sure you wash it really well to remove any dirt or grit that may be hidden between the leaves. Carefully drain and lay out on a clean tea towel, gather the edges together lightly and, if space allows swing it backwards and forwards to get rid of excess liquid. Of course a salad spinner is great for this.

CHOPPING CUCUMBER INTO SMALL DICE

Sometimes also called brunois, these are little 5mm cubes. Using a large, sharp knife, cut the cucumber across the middle, then again into strips about 5mm wide. Cut again into 5mm sticks and then once again cut across to make 5mm dice. (Follow the same method for any long vegetable.)

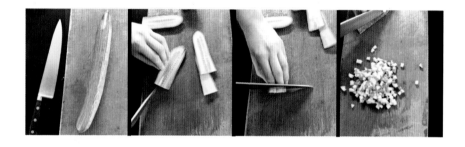

SHUCKING OYSTERS

This means to open oysters. You will need an oyster knife which has a short, strong blade (see page 18) that can get under the tough hinge of the oyster and lever it off.

TOASTING NUTS

More often than not I prefer to toast nuts before adding them to a dish as it gives a fuller flavour. Toasting walnuts, for example, sets them at a new level. I find the best way to toast them evenly is to scatter them on a baking tray and place in the oven for a few minutes until lightly golden all over. I always set a timer when following this method as they can quickly burn, which will make them bitter and unusable. You can of course toast them in a dry pan, but you need to stir them frequently to brown them evenly all over.

SEPARATING AN EGG

Have ready two small bowls. Crack the egg across the middle, holding it over one of the bowls. Carefully pull the two halves of the shell apart, sliding the yolk into one shell half as you go. Tip the yolk into the other shell half and the egg white should drop away underneath into the bowl. Place the yolk in the other bowl. Alternatively, drop the egg yolk onto your closed fingers. Shake your fingers gently and the egg white will again drop away from the yolk between your fingers.

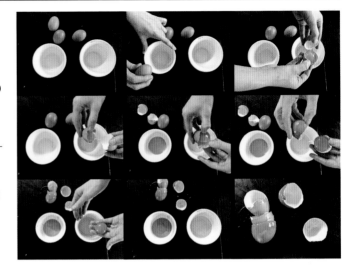

POACHING AN EGG

A tricky one. As everyone says, the fresher the egg, the better, but most of us don't have access to really fresh eggs all the time. Don't add salt to the water as the egg will become pitted; and don't add vinegar unless you want your egg tasting of vinegar!

Bring a small pan full of water to the boil. Break an egg into a cup or small bowl. Gently stir the water with a spoon to create a vortex: nothing dramatic, just enough to make a dip in the centre of the water. Slowly pour the egg into the centre – it will gently float around. When the water reaches the boil again, reduce to a simmer until the egg is cooked to your liking. I prefer mine really runny, which takes about 3–4 minutes, but cook them for however long you like them. Lift out with a slotted spoon and briefly drain on a clean tea towel or kitchen paper to get rid of excess water before serving.

You can also get an egg to this point, then once it is just cooked, lift it out into a bowl of cold water to stop it cooking any further. When you're ready to serve, bring another large pan of water to the boil and lower the egg in to reheat. This is handy if you want to cook poached eggs for a few people; it saves you stressing in the kitchen trying to get the perfectly cooked egg.

PEELING AN APPLE

Peeling an apple from top to bottom makes it really easy. But if you're desperate to see whom you'll marry and you need one long piece of peel to throw over your left shoulder to see what initial it lands in the shape of, peel from the top, spinning the apple as you do it.

CORING AN APPLE

If you need to core an apple all the way through, there is an apple corer available that bores a hole through the fruit when you twist it. This creates a perfect tunnel in the apple to hold stuffing. Otherwise, peel if needed, cut into quarters and use a knife to cut the hard core out of the middle. Then slice or chop as required.

PEELING & SEGMENTING A CITRUS FRUIT

Cut off a thin slice from each end of the citrus fruit to expose the flesh beneath. Place upright on a board and, using a large, sharp knife, peel off strips of the zest from top to bottom, removing all the bitter white pith as you go. Holding the peeled fruit over a bowl to catch the juice, cut the segments away by cutting down on either side of each piece of membrane and tipping the segments into the bowl below. Once you have removed all the segments, squeeze the remaining membrane to remove any juice remaining.

PEELING A PINEAPPLE

With a serrated bread knife, cut off the top and bottom of the pineapple, then stand the fruit upright on a board. Slice away the skin in downward movements, turning as you go.

PEELING & DESEEDING A POMEGRANATE

The easiest and cleanest way to peel and remove the seeds of a pomegranate. With a small, sharp knife, score all the way round the top of the fruit and pull off a lid of peel. This will reveal the separate sections of the pomegranate below, separated by membrane. On the outside, but following the lines of the membrane, score the skin from top to bottom and repeat around the whole fruit. Then break the pomegranate apart in its sections, peel off any membrane or bitter white pith and drop the seeds into a bowl.

PEELING & CORING A PEAR

Peel a pear in long strokes from top to bottom. If you need to stuff the pear whole, use a teaspoon to bore upwards through the base of the fruit and scoop out the core. Otherwise, cut the pear in half lengthways and use a teaspoon to scoop out the core from the halves.

MAKING BREADCRUMBS

If it's a crusty loaf, use a serrated bread knife to slice off the crusts on all sides. If it's a soft loaf with soft crusts, you can use the whole thing. Cut the loaf into thick slices, then cut again to make chunky strips and cut across again to make large cubes (alternatively pull the bread into large pieces). Place the cubes or pieces into a food processor or blender and whiz until you have breadcrumbs of the fineness required.

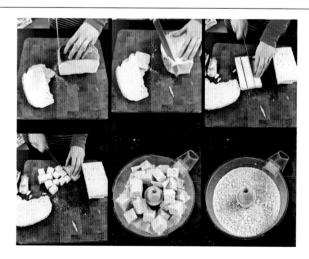

SLICING ON A MANDOLIN

See also under 'Mandolin' on page 18.

Mandolin is brilliant for slicing vegetables wafer-thinly. However as the blade is super sharp, take great care to keep your fingers out of its way. Adjust the width of the blade to the required thickness, then carefully slice your vegetable by moving it up and down over the mandolin blade.

MELTING CHOCOLATE OVER A BAIN-MARIE

A bain-marie (French for 'water bath') enables heat to be moderated. For example, you need to melt chocolate carefully so as not to burn it, and this is the safest method. Tip finely chopped chocolate into a heat-proof bowl and place the bowl over a pan of simmering water. You don't want to get the chocolate too hot, so remove the bowl from the heat immediately and stir occasionally until melted.

REMOVING SEEDS FROM A VANILLA POD

Using a small, sharp knife (or pair of scissors), cut the vanilla pod in half lengthways. Scrape away the seeds from each half from top to bottom.

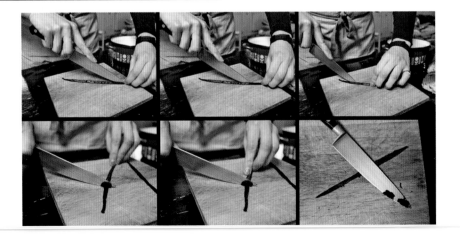

WHAT DOES IT ALL MEAN?

Are you flummoxed by the terms baking blind, sauté and refresh? Once you understand, you'll be away.

SWEATING OR COOKING WITHOUT COLOUR

This is the method, which refers to cooking chopped vegetables (usually onion), where you fry over a fairly low heat (stirring occasionally) and gently cook the ingredients without colouring – as opposed to making them golden or caramelising them which changes the flavour. You sweat out any moisture until the pieces are almost translucent. Cooking them slowly like this really sweetens them and deepens the flavour of the final result.

SAUTÉING

To sauté (French for jump) means to fry (a few ingredients at a time) briskly, stirring and turning the ingredients frequently, in a moderately hot, lightly greased pan. The aim is to brown the food on the outside, enrich the flavour and fry just long enough to cook the inside and seal in moisture. (Stir-frying is similar to sautéing.)

SEARING OR PAN FRYING

Usually this means to fry over a high heat to make the food brown well all over. It generally refers to meat. Searing creates a tasty caramelised flavour on the surface of what you are cooking and helps to create a sauce deep in flavour.

COOKING UNTIL TENDER

To cook until tender means to cook until the ingredients are cooked through to the required degree to be ready to eat.

RESTING MEAT

You may be asked to rest meat for a while before serving (often up to an hour if cooking a roast). It really does make a difference and tenderises the meat as it sits. To keep it warm, wrap loosely in foil and keep in a warm place, such as a turned-off oven or just above on the hob where it is warm from the oven below.

KEEPING WARM

Sometimes you need to keep cooked items of food warm (sometimes improving them; see Resting Meat below left) while you finish cooking the rest of the meal. Wrap the items loosely in foil and keep in a warm place; such as a turned-off oven or just above on the hob where it is warm from the oven below. If you're concerned they have become too cool, pop into a hot oven for a couple of minutes to warm through again. (Be careful, though, as you don't want to overcook them or let them dry out.) If keeping large items of food warm for a longer length of time, like roast meat, wrap in foil and then cover in a towel or something similar to insulate them.

DE-GLAZING

When food is seared, lots of yummy bits stick to the pan that can really add to the flavour of any sauce you are making. Adding liquid to the pan on a high heat will make the liquid boil up and take those bits with it.

FLAMBÉEING

This term describes the process that occurs when you add alcohol to a dish you are cooking and ignite it with a naked flame. The alcohol will burn off and its effect will be flavoursome but less harsh.

REDUCING A SAUCE

To reduce is to boil or simmer a liquid until it reduces in quantity as it evaporates and the resulting sauce will become thicker and more intensely flavoured.

MODERATE HEAT

A medium heat. Not hot, not cool.

SIMMER TO BOILING

To simmer is to cook gently in liquid over a low heat where only a few bubbles rise to the surface. Once you raise the heat and you have lots more faster-moving, bigger bubbles, this is called boiling. A rolling boil means just that: you will see the liquid literally rolling over itself as it cooks.

POACHING

Poaching means to cook in deep liquid, where the food is totally submerged and the liquid is just above a simmer.

BLANCHING

To blanch means to par-cook, cool down and reheat again later. If, for example, you blanch French beans, you cook the beans in water until they are only just cooked, then you drain, refresh (see below) and reheat in more water later on. This is what busy chefs do and it's a really handy tip to help save time when cooking a meal. Have the vegetables blanched ready and then dip them into a pan of boiling water just before serving and they will take only a short moment to heat through, ready to drain again and serve.

REFRESHING

Refreshing is a process by which you can halt the cooking of, say, steamed or boiled vegetables (or eggs), cooling them down quickly (maybe to reheat later – see 'Blanching' above). So, once your food is ready, drain immediately and then refresh under lots of cold running water or submerge in a large bowl of iced water until cold. Drain again.

ZESTING

Zesting is the method of removing the zest from citrus fruit, in little pieces, without attaching any of the bitter white pith below it. Use the fine side of a grater, and keep turning the fruit around as you grate. You can also buy a small gadget for this that pulls the zest off in very fine strands.

BEATING

Beating is when you literally beat the hell out of what you are making. This is a forceful method and sometimes is the only way to incorporate two or more ingredients. It helps aireate and can make something smoother the more it is beaten. To beat lightly means beating briefly to combine, like when you beat eggs together.

WHISKING

If making meringue sometimes it refers to beating the egg whites but you actually need a whisk to whisk as much air into them as possible in the shortest amount of time. Light whisking usually means just to whisk briefly to incorporate.

FOLDING

This refers to the motion you create when trying to combine two thick food components together. Using a large metal spoon, lift and twist and fold over the two ingredients — for instance, when incorporating flour into a cake mixture. Done carefully, it is the best way to blend the two evenly and helps to keep the volume.

SOFT PEAKS

The more you cook, the more you'll understand what a soft peak is. It's when you whisk something like cream or egg white until you have soft, limp, thick folds of mixture, not yet cloud-like. Soft lobes of silky whipped cream are very sexy indeed. Over-whipped cream is revolting and is more difficult to incorporate into a dish. Over-whisked egg white will start to appear grainy and will lose its air strength for what you are cooking.

RIBBONS

When you beat egg and sugar together for a long time, like when making zabaglione, you need to create as much air and volume as possible. It takes a while, you'll know you're at the right point when lifting the whisk and moving it backwards and forwards creates ribbons of mixture that sit on the surface and hold there for a few seconds before sinking and disappearing.

EGG WASH

Lightly beaten egg brushed over a dish that is to be baked is known as an egg wash. You can use the whole egg or just the white or just the yolk (this will give an intense, deep glaze). A tiny pinch of salt will help to break the egg down so that it is easier to use. Add a little milk to make a thinner glaze.

INVERTING

To turn something out the opposite way to which it was cooked. Using a heat-proof cloth to hold the pan or tin, hold a large plate or tray (larger than the item) over the top and turn over. Remove the pan or tin, leaving the inverted food on the plate.

RECIPES MOST USEFUL

SALAD DRESSING

For me a good basic salad dressing can be just extra-virgin olive oil, a squeeze of lemon juice and salt and pepper.

The vinegar you use is up to you (though don't think about using malt vinegar here as it's too harsh). For a sticky sweetness use balsamic, or for a slightly nutty, almost smoky flavour, try sherry vinegar. Wine vinegar (red or white), cider vinegar or rice vinegar can also be used.

Additions to this could be a little crushed garlic, a smidge of mustard (wholegrain or Dijon) or a trickle of honey for sweetness.

If you want a lighter-flavoured dressing, use a mix of olive oil and vegetable oil such as groundnut; for something special add a few drops of walnut oil.

Place a pinch of salt into a bowl, whisk in the vinegar or lemon juice, add a few grindings of black pepper and finally whisk in the olive oil. Taste and adjust the seasoning if needed.

4 tablespoons
 extra-virgin olive oil
1 tablespoon vinegar or
 freshly squeezed
 lemon juice
sea salt and freshly
 ground black pepper

VEGETABLE STOCK

The vegetable combination for this stock doesn't have to be strictly adhered to: vary it according to the flavour you fancy. I'm fond of popping a star anise in sometimes to infuse happily – it's Ramsay inspired and adds a subtle aniseed edge, but it's not crucial.

Place all the vegetables, herbs and spices into a large, deep pot. Cover well with water and simmer gently for 1–2 hours.

Stir in the wine or vermouth (if using), remove from the heat and leave to cool completely and infuse thoroughly.

Strain the stock into the bowl. I usually strain in a colander first and then through a fine sieve.

2 leeks, roughly chopped
6 carrots, roughly chopped
5 celery sticks,
 roughly chopped
2 onions, roughly chopped
1 whole garlic bulb, cut in
 half across its middle
1 lemon, cut into wedges
6 fresh bay leaves
handful of parsley stalks

few sprigs of thyme
1 sprig of tarragon
sprinkling of white or
 black peppercorns
1.8 litres cold water
1 fennel bulb (optional)
1–2 star anise (optional)
200ml white wine or
 vermouth (optional)

CHICKEN STOCK

Use a raw chicken or the cooked carcass and giblets left over from a roast to make a tasty stock, far superior to one made from any bought cube. A sprig of tarragon or a couple garlic cloves would give a gorgeous sweetness.

Chop the chicken carcass into 3 or 4 pieces and place it in a large, deep pot with the other ingredients and ensure everything is covered with water.

Bring slowly to the boil, removing any scum that rises to the surface with a slotted spoon.

Lower the heat to a bare simmer. Simmer for 2–2½ hours. Strain the stock through a fine sieve into a bowl (as with the vegetable stock above, I usually find it easier to strain it through a colander first and then a fine sieve) and leave to go completely cold before refrigerating.

1 raw or cooked
 chicken carcass
2 large carrots,
 roughly chopped
1 leek, roughly chopped
1 large onion,
 roughly chopped
1 celery stick,
 roughly chopped

1 sprig of thyme
1 fresh bay leaf
few whole black
 peppercorns
4–6 parsley stalks
1.8 litres cold water

FLUFFY RICE

This gives you perfectly cooked, light and fluffy rice every time.

Pour the rice into a sieve and wash under cold running water until the water runs clear.

Tip the rice into a pan and pour on enough cold water to come up to the first knuckle on your finger. Although this method sounds odd, it always works, whatever size fingers you have! (I've used this method for up to 6–8 portions.)

Add a pinch of salt, and cover tightly with a lid. If your lid doesn't fit tightly, line it with a piece of foil to make a tight seal.

Bring to the boil, then reduce the heat and simmer for 12–14 minutes. Check after 12 minutes: if all the water has been absorbed, your rice should be cooked. If not, place the pan back on the heat for a couple more minutes. Fluff up with a fork, cover again and leave to stand, off the heat, for 5 minutes before serving.

60–75g basmati or jasmine rice per person
salt

SPELT SODA BREAD

The easiest, tastiest bread I know. Makes 1 large loaf. I add a little treacle to the dough to give it a rich, nutty sweetness.

Preheat your oven to 200°C/gas mark 6.

Mix the flours, salt, soda and tartar in a large bowl. Toss in the butter, cut into cubes and rub into the flour until the texture resembles fine breadcrumbs. Stir the treacle (or honey) into the buttermilk or yogurt, then gradually add it to the flour mixture, and using a fork, bring together until a soft dough results. Form into a smooth ball and place on a greased baking tray.

With a knife, cut a criss-cross slash on the top and bake for about 30–35 minutes or until the loaf sounds hollow when tapped. Place on a wire rack to cool.

350g white flour
500g spelt or wholemeal flour, plus extra for dusting
1½ teaspoons salt
2 level teaspoons bicarbonate of soda
2 level teaspoons cream of tartar
100g unsalted butter, softened

1 tablespoon treacle or honey
725ml buttermilk or natural low-fat yogurt (not strained Greek yogurt as it's too thick)

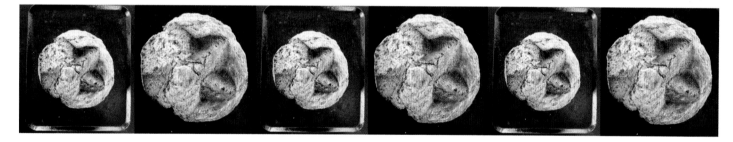

MAYONNAISE

It's fine to use bottled mayonnaise, but once you've tasted homemade and realise how easy it is to make, you'll never look back. The oil you use will depend on what flavour you need. Using all olive oil will give you a gutsy, strong mayonnaise. Sunflower or groundnut oil will be much lighter in flavour. Try a mix of both. Add chopped fresh herbs or crushed garlic at your pleasure.

Place the egg yolks, mustard and lemon juice in a bowl and whisk until thickened slightly. Keep whisking briskly and gradually add the oil in a slow, thin stream, whisking all the time until you have a thick cream. Season to taste.

Alternatively, make the mayonnaise in a food processor following the method outlined above.

Mayonnaise Rescue
If your mayonnaise separates and curdles, don't panic. Place a new egg yolk in another bowl and slowly whisk in the curdled mixture.

Saffron Mayonnaise (great with fish)
Place a pinch of saffron strands in a small bowl, pour over 1 tablespoon boiling water and leave to infuse for 10 minutes. Make the mayonnaise as above, adding the infused saffron at the end.

2 egg yolks
1 teaspoon Dijon mustard
1 tablespoon lemon juice or white wine vinegar
200ml sunflower, groundnut or olive oil or a mixture
sea salt and freshly ground black pepper

SHORTCRUST PASTRY

Sift the flour into a large bowl and add the salt. Cut the butter into cubes and add to the bowl. Using the tips of your fingers, rub the butter into the flour until you have a mixture that resembles fine breadcrumbs.

Trickle a little cold water (a good guide is to allow 1 teaspoon water per 25g flour). Using a fork, stir in the water, then bring the mixture together to form a firm dough.

Alternatively, place the flour, salt and butter in the bowl of a food processor and whiz to form breadcrumbs. With the motor running, trickle in the water, continuing to mix for just enough time to form a dough. Don't over-mix.

Enriched Shortcrust Pastry
To the above recipe, add 1 egg yolk and a little less water to make the dough.

Makes enough for a 25cm tart tin
250g plain flour
pinch salt
125g unsalted butter

SWEETCRUST PASTRY

Sift the flour into a large bowl and add the salt. Cut the butter into cubes and add to the bowl. Using the tips of your fingers, rub the butter into the flour until you have a mixture that resembles fine breadcrumbs, then stir in the sugar. Pour in the water and egg yolks and mix in with a fork, then use your fingers to form the pastry into a dough.

Alternatively, place the flour, salt and butter in the bowl of a food processor and whiz to form breadcrumbs. With the motor running, trickle in the egg yolks and water continuing to mix for just enough time to form a ball of dough. Don't over-mix.

Makes enough for a 25 cm tart tin
250g plain white flour
pinch of salt
125g unsalted butter
3 tablespoons
 caster sugar
2 tablespoons cold water
2 egg yolks

LINING A TART TIN

On a lightly floured surface, roll out the pastry thinly with a rolling pin, so it's a little bigger than the tin. Lightly flour the rolling pin and roll the pastry up loosely around it, then unroll over the tin.

Push the pastry into the corners of the tin and cut off the excess with a knife. With your fingertips, gently pinch up the edges by a couple of millimetres again to make a neat edge.

BAKING BLIND

You'll need to bake pastry blind when making a tart that requires a cooked or semi-cooked, crisp pastry base (where a completely cooked filling is placed in the tart shell, or one that doesn't take long to cook). You pre-bake the pastry shell weighted down with baking beans (see page 16), then the beans are removed in their paper and the pastry shell is returned to the oven to finish cooking.

Prick the base of the raw pastry all over with a fork. Cut a piece of parchment paper slightly bigger than the tin, place inside the pastry shell and fill to the rim with baking beans. Then place in a preheated oven at 190°C/gas mark 5 and bake for 10 minutes. Remove the paper and beans and cook for a further 5–10 minutes for a par-baked shell, or 10–15 minutes for a fully cooked shell.

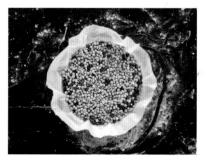

AUTUMN

WHITE BEAN SOUP WITH PARSLEY & ROAST ALMOND PESTO.
POLPETTE DI TONNO WITH BAKED BAY TOMATOES.
BLACKBERRY SEMIFREDDO ICE-CREAM SANDWICHES.

60 min   Preheat your oven to 180°C/gas mark 4. For the starter, scatter the almonds for the pesto on a baking sheet and roast for 5–10 minutes until dark golden brown. Keep an eye on them so they don't burn. Tip onto a plate and leave to cool. Turn the temperature up to 200°C/gas mark 6.

Begin the main course. Arrange the whole tomatoes in a baking dish in a single layer. Place the whole (unpeeled) garlic cloves and bay leaves in between them. Drizzle with half of the oil and sprinkle with salt, pepper and oregano. Bake in the oven for 45–50 minutes until really soft.

Place the breadcrumbs for the polpette in a bowl, pour over the milk and leave to soak for 10 minutes.

50 min   Now for the dessert. Place half of the blackberries in a small pan with the crème de mure (or cassis) and sugar. Bring to the boil, and then remove from the heat and leave to cool.

To make the soup, finely chop the onion and crush the garlic. Heat the oil in a large pan, add the onion and garlic and cook without colouring for 5–10 minutes until the onion is soft. Drain and rinse the beans, add to the pan with the stock and bring to the boil. Remove from the heat and leave to cool slightly, and then blend half of the soup until smooth. Return to the pan and season well.

40 min   Remove the ice cream from the freezer and leave to soften in the fridge for 20-30 minutes. Back to the main course. Squeeze out the excess milk from the breadcrumbs and place in a large bowl. Finely chop the tuna and add to the bowl with the breadcrumbs. Finely grate the Pecorino or Parmesan and finely chop the parsley. Add to the bowl with the currants, pine nuts, lemon zest and beaten egg. Season with salt and black pepper – go easy on the salt because the Parmesan is quite salty already – and combine thoroughly.

30 min   To make the pesto for the starter, place the parsley leaves and roasted almonds in a food processor. Add a good slug of the oil and blitz until roughly chopped – you want it to be quite rough in texture. Scrape into a bowl and stir in the remaining oil. Finely grate the Parmesan or Pecorino, stir into the pesto and season to taste.

20 min   Tip some flour onto a dinner plate and, with wet hands, shape the mixture into 18 balls. Roll each one lightly in flour. To cook the polpette, heat the remaining oil in a large non-stick frying pan over a moderate heat. Add the polpette – you will probably need to cook them in batches – and fry, turning occassionally, for 8–10 minutes or until cooked through. Cover with foil to keep warm.

10 min   To finish the dessert, stir the remaining berries into the blackberry compote. Scrape the ice cream into a bowl and carefully fold in the berries and compote. Return to the freezer. Pop the tray of cooked polpette into the oven to warm while you eat the starter.

To serve the starter, warm the soup and ladle into bowls. Stir a small spoonful of pesto into each bowl and place the rest on the table so everyone can help themselves. (Any leftover pesto could be used as pasta sauce.) Serve with crusty bread.

To serve the main course, place 3 polpette on each plate and accompany with 2 baked tomatoes on the side. Drizzle with the herby cooking juices and add a bay leaf and softened garlic clove to each plate, so your guests can squeeze out the flesh to eat with their tomatoes.

To serve the dessert, scoop a good spoonful of the blackberry semifreddo between 2 waffle wafers.

<u>White Bean Soup with Parsley & Roast Almond Pesto</u>
1 onion
2 garlic cloves
2 tablespoons extra-virgin olive oil
2 x 400g tins white beans (see page 8)
1 litre chicken or vegetable stock
50g whole almonds, skin on
1 bunch of flat-leaf parsley leaves (about 70g)
200ml extra-virgin olive oil
50g Parmesan or Pecorino cheese
sea salt and freshly ground black pepper
crusty bread, to serve

<u>Polpette di Tonno with Baked Bay Tomatoes</u>
12 ripe tomatoes
6 garlic cloves
6 fresh bay leaves
6 tablespoons olive oil
2 teaspoons dried oregano
50g fresh white breadcrumbs (see page 27)
100ml milk
600g sustainably caught line tuna, skinned and chopped
 finely or firm white fish
50g Pecorino or Parmesan
a handful of flat-leaf parsley (about 70g)
2 tablespoons currants
2 tablespoons pine nuts
finely grated zest of 1 lemon
1 egg
plain flour, for dusting
sea salt and freshly ground black pepper

<u>Blackberry Semifreddo Ice-Cream Sandwiches</u>
500g good vanilla ice cream
350g blackberries
2 tablespoons crème de mure (or cassis), optional
1 tablespoon golden caster sugar
12 waffle wafers

WHITE BEAN SOUP WITH PARSLEY & ROAST ALMOND PESTO

This pesto comes from chef Carla Tomasi who shared this recipe with me when we both worked for the same cookery school, Tasting Places. It's a gem of a recipe with the darkly roasted almonds and works beautifully on pasta too, with grated Pecorino.

Preheat your oven to 180°C/gas mark 4. Place the almonds for the pesto on a baking sheet and roast in the oven for 5–10 minutes until dark golden brown (but not burnt!). Tip onto a plate and leave to cool.

Meanwhile, finely chop the onion and crush the garlic. Heat the oil in a large pan, add the onion and garlic and cook without colouring for 5–10 minutes until the onion is soft. Drain and rinse the beans, add to the pan with the stock and bring to the boil. Remove from the heat and leave to cool slightly, and then blend half of the soup until smooth. Return to the pan and season well.

To make the pesto, place the parsley leaves and roasted almonds in a food processor. Add a good slug of the oil and blitz until roughly chopped – you want it to be quite rough in texture. Scrape into a bowl and stir in the remaining oil. Finely grate the Parmesan or Pecorino, stir into the pesto and season to taste.

Reheat the soup and ladle into soup bowls. Add a small spoonful of pesto to each bowl and serve the rest separately so everyone can help themselves. Accompany with crusty bread.

1 onion
2 garlic cloves
2 tablespoons
 extra-virgin olive oil
2 x 400g tins white beans
 (see page 8)
1 litre chicken or
 vegetable stock
sea salt and freshly
 ground black pepper
crusty bread, to serve

For the pesto
50g whole almonds,
 skin on
1 bunch of flat-leaf
 parsley leaves
 (about 70g)
200ml extra-virgin
 olive oil
50g Parmesan or Pecorino
 cheese

POLPETTE DI TONNO WITH BAKED BAY TOMATOES

You need ripe tomatoes for this recipe otherwise it's not worth making. I love bay as a herb and have just bought myself a tree. It's useful to keep fresh leaves in the fridge or freezer. This is a recipe from my friend Maxine Clark and it will always remind me of working with her in Sicily.

Preheat your oven to 200°C/gas mark 6.

Place the breadcrumbs in a bowl, pour over the milk and leave to soak for 10 minutes.

Arrange the whole tomatoes in a baking dish in a single layer. Place the whole (unpeeled) garlic cloves and bay leaves in the gaps between the tomatoes. Drizzle the tomatoes with the oil and sprinkle with salt, pepper and oregano. Bake in the oven for 45–50 minutes until really soft.

Squeeze out the excess milk from the breadcrumbs and place in a large bowl. Finely chop the fish and add to the bowl with the breadcrumbs. Finely grate the Pecorino or Parmesan and finely chop the parsley. Add to the bowl with the currants, pine nuts, lemon zest and beaten egg. Season with salt and black pepper and combine thoroughly. With wet hands, shape the mixture into 18 little balls and dust lightly in flour.

To cook the polpette, heat the oil in a large non-stick frying pan over a moderate heat. Add the polpette – you will probably need to cook them in batches – and fry, turning occasionally, for 8–10 minutes or until cooked through. Cover with foil to keep warm while you cook the rest.

To serve, place 3 polpette on each plate and accompany with 2 baked tomatoes on the side. Drizzle with the herby cooking juices and add a bay leaf and softened garlic clove to each plate, so your guests can squeeze out the flesh to eat with their tomatoes.

3 slices white bread for breadcrumbs (see page 27) or 50g fresh white breadcrumbs
100ml milk
600g sustainably sourced line-caught tuna, skinned
50g Pecorino or Parmesan cheese
a handful of flat-leaf parsley (about 70g)
2 tablespoons currants
2 tablespoons pine nuts
finely grated zest of 1 lemon
1 egg, beaten
plain flour, for dusting
3 tablespoons olive oil

For the tomatoes
12 ripe tomatoes
6 garlic cloves
6 fresh bay leaves
3 tablespoons olive oil
2 teaspoons dried oregano
sea salt and freshly ground black pepper

BLACKBERRY SEMIFREDDO ICE-CREAM SANDWICHES

Blackberries will always remind me of my Dad when he and I would go blackberry picking. Semifreddo means semi-frozen. Make this about an hour or two before you need it. You don't want the berries and compote to freeze completely as they will go rock hard.

Remove the ice cream from the freezer and leave to soften in the fridge for 20–30 minutes.

Place half of the blackberries in a small pan with the crème de mure (or cassis) and sugar. Bring to the boil, and then remove from the heat and leave to cool.

When the ice cream has softened, gently stir in the blackberry compote with the remaining berries and return to the freezer.

To serve, scoop a good spoonful of semifreddo between 2 waffle wafers or spoon into a glass and serve the wafers on the side.

500g good vanilla ice cream
350g blackberries
2 tablespoons crème de mure (or cassis), optional
1 tablespoon golden caster sugar
12 waffle wafers

EGG POTS WITH WILD MUSHROOMS.
PARMESAN LAMB PATTIES ON ROCKET, PEAR & TOASTED ALMOND SALAD.
FIG, HONEY & BASIL TART.

60 min Preheat your oven to 180°C/gas mark 4. For the starter, cut the baguette in half across the middle, and then slice lengthways into thin slices. Arrange the bread on a baking tray in a single layer and bake in the oven until crisp – about 5–7 minutes.

Slice the lamb fillets for the main course across into 1cm slices. Place the meat in the bowl of a food processor and use the pulse button to chop the lamb finely (it needs to be finely chopped, not blitzed to a paste, so don't overdo it.)

50 min Scrape the lamb into a bowl, then grate the onion into the bowl. Crush the garlic. Pull the leaves from the thyme sprigs. Chop the Parmesan into tiny cubes, about 5mm square. Combine everything together and season well. Mix again and shape into 12 patties.

40 min Back to the starter. Beat the whole eggs and yolks together in a bowl with the cream and pass through a fine sieve into a jug (this will make a much smoother custard). Remove the leaves from the tarragon and chop. Add to the egg and cream mixture and season with salt, pepper and a pinch of nutmeg. Slice the mushrooms. Melt the butter in a large frying pan over a moderate heat, add the mushrooms and sauté for about 8–10 minutes until just tender. Increase the heat, add the lemon juice, season well and cook until all the liquid has evaporated.

30 min Divide the mushroom mixture between 6 150ml ramekins or cups. Stand them in a roasting tin. Carefully pour the custard mixture over the mushrooms. Boil a kettle of water and transfer the tin to the oven. Very carefully fill the tin with boiling water so it comes halfway up the sides of the ramekins or cups. Bake for about 10–15 minutes, or until the custard is just cooked but still a bit wobbly in the centre.

20 min For the main course, heat 2 tablespoons oil in a large frying pan over a medium-to-low heat. Add the almonds and fry until toasted, stirring regularly. Add a pinch of each sea salt flakes and smoked paprika and tip into a bowl. Set aside. (Keep the pan to one side for later.) Now for the dessert. Roll out the pastry to form a rectangle, 30 x 35cm, and transfer to a baking sheet. Gently prick the pastry all over with a fork – just to dent it (not pierce it) to stop the pastry inflating in the oven. Slice the figs and arrange in a single layer on top of the pastry. Make a lip by turning the pastry over by a couple of centimetres. Drizzle the figs with the honey, sprinkle evenly with sugar and dot with butter. Pick off the basil leaves and tuck one under each slice of fig.

Remove the mushroom pots from the oven and increase the temperature to 200°C/gas mark 6.

Place the fig tart in the oven and bake for 20–25 minutes until the pastry is golden and the fruit is bubbling. (You can cook the tart while you eat your starter and main course.)

10 min To cook the lamb patties, add the remaining oil to the frying pan and fry the patties over a moderate heat for 2–3 minutes on each side – you may need to fry them in batches and then transfer them to a plate while you cook the rest. Cover with foil to keep warm while you eat your starter.

To serve the starter, place each ramekin or cup on a saucer, insert a long piece of toast into each and serve immediately.

To serve the main course, place a handful of rocket on each plate. Slice the pears, removing the core (see page 27), and scatter the slices around the plate. Top with 2 patties. Then return the frying pan to a high heat, tip in the roasted almonds and squeeze in the lemon juice. Toss well for a few seconds, and then spoon the almonds over the salad.

To serve the dessert, cut the tart into 6 slices and transfer to your serving plates.

Egg Pots with Wild Mushrooms
2 whole eggs, plus 4 yolks
600ml double cream
2 sprigs of tarragon
grated nutmeg, to taste
300g mixture of wild, field and chestnut mushrooms, cleaned (see page 23)
40g butter
juice of ½ lemon
1 small baguette
sea salt and freshly ground black pepper

Parmesan Lamb Patties on Rocket, Pear & Toasted Almond Salad
750g whole lamb neck fillets (2–3, depending on size), trimmed of excess fat and sinew
1 red onion
1 garlic clove
2 sprigs of thyme
70g piece of Parmesan cheese
4 tablespoons olive oil
100g whole almonds, skin on
a pinch of smoked paprika
juice of ½ lemon
4 bunches of rocket (about 300g)
2 ripe pears
sea salt flakes and freshly ground black pepper

Fig, Honey & Basil Tart
500g shortcrust pastry
9 figs
2 tablespoons runny honey
25g demerara sugar
25g butter
1 small bunch of basil

EGG POTS WITH WILD MUSHROOMS

The tarragon gives a good pungent kick to the mushrooms and creamy custard.

Preheat your oven to 180°C/gas mark 4.

Beat the whole eggs and yolks together in a bowl with the cream and pass through a fine sieve into a jug (this will make a much smoother custard). Remove the leaves from the tarragon and chop. Add to the egg and cream mixture and season with salt, pepper and a pinch of nutmeg.

Slice the mushrooms. Melt the butter in a large frying pan over a moderate heat, add the mushrooms and sauté for about 8–10 minutes until just tender. Increase the heat, add the lemon juice, season well and cook until all the liquid has evaporated.

Divide the mushroom mixture between 6 150ml ramekins or cups. Stand them in a roasting tin. Carefully pour the custard mixture over the mushrooms. Boil a kettle of water and transfer the tin to the oven. Very carefully fill the tin with boiling water so it comes halfway up the sides of the ramekins or cups.

Bake for 10–15 minutes, or until the custard is just cooked but still a bit wobbly in the centre.

Meanwhile, cut the baguette in half across the middle, and then slice lengthways into thin slices. Arrange the bread on a baking tray in a single layer and bake in the oven until crisp – about 5–7 minutes.

To serve the egg pots, place each ramekin or cup on a little saucer, insert a long piece of toast into each and serve immediately.

2 whole eggs, plus 4 yolks
600ml double cream
2 sprigs of tarragon
grated nutmeg, to taste
300g mixture of wild,
 field and chestnut
 mushrooms, cleaned
 (see page 23)
40g butter
juice of ½ lemon
1 small baguette
sea salt and freshly
 ground black pepper

PARMESAN LAMB PATTIES ON ROCKET, PEAR & TOASTED ALMOND SALAD

Once cooked the Parmesan creates little melting nuggets of cheese.

Slice the lamb fillets across into 1cm slices. Place the meat in the bowl of a food processor and use the pulse button to chop the lamb finely (it needs to be finely chopped, not blitzed to a paste, so don't overdo it).

Scrape the lamb into a bowl. Grate the onion into the bowl with the lamb. Crush the garlic. Pull the leaves from the thyme sprigs. Chop the Parmesan into tiny cubes, about 5mm square. Combine everything together and season well. Mix again and shape into 12 equal-sized patties.

Heat 2 tablespoons of the oil in a large frying pan over a medium-to-low heat. Add the almonds and fry until toasted, stirring regularly. Add a pinch of each sea salt flakes and smoked paprika and tip into a bowl. Set aside.

Add the remaining oil to the pan and fry the patties over a moderate heat for 2–3 minutes on each side – you will probably need to fry them in batches and then transfer them to a plate while you cook the rest. Remove the last of the patties from the pan, tip in the roasted almonds, increase the heat and squeeze in the lemon juice. Toss well for a few seconds.

To prepare the salad, wash and dry the rocket leaves and slice the pears, removing the core (see page 27). Place a handful of rocket on each of 6 dinner plates and scatter with the sliced pears. To serve, place 2 patties on top of each plate of salad, spoon over some of the almonds and serve straight away.

750g whole lamb neck fillets (2–3 depending on size), trimmed of excess fat or sinew
1 red onion
1 garlic clove
2 sprigs of thyme
70g piece of Parmesan cheese
4 tablespoons olive oil
100g whole almonds, skin on
a pinch of smoked paprika
juice of ½ lemon
4 bunches of rocket (about 300g)
2 ripe pears
sea salt flakes and freshly ground black pepper

FIG, HONEY & BASIL TART

In this menu you have enough cream already but, if you were cooking this another time, you could dot the tart with mascarpone at the table or accompany it with single cream.

Preheat your oven to 200°C/gas mark 6.

Roll out the pastry to form a rectangle, 30 x 35cm, and transfer to a baking sheet. Gently prick the pastry all over with a fork – just to dent it (not pierce it) to stop the pastry inflating while it is in the oven. Slice the figs and arrange in a single layer on top of the pastry. Make a lip by turning the edges of the pastry over by a couple of centimetres.

Drizzle the figs with the honey, sprinkle evenly with sugar and dot with butter. Pick off the basil leaves and tuck one under each slice of fig. Bake in the oven for 20–25 minutes until the pastry is golden and the fruit is bubbling.

500g shortcrust pastry
9 figs
2 tablespoons runny honey
25g demerara sugar
25g butter
1 small bunch of basil

RED ONION SOUP WITH GOAT'S CHEESE CROÛTES.
ORANGE & ALMOND STUFFED PORK WITH SWEET POTATO & ROSE HARISSA MASH.
AFFOGATO AL CAFFÈ.

60 min Preheat your oven to 190°C/gas mark 5. Pierce the whole sweet potatoes all over with a fork and bake in the oven for 35–45 minutes, or until tender. Meanwhile, spread the ground almonds on a baking sheet and toast in the bottom of the oven for 10 minutes until evenly golden. Tip into a bowl to cool.

To make the soup, finely slice the onions and crush the garlic. Heat the oil in a large saucepan, add the onions, garlic and fennel seeds and cook over a low heat for 5–7 minutes. When the onions begin to soften, sprinkle with a little salt, cover and cook over a very low heat for 35–40 minutes until really soft. Stir occasionally to check the onions aren't sticking.

50 min Meanwhile, make the stuffing and marinade for the pork. Finely grate the zest of all 4 oranges. Peel and segment 2 of the oranges (see page 26) and squeeze the juice of the other 2 into a jug. Add the olive oil to the orange juice, season with salt and pepper and set aside. Cut the garlic into fine slivers. Finely chop the parsley. Add the orange zest to the ground almonds, along with the drained orange segments, the garlic slivers, honey, parsley and oregano. Mix well and season.

40 min Slice each pork fillet lengthways, almost but not quite all the way through, and open out like a book. Divide the almond mixture between the fillets. Bring the edges of the meat together and tie with string at 2.5cm intervals. Place the fillets in a shallow dish and pour over the orange and olive oil mixture.

30 min Heat a roasting tin and seal the fillets all over for 3–4 minutes. (Keep the marinade to one side for later.) Transfer the fillets to the oven and roast for 8–10 minutes or until cooked, then transfer the fillets to a plate, cover with foil and set aside to rest. (Keep the roasting tin for later.)

20 min The onions for the soup should now be soft. Increase the heat, add the vinegar and boil briskly for 1–2 minutes until reduced by half. Add the bay leaf, thyme, red wine and stock. Bring to the boil and simmer for 10–15 minutes.

The sweet potatoes should now be tender. Remove them from the oven and leave to cool slightly before peeling. To make the mash, place the sweet potato flesh in a pan, mash well with a fork and season.

10 min To make the croûtes, cut the baguette into slices on the angle and arrange in a single layer on a baking sheet. Spread each slice with the thinnest scraping of Gentleman's Relish (if using), and then with some goat's cheese. Place in the oven and bake for about 5–8 minutes or until bubbling.

To serve the starter, season the soup and ladle into soup bowls. Accompany with the goat's cheese croûtes.

To make the sauce for the pork, add the reserved marinade to the roasting tin and bring to the boil. Whisk in the butter and season to taste with salt and pepper. Place the pan of sweet potato mash on the heat and warm through, stir in the harissa and check for seasoning.

To serve the main course, slice the pork fillets. Place a spoonful of the harissa mash on each plate, top with a few slices of pork and spoon over the sauce.

Serve the dessert, place a ball of ice cream in 6 heatproof glasses. Pour over the hot, freshly made espresso coffee and serve immediately with the biscuits on the side.

Red Onion Soup with Goat's Cheese Croûtes
3 large red onions
1 garlic clove
3 tablespoons olive oil
1 teaspoon fennel seeds, crushed
2 tablespoons red wine vinegar
2 bay leaves
2 sprigs of thyme
150ml red wine
600ml vegetable or chicken stock
sea salt and freshly ground black pepper

Goat's Cheese Croûtes
1 baguette
Gentleman's Relish (optional)
75g creamy soft goat's cheese

Orange & Almond Stuffed Pork with Sweet Potato & Rose Harissa Mash
100g ground almonds
4 sweet potatoes
4 large oranges
4 tablespoons olive oil
4 garlic cloves
couple of sprigs of flat-leaf parsley
2 tablespoons runny honey
½ teaspoon dried oregano
2 pork fillets (about 400–500g each), trimmed of excess fat and sinew
25g butter
1 tablespoon rose harissa
sea salt and freshly ground black pepper

Affogato al Caffè
500g vanilla ice cream
6 shots of freshly made espresso coffee
12 shortbread fingers or long biscotti

RED ONION SOUP WITH GOAT'S CHEESE CROÛTES

The slow cooking of the onions makes them sweet and soft – they melt in the mouth.

Finely slice the onions and crush the garlic. Heat the oil in a large saucepan, add the onions, garlic and fennel seeds and cook gently for 5–7 minutes. When the onions begin to soften, sprinkle with a little salt, cover and cook over a very low heat for 35–40 minutes until really soft. Stir occasionally to check the onions aren't sticking.

Increase the heat, add the vinegar and boil briskly for 1–2 minutes until reduced by half. Add the bay leaf, thyme, red wine and stock. Bring to the boil and simmer for 10–15 minutes.

Preheat your oven to 190°C/gas mark 5.

To make the croûtes, cut the baguette into slices on the angle and arrange in a single layer on a baking sheet. Spread each slice with the thinnest scraping of Gentleman's Relish (if using), and then with some goat's cheese. Place in the oven and bake for about 5–8 minutes or until bubbling.

To serve, season the soup and ladle into soup bowls. Accompany with the goat's cheese croûtes on the side.

3 large red onions
1 garlic clove
3 tablespoons olive oil
1 teaspoon fennel seeds, crushed
2 tablespoons red wine vinegar
2 bay leaves
2 sprigs of thyme
150ml red wine
600ml vegetable or chicken stock
sea salt and freshly ground black pepper

For the croûtes
1 baguette
Gentleman's Relish (optional)
75g creamy soft goat's cheese

ORANGE & ALMOND STUFFED PORK WITH SWEET POTATO & ROSE HARISSA MASH

Rose harissa is warm and perfumed and gives a delicious zing to the mash.

Preheat your oven to 190°C/gas mark 5. Spread the ground almonds on a baking sheet and toast in the oven for 10 minutes or until evenly golden. Tip into a bowl to cool.

Pierce the whole sweet potatoes all over with a fork and bake in the oven for 35–45 minutes until tender.

Finely grate the zest of all 4 oranges. Peel and segment 2 of the oranges (see page 26) and squeeze the juice of the other 2 into a jug. Add the olive oil to the orange juice, season with salt and pepper and set aside. Cut the garlic into fine slivers. Finely chop the parsley. Add the orange zest to the ground almonds, along with the drained orange segments, the garlic slivers, honey, parsley and oregano. Mix well and season.

Slice each pork fillet lengthways, almost but not all the way through, and open out like a book. Divide the almond mixture between the fillets. Bring the edges of the meat together and tie with string at 2.5cm intervals. Place the fillets in a shallow dish and pour over the orange and olive oil mixture.

When the sweet potatoes are ready, remove from the oven and leave to cool slightly before peeling. To make the mash, place the sweet potato flesh in a pan, mash thoroughly with a fork and season well.

Heat a roasting tin and seal the fillets all over for 3–4 minutes. (Keep the marinade to one side for later.) Transfer the fillets to the oven and roast for 8–10 minutes or until cooked through. Remove from the oven and transfer the pork fillets to a plate. Cover with foil to keep warm and set aside to rest.

To make the sauce, add the marinade to the roasting tin and bring to the boil. Whisk in the butter and season to taste with salt and pepper. Place the pan of sweet potato mash on the heat and warm through, stir in the harissa and check for seasoning.

To serve, slice the pork fillets. Place a spoonful of the harissa mash on each plate, top with a few slices of pork and spoon over the sauce.

100g ground almonds
4 sweet potatoes
4 large oranges
4 tablespoons olive oil
4 garlic cloves
couple of sprigs of
 flat-leaf parsley
2 tablespoons
 runny honey
½ teaspoon dried oregano
2 pork fillets (about
 400–500g each),
 trimmed of excess fat
 and sinew
25g butter
1 tablespoon rose harissa
sea salt and freshly
 ground black pepper

AFFOGATO AL CAFFÈ

A grown-up coke float!

Place a ball of ice cream in 6 heatproof glasses. Pour over the hot, freshly made espresso coffee and serve immediately with the biscuits on the side.

500g vanilla ice cream
6 shots of freshly made
 espresso coffee
12 shortbread fingers
 or long biscotti

ROAST TOMATOES WITH ANCHOVIES & MINT.
OVEN-BAKED MUSHROOM RISOTTO WITH WALNUT & WILD MUSHROOM GREMOLATA.
FRESH FIG & FIG ROLL CRUMBLE.

60 min   Preheat your oven to 180°C/gas mark 4. Begin with the main course. Place the porcini in a heatproof measuring jug and pour over 400ml boiling water. Leave to soak for 15 minutes. Scatter the walnuts on a baking tray and cook in the oven for 5–6 minutes until golden. Finely chop the onion and celery and slice the field mushrooms. Remove the leaves from the tarragon and chop finely.

50 min   Now for the starter. Remove the leaves from the mint. Roughly chop the garlic. Lift the anchovies and sundried tomatoes from their oil (but reserve the oil). Place the mint, garlic, anchovies and sundried tomatoes in the bowl of a food processor and blitz until finely chopped. Gradually add the oil from the tin of anchovies through the feeder tube with 4 tablespoons of oil from the sundried tomatoes. Scrape into a bowl and season with pepper and salt, if needed – go easy on the salt because the anchovies will be quite salty already.

Cut the tomatoes across their middle and lay, cut-side up, in a single layer in a baking dish. Spoon the dressing over the tomatoes and transfer to the oven. Bake for 45 minutes or until very tender.

40 min   Back to the main course. Pour the stock into a pan and bring to a simmer. Meanwhile, melt 50g of the butter in a large, heavy-based casserole, add the onion and celery and cook for 5–6 minutes without colouring until soft. Drain the porcini over a fine sieve, reserving the liquor, and chop finely. Add the chopped porcini and sliced field mushrooms to the pan and cook, stirring occasionally, for a further 5 minutes.

30 min   Add the rice and tarragon and stir-fry for about a minute. Stir in the stock and reserved mushroom liquor and season with pepper. Cover with a lid and place in the oven for 25–30 minutes, stirring after 15 minutes.

To make the dessert, chop the pistachios roughly. Cut the figs in half and lay in an oven-proof dish in a single layer. Finely grate the orange zest over the figs, sprinkle evenly with sugar and squeeze over the orange juice. Crumble the Fig Rolls into small pieces and scatter over the figs with the chopped pistachios. Cover with foil and bake in the oven for 15 minutes, and then remove the foil and continue to cook for a further 10 minutes or until golden and bubbling.

20 min   Meanwhile, finish preparing the ingredients for the main course. Cut the Tallegio into 1cm cubes. Remove the leaves from the parsley and chop finely. Finely chop the garlic. Finely grate the zest from the lemon and squeeze the juice. Crush the walnuts roughly with your fingers. Chop the girolles roughly if large.

10 min   Remove the risotto from the oven when the rice is just tender and all the liquid has been absorbed. Stir in the lemon juice, mascarpone, chopped Tallegio and Parmesan. Season, cover again and set aside.

Melt the remaining butter in a large frying pan, add the girolles and cook, tossing occasionally, for 2–3 minutes or until soft. Season with salt and pepper and stir in the lemon zest, parsley, garlic and walnuts.

To serve the starter, warm the flatbread in the oven for a few minutes. Arrange 4 tomato halves on each of 6 starter plates, drizzle over the cooking juices and serve with the flatbread on the side.

To serve the main course, place a large spoonful of the risotto on each of 6 soup plates, scatter over a little of the girolle mixture and serve immediately with extra grated Parmesan on the side.

To serve the dessert, divide the fig crumble between your dessert dishes and accompany with a spoonful of yogurt.

Roast Tomatoes with Anchovies & Mint
15g mint leaves
1 garlic clove
1 x 50g tin anchovies in olive oil
50g sundried tomatoes in olive oil (drained weight)
12 ripe tomatoes
sea salt and freshly ground black pepper
flatbread, to serve

Oven-baked Mushroom Risotto with
Walnut & Wild Mushroom Gremolata
15g dried porcini mushrooms
100g walnuts
1 onion
2 celery sticks
400g field mushrooms
15g tarragon leaves
1 litre chicken or vegetable stock
85g butter
400g risotto rice (such as Carnaroli or Arborio)
200g Tallegio cheese
15g flat-leaf parsley
2 garlic cloves
1 lemon
150g girolles or other wild mushrooms, cleaned
 (see page 23)
100g mascarpone
50g Parmesan cheese grated, plus extra to serve
sea salt and freshly ground black pepper

Fresh Fig & Fig Roll Crumble
50g shelled pistachios
12 fresh figs
1 large orange
50g muscovado sugar
1 packet of Fig Rolls
Greek yogurt, to serve

ROAST TOMATOES WITH ANCHOVIES & MINT

The tomatoes cook down and become sweet and intensely flavoured.

Preheat your oven to 180°C/gas mark 4.

Remove the leaves from the mint. Roughly chop the garlic. Lift the anchovies and sundried tomatoes from their oil (but reserve the oil). Place the mint, garlic, anchovies and sundried tomatoes in the bowl of a food processor and blitz until finely chopped. Gradually add the oil from the tin of anchovies through the feeder tube with 4 tablespoons oil from the sundried tomatoes.

Scrape into a bowl and season with pepper and salt, if needed – go easy on the salt because the anchovies will be quite salty already.

Cut the tomatoes across their middle and lay, cut-side up, in a single layer in a baking dish. Spoon the dressing over the tomatoes and transfer to the oven. Bake for 45 minutes or until very tender.

To serve the tomatoes, warm the flatbread in the oven for a few minutes. Arrange 4 tomato halves on each of 6 starter plates, drizzle over the cooking juices and serve with the flatbread on the side.

15g mint leaves
1 garlic clove
1 x 50g tin anchovies
 in olive oil
50g sundried tomatoes in
 olive oil (drained weight)
12 ripe tomatoes
sea salt and freshly
 ground black pepper
flatbread, to serve

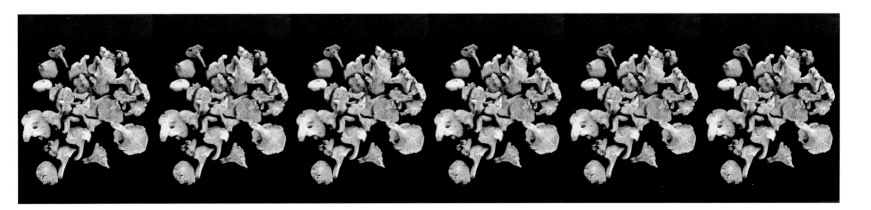

OVEN-BAKED MUSHROOM RISOTTO WITH WALNUT & WILD MUSHROOM GREMOLATA

Gremolata is an Italian garnish made from parsely, chopped garlic and slivers of lemon zest and it gives a freshness to this creamy dish.

Preheat your oven to 180°C/gas mark 4.

Place the porcini in a heatproof measuring jug and pour over 400ml boiling water. Leave to soak for 15 minutes. Scatter the walnuts on a baking tray and cook in the oven for 5–6 minutes until golden. Finely chop the onion and celery. Slice the field mushrooms. Remove the leaves from the tarragon and finely chop.

Pour the stock into a pan and bring to a simmer. Meanwhile, melt 50g of the butter in a large, heavy-based casserole, add the onion and celery and cook for 5–6 minutes without colouring until soft. Drain the porcini over a fine sieve, reserving the liquor, and chop finely. Add the chopped porcini and sliced field mushrooms to the pan and cook, stirring occasionally, for a further 5 minutes. Add the rice and tarragon and stir-fry for about a minute. Stir in the stock and reserved mushroom liquor and season with pepper. Cover with a lid and place in the oven for 25–30 minutes, stirring after 15 minutes.

Meanwhile, cut the Tallegio into 1cm cubes. Remove the leaves from the parsley and chop finely. Finely chop the garlic. Finely grate the zest from the lemon and squeeze the juice. Crush the walnuts roughly with your fingers. Chop the girolles roughly if large.

Remove the risotto from the oven when the rice is just tender and all the liquid has been absorbed. Stir in the lemon juice, mascarpone, chopped Tallegio and Parmesan. Season, cover again and set aside while you cook the girolles.

Melt the remaining butter in a large frying pan, add the girolles and cook, tossing occasionally, for 2–3 minutes or until soft. Season with salt and pepper and stir in the lemon zest, parsley, garlic and walnuts.

To serve, place a large spoonful of the risotto on each of 6 soup plates, scatter over a little of the girolle mixture and serve immediately with extra grated Parmesan on the side.

15g dried porcini mushrooms
100g walnuts
1 onion
2 celery sticks
400g field mushrooms
15g tarragon leaves
1 litre chicken or vegetable stock
85g butter
400g risotto rice (such as Carnaroli or Arborio)
200g Tallegio cheese
15g flat-leaf parsley
2 garlic cloves
1 lemon
150g girolles or other wild mushrooms, cleaned (see page 23)
100g mascarpone
sea salt and freshly ground black pepper
50g Parmesan cheese grated, plus extra to serve

FRESH FIG & FIG ROLL CRUMBLE

The crumbled fig rolls give an extra chewy twist.

Preheat your oven to 180°C/gas mark 4. Chop the pistachios roughly. Cut the figs in half and lay in an oven-proof dish in a single layer. Finely grate the zest from the orange over the figs. Sprinkle evenly with the sugar and squeeze over the orange juice. Crumble the Fig Rolls into small pieces and scatter over the figs with the chopped pistachios.

Cover with foil and bake in the oven for 15 minutes, and then remove the foil and continue cooking for a further 10 minutes or until golden and bubbling.

Serve warm with Greek yogurt on the side.

50g shelled pistachios
12 fresh figs
1 large orange
50g muscovado sugar
1 packet of Fig Rolls
Greek yogurt, to serve

SALAD OF APPLES & PEARS, BLUE CHEESE & WATERCRESS.
OPEN ROAST GARLIC & FIELD MUSHROOM LASAGNE WITH MOLLICA.
PLUM & PRUNE MAPLE SYRUP OAT CRUMBLE.

60 min Preheat your oven to 190°C/gas mark 5. Place the whole (unpeeled) garlic bulb in a small roasting tin, rub all over with 1 tablespoon of the olive oil and roast in the oven for about 30 minutes or until soft.

Scatter the walnuts and pine nuts for the starter on a baking tray and roast in the oven for 5–6 minutes or until golden. Tip onto a plate to cool.

Meanwhile, get on with the crumble. Cut the plums in half and remove the stones. Combine the plum halves and prunes in a large, deep baking dish (or individual dishes). Add the maple syrup and a couple of tablespoons of the muscovado sugar, splash with 2 tablespoons water and toss well together.

50 min To make the crumble topping, melt the butter in a small pan, stir in the oats and the remaining muscovado sugar and add a pinch of cinnamon. Sprinkle over the plums and bake in the oven for 40–45 minutes until bubbling and golden.

40 min Make a dressing for the starter by combining the lemon juice and olive oil in a small bowl and season well.

Prepare the filling for the lasagne. Finely chop the onion and deseed and finely chop the chilli. Cut the fennel into quarters lengthways, cut out and remove the tough core and slice the rest. Slice the mushrooms, chop the herbs and finely grate the Pecorino.

30 min Melt the butter in a large frying pan over a low heat. Add the onion and chilli and cook for 2–3 minutes without colouring. Put in the fennel slices and cook over a moderate heat for about 5–8 minutes or until the fennel has softened. Add the mushrooms and stew until soft. Remove the garlic from the oven, leave to cool for about

10 minutes, and then squeeze out the flesh from each clove into a bowl and mash well with a fork. Set aside.

To make the mollica, cut the crusts off the bread and blitz in a food processor to make fine breadcrumbs. Heat the remaining olive oil in a small frying pan. Add the breadcrumbs and fry over a moderate heat, stirring occasionally, until golden brown. Be careful not to burn them!

20 min Once the mushrooms are soft, turn up the heat, crumble in the chestnuts and add the herbs, mashed garlic, vermouth and lemon juice. Stir-fry over a moderate heat until the pan is nearly dry. Add the crème fraîche, bring to the boil and season well with salt and pepper.

10 min Cut each lasagne sheet into 2 squares. Bring a very large pan of salted water to the boil and slide in the lasagne sheets, one at a time, so they don't stick together; cook for 3–5 minutes or until *al dente*. Drain in a colander.

Assemble the starter at the last minute. Core and thinly slice the pears and apples (see page 27), and place in a large serving bowl. Add the watercress and scatter in the toasted nuts. Pour the dressing over the top and toss well together. To serve, slice the cheese into thin shavings and scatter over the salad. Accompany with the grapes on the side.

To assemble the lasagne, place a sheet of pasta on each plate, top with a spoonful of the mushroom mixture and repeat with the rest of the pasta and mushrooms so you end up with 6 little stacks, each 3 sheets high. To serve, sprinkle the tops with a little mollica and Pecorino, and hand the rest around separately so everyone can help themselves.

Serve the warm crumble with yogurt on the side.

Salad of Apples & Pears, Blue Cheese & Watercress
50g walnuts
50g pine nuts
juice of ½ lemon
4 tablespoons extra-virgin olive oil
2 juicy pears
2 crisp apples
1 small bunch of watercress
100g blue cheese, such as British Stichelton or Stilton
1 small bunch of Muscat grapes or other black grapes
sea salt and freshly ground black pepper

Open Roast Garlic & Field Mushroom Lasagne with Mollica
1 garlic bulb
4 tablespoons olive oil
1 red onion
1 red chilli
1 fennel bulb
750g flat field mushrooms, cleaned (see page 23)
10g tarragon leaves
1 small bunch of flat-leaf parsley
100g Pecorino cheese
75g butter
4 slices of country bread, for the breadcrumbs (see page 27)
250g cooked chestnuts (available vacuum-packed or in tins)
50ml white vermouth
juice of ½ lemon
200ml crème fraîche
9 rectangular fresh lasagne sheets
sea salt and freshly ground black pepper

Plum & Prune Maple Syrup Oat Crumble
6 ripe plums
12 stoned prunes
6 tablespoons maple syrup (or honey)
75g dark muscovado sugar
100g butter
200g porridge oats
pinch of ground cinnamon
yogurt, to serve

SALAD OF APPLES & PEARS, BLUE CHEESE & WATERCRESS

I'm a great fan of a new unpasteurised, Stilton-style cheese from Neal's Yard Dairy called Stichelton (the old Saxon name for the town of Stilton). Smooth, buttery and salty, it is lighter and less dense than Stilton.

Preheat your oven to 190°C/gas mark 5.

Scatter the walnuts and pine nuts on a baking tray and roast in the oven for 5–6 minutes or until golden. Tip onto a plate to cool.

Make a dressing with the lemon juice and olive oil and season well. Core and thinly slice the pears and apples (see pages 26 and 27), and place in a large serving bowl. Add the watercress and scatter in the toasted nuts. Pour the dressing over the top and toss well together.

To serve, slice the cheese into thin shavings and scatter over the salad. Accompany with the grapes on the side, so everyone can help themselves.

50g walnuts
50g pine nuts
juice of ½ lemon
4 tablespoons
 extra-virgin olive oil
2 juicy pears
2 crisp apples
1 small bunch
 of watercress
100g blue cheese,
 such as British Stichelton
 or Stilton
1 small bunch of
 Muscat grapes or other
 black grapes
sea salt and freshly
 ground black pepper

OPEN ROAST GARLIC & FIELD MUSHROOM LASAGNE WITH MOLLICA

Mollica is simply breadcrumbs fried until crispy in olive oil. Frequently used in Sicilian cooking as a topping for pasta, and even pizza, they add a lovely crunchy texture to this creamy pasta dish.

Preheat your oven to 190°C/gas mark 5.

Place the whole (unpeeled) garlic bulb in a small roasting tin, rub all over with 1 tablespoon of the olive oil and roast in the oven for about 30 minutes or until soft. Leave to cool for 10 minutes, and then squeeze out the flesh from each clove into a bowl and mash well with a fork. Set aside.

Finely chop the onion and deseed and finely chop the chilli. Cut the fennel into quarters lengthways, cut out and remove the tough core and slice the rest. Slice the mushrooms, chop the herbs and finely grate the Pecorino.

Melt the butter in a large frying pan over a low heat. Add the onion and chilli and cook for 2–3 minutes without colouring. Put in the fennel slices and cook over a moderate heat for about 5–8 minutes or until the fennel has softened. Add the mushrooms and stew until soft.

Meanwhile, make the mollica. Cut the crusts off the bread and blitz in a food processor to make fine breadcrumbs. Heat the remaining olive oil in a small frying pan. Add the breadcrumbs and fry over a moderate heat, stirring occasionally, until golden brown. Be careful not to burn them!

Once the mushrooms are soft, crumble the chestnuts into the pan and add the herbs, mashed garlic, vermouth and lemon juice. Stir-fry over a moderate heat until the pan is nearly dry. Add the crème fraîche, bring to the boil and season well with salt and pepper.

Cut each lasagne sheet into 2 squares. Bring a very large pan of salted water to the boil and slide in the lasagne sheets, one at a time, so they don't stick together, cook for 3–5 minutes or until *al dente*. Drain in a large colander.

To assemble the lasagne, place one sheet of pasta on each plate, top with a spoonful of the mushroom mixture and repeat with the rest of the pasta and mushrooms. You should end up with 6 little stacks, each 3 sheets high.

To serve, sprinkle the tops with a little mollica and Pecorino and serve the rest at the table so everyone can help themselves.

1 garlic bulb
4 tablespoons olive oil
1 red onion
1 red chilli
1 fennel bulb
750g flat field mushrooms, cleaned (see page 23)
10g tarragon leaves
small bunch of flat-leaf parsley
100g Pecorino cheese
75g butter
4 slices of country bread, for the breadcrumbs (see page 27)
250g cooked chestnuts (available vacuum-packed or in tins)
50ml white vermouth
juice of ½ lemon
200ml crème fraîche
9 rectangular fresh lasagne sheets
sea salt and freshly ground black pepper

PLUM & PRUNE MAPLE SYRUP OAT CRUMBLE

What makes this delicious is the combination of the sharpness of the plums and the stickiness of the prunes under the oaty crust.

Preheat your oven to 180°C/gas mark 4.

Cut the plums in half and remove the stones. Combine the plum halves and prunes in a large, deep baking dish (or individual dishes). Add the maple syrup and a couple of tablespoons of the muscovado sugar, splash with 2 tablespoons water and toss well together.

To make the topping, melt the butter in a small pan, stir in the oats and the remaining muscovado sugar and add a pinch of cinnamon. Sprinkle over the plums and bake in the oven for 40–45 minutes until bubbling and golden. Serve with the yogurt.

6 ripe plums
12 stoned prunes
6 tablespoons maple
  syrup (or honey)
75g dark muscovado
  sugar
100g butter
200g porridge oats
pinch of ground cinnamon
yogurt, to serve

AVOCADO MASH WITH ROAST CHERRY TOMATOES & TORTILLA CRISPS.
DUCK BURGERS WITH ROAST PLUMS & SWEET POTATOES.
POIRE BELLE HÉLÈNE.

60 min   Preheat your oven to 200°C/gas mark 6. Begin with the starter. Place the whole peppers in a roasting tin and roast for 20–30 minutes or until charred all over and very tender. Remove from the oven and cover with a damp cloth (see page 24).

To make the duck burgers, remove the skin from the duck legs with a sharp knife and cut away the flesh from the bones in large chunks. Chop the flesh into 5mm cubes and place half of the meat in the bowl of a food processor with the breadcrumbs and dried cranberries. (Keep the rest of the diced meat to one side.)

50 min   Cut the sweet potatoes in half lengthways, and score the cut side like a harlequin with a small, sharp knife. Place cut-side up on a large baking tray and drizzle with 2–3 tablespoons of the olive oil. Season with sea salt flakes. Bake in the top of the oven for 45 minutes or until tender and lightly golden in places.

Meanwhile, chop the sage and lovage (or celery leaves), add them to the food processor with the duck mixture and blitz until roughly chopped, almost to a paste. Tip into a bowl and add the reserved diced meat and some salt and pepper. Finely grate in the zest from the orange. Finely chop the onion and add to the bowl.

40 min   Trim the liver and remove the tough membrane in the centre of each piece with a small, sharp knife. (This doesn't take long; you can usually see them as they are white.) Chop the liver into 5mm cubes and combine thoroughly with the duck leg mixture in the bowl.

For the dessert, place a sliver of lemon zest in a large pan and squeeze in the lemon juice. Pour in 1 litre water, add the sugar and place the pan over a lowish heat to dissolve the sugar. Cut the vanilla pod (if using) in half lengthways and scrape the seeds into the pan. Add the split pod.

30 min   Peel the pears and, keeping them whole, slide them into the pan. Bring to the boil, and then poach gently for 30–40 minutes, or until tender when pierced with the point of a knife.

20 min   Tip the whole plums into a small roasting tin or oven-proof dish. Place in the middle of the oven and roast for about 20–30 minutes, or until the skins split open, the flesh is tender and the juices start to ooze out. Remove from the oven and taste the juice to see if you think it needs sweetening. If necessary, sprinkle with a little caster sugar and return to the oven for a further 5 minutes.

Meanwhile, roast the tomatoes for the starter. Mix the olive oil in a small bowl with the chilli flakes and season well. Place the cherry tomatoes and olives in a roasting tray, drizzle with the chilli oil and roast in the bottom of the oven for 10–15 minutes, or until the tomatoes are very soft and lightly charred, but still holding together.

10 min   Cut the tortillas, if using, into thin strips and spread out on 2 baking sheets. Place in the oven and bake for 3–4 minutes until crisp.

To make the avocado mash, squeeze the juice from the limes into a serving bowl. Remove the stones from the avocados and scoop the flesh into the bowl with a large spoon, scraping close to the skin. Season with sea salt flakes and freshly ground black pepper. Mash the avocados with a fork, keeping the texture quite chunky. Peel the peppers and remove the seeds, and then slice the flesh into small strips. Stir into the avocado mash. Top with about half of the soured cream.

To serve the starter, pull the tomatoes from the vine (use a fork if they are too hot to handle) and arrange them on top of the avocado mash. Scatter with the olives and add the

cooking juices from the tin. Accompany with the remaining soured cream and the tortilla crisps (or crusty bread).

To cook the burgers for the main course, heat 1 tablespoon of the olive oil in a large frying pan over a moderate heat. (I would leave this until after you have finished eating your starter.) Roughly divide the duck mixture into 12 burgers and place in the pan – you will probably need to do this in batches. Fry for about 3–4 minutes on each side, so that the burgers are crispy and brown on the outside and just tender in the centre. Transfer the cooked burgers to a plate while you cook the rest, adding a little more oil to the pan if necessary.

To serve the main course, place 2 sweet potato halves on each plate, top with 2 duck burgers and spoon a couple of plums with any of the cooked juices over the top.

To make the chocolate sauce for the dessert, heat the dark brown sugar and cream in a small pan and stir until the sugar has dissolved. Remove the pan from the heat, break in the chocolate and stir until melted.

To serve the dessert, cut a sliver from the bottom of each pear so it can stand upright on a plate. Accompany with the vanilla ice cream and hot chocolate sauce, and a little of the poaching syrup.

<u>Avocado Mash with Roast Cherry Tomatoes & Tortilla Crisps</u>
2 red Romano or other red peppers
2 tablespoons olive oil
pinch of dried chilli flakes
300g cherry tomatoes on the vine
handful of kalamata olives
6 flour tortillas (or good crusty bread)
juice of 2–3 limes
3 ripe avocados (I use Hass)
150ml soured cream
sea salt flakes and freshly ground black pepper

<u>Duck Burgers with Roast Plums & Sweet Potatoes</u>
6 small sweet potatoes
3–4 tablespoons olive oil
12 whole plums
a little caster sugar, for sprinkling
2 duck legs
50g fresh breadcrumbs (see page 27)
25g dried cranberries
a few sage leaves
25g lovage (or celery leaves and soft celery sticks
 from the heart of a celery head)
1 orange
1 red onion
350g duck liver
sea salt flakes and freshly ground black pepper

<u>Poire Belle Hélène</u>
1 lemon
100g caster sugar
1 vanilla pod (optional)
6 large pears
2 tablespoons dark brown or molasses sugar
3 tablespoons double cream
150g dark chocolate, not too bitter
vanilla ice cream, to serve

AVOCADO MASH WITH ROAST CHERRY TOMATOES & TORTILLA CRISPS

The creamy avocado and tomatoes with a hint of chilli is simple, yet delicious.

Preheat your oven to 200°C/gas mark 6.

Place the whole peppers in a roasting tin and roast for 20–30 minutes or until charred all over and very tender. Remove from the oven and cover with a damp cloth (see page 24).

Mix the olive oil in a small bowl with the chilli flakes and season well. Place the cherry tomatoes and olives in a roasting tray, drizzle with the chilli oil and roast for 10–15 minutes, or until the tomatoes are very soft and lightly charred, but still holding together.

Cut the tortillas, if using, into thin strips and spread out on 2 baking sheets. Place in the oven and bake for 3–4 minutes until crisp.

Squeeze the juice from the limes into a serving bowl. Remove the stones from the avocados and scoop the flesh into the bowl with a large spoon, scraping close to the skin. Season with sea salt flakes and freshly ground black pepper. Mash the avocados with a fork, keeping the texture quite chunky. Peel the peppers and remove the seeds, and then slice the flesh into small strips. Stir into the avocado mash. Top with about half of the soured cream.

Pull the tomatoes from the vine (use a fork if they are too hot to handle) and arrange them on top of the avocado mash. Scatter with the olives and scrape in any of the cooking juices from the tin.

Serve the remaining soured cream on the side, along with the tortilla crisps (or crusty bread).

2 red Romano or
  other red peppers
2 tablespoons olive oil
pinch of dried chilli flakes
300g cherry tomatoes
  on the vine
handful of kalamata
  olives
6 flour tortillas
  (or good crusty bread)
juice of 2–3 limes
3 ripe avocados
  (I use Hass)
150ml soured cream
sea salt flakes and freshly
  ground black pepper

DUCK BURGERS WITH ROAST PLUMS & SWEET POTATOES

The sharpness of the roast plums cuts through the richness of the duck.

Preheat your oven to 200°C/gas mark 6. Cut the sweet potatoes in half lengthways, and score the cut side like a harlequin with a small, sharp knife. Place cut-side up on a large baking tray and drizzle with 2–3 tablespoons of the olive oil. Season with sea salt flakes. Bake for 45 minutes or until tender and lightly golden in places.

Tip the whole plums into a small roasting tin or oven-proof dish. Place in the oven and roast for about 20–30 minutes, or until the skins split open, the flesh is tender and the juices start to ooze out. Remove from the oven and taste the juice to see if you think it needs sweetening. If necessary, sprinkle with a little caster sugar and return to the oven for a further 5 minutes.

Meanwhile, remove the skin from the duck legs with a sharp knife and cut away the flesh from the bones in large chunks. Chop the flesh into 5mm cubes and place half of the meat in the bowl of a food processor with the breadcrumbs and dried cranberries. (Keep the rest of the diced meat to one side.)

Chop the sage and lovage (or celery leaves), add them to the processor and blitz until roughly chopped, almost to a paste. Tip into a bowl and add the reserved diced meat and some salt and pepper. Finely grate in the zest from the orange. Finely chop the onion and add to the bowl.

Trim the liver and remove the tough membrane in the centre of each piece with a small, sharp knife. (This doesn't take long; you can usually see them as they are white.) Chop the liver into 5mm cubes and mix thoroughly with the duck leg mixture in the bowl.

To cook the burgers, heat 1 tablespoon of the olive oil in a large frying pan over a moderate heat. Roughly divide the duck mixture into 12 burgers and drop into the pan – you will need to cook them in batches. Fry for about 3–4 minutes on each side, so that the burgers are crispy and brown on the outside and just tender in the centre. Transfer the cooked burgers to a plate while you cook the rest, adding a little more oil to the pan if necessary.

To serve, place 2 sweet potato halves on each plate, top with 2 duck burgers and spoon a couple of plums with any of the cooked juices over the top.

6 small sweet
  potatoes, scrubbed
3–4 tablespoons olive oil
12 whole plums
a little caster sugar,
  for sprinkling
2 duck legs
50g fresh breadcrumbs
  (see page 27)
25g dried cranberries
a few sage leaves
25g lovage (or celery
  leaves and soft celery
  sticks from the heart of a
  celery head)
1 orange
1 red onion
350g duck liver
sea salt flakes and freshly
  ground black pepper

POIRE BELLE HÉLÈNE

This classic combination of poached pear and chocolate sauce was divised by Auguste Escoffier in 1864, in celebration of the operetta La Belle Hélène.

Place a sliver of lemon zest in a large pan and squeeze in the lemon juice. Pour in 1 litre water, add the sugar and place over a lowish heat to dissolve the sugar. Cut the vanilla pod (if using) in half lengthways and scrape the seeds into the pan. Add the split pod.

Meanwhile, peel the pears. Keeping them whole, slide the pears into the pan. Bring to the boil, and then poach gently for 30–40 minutes, or until tender when pierced with a knife.

To make the chocolate sauce, heat the dark brown sugar and cream in a pan and stir until the sugar has dissolved. Remove from the heat, break in the chocolate and stir until melted.

To serve, cut a sliver from the bottom of each pear so it can stand upright on a plate. Accompany with the vanilla ice cream, hot chocolate sauce, and a little of the poaching syrup.

1 lemon
100g caster sugar
1 vanilla pod (optional)
6 large pears
2 tablespoons dark brown
 or molasses sugar
3 tablespoons
 double cream
150g dark chocolate,
 not too bitter
vanilla ice cream,
 to serve

BAKED BEETROOT & TOMATO SALAD.
PORK & FIG SPIEDINI WITH ORANGE SPICE DRESSING & WHITE BEAN & ROCKET MASH.
SCHIACCIATA CON L'UVA (GRAPE BREAD) WITH GORGONZOLA DOLCE.

60 min   Preheat your oven to 200°C/gas mark 6. Trim the beetroots, removing the stringy roots but leaving 5cm of stalk on top. Scrub really well, wrap in foil and bake in the oven for 30–40 minutes until tender.

Now for the dessert. Tip the raisins into a small bowl, pour over the wine and set aside.

Place the bread mix in a large bowl and add a pinch of salt. Make a well in the centre and pour in the oil and 320ml lukewarm water (the amount of water will vary depending on the make of your mix, so refer to the packet instructions). Mix together with a fork until a dough starts to form, and then tip out onto your work surface and knead well for 5 minutes. Place the dough back in the bowl, cover with clingfilm and set aside to rest for 5 minutes.

50 min   Remove the grapes from their stalks, halve and tip into a large bowl. Crush the walnuts roughly using a rolling pin and add to the bowl with the grapes. Mix together. Crush the fennel seeds (if using) in a pestle and mortar and add to the bowl. Grease a large baking tray.

Cut the dough in half and roll out each half to form a 23cm circle. Place one circle of dough on the baking tray. Drain the raisins and combine with the grape and walnut mixture. Spread half of this mixture evenly over the dough base. Top with the second circle of dough and scatter with the rest of the grape, walnut and raisin mixture. Cover loosely with clingfilm or a tea towel and leave for about 20–30 minutes until doubled in size.

40 min   To make the marinade for the pork, finely grate the zest from the orange, squeeze the juice and place together in a large bowl. Add the thyme to the bowl with the spices and 3 tablespoons olive oil. Cut the pork fillets into rounds about 1cm thick. Cut each fig into 4 wedges. Add the pork and figs to the marinade, season with salt

and pepper and toss well together. Set aside to marinate for 15–20 minutes.

Meanwhile, soak 12 long wooden skewers in warm water. Open the tins of butter beans, rinse and drain well.

30 min   To make the dressing for the starter, mix together the maple syrup, vinegar, mustard and oil in a large serving bowl. Crush the caraway seeds in a pestle and mortar and add to dressing with some salt and pepper. Chop the tomatoes into large chunks and add to the serving bowl. Wash and dry the spinach. Remove the leaves from the herbs and chop roughly; set aside.

20 min   Remove the cooked beetroots from the oven, cut each one into 6 wedges (no need to peel first) and add to the bowl with the tomatoes. Increase the oven temperature to 220°C/gas mark 7.

Place the grape bread on the middle shelf of the oven and cook for about 30 minutes, or until the bread is golden brown and sounds hollow when tapped on the base.

Preheat the grill to high. Thread the slices of pork by weaving each piece onto a wooden skewer. Add a couple of fig wedges to each one and place the skewers on a large baking tray. Drizzle over any of the remaining marinade.

10 min   Place the pork skewers under the grill for 5–8 minutes or until the meat is tender and cooked through. Meanwhile, make the white bean mash. Crush the garlic. Heat 100ml olive oil with the garlic in a pan over a low heat. Place the drained butter beans in a food processor and blend until smooth, then tip into the garlic oil and stir well to combine. Cook over a low heat for 5 minutes, stirring occasionally, until heated through. Stir in the Parmesan and rocket or salad leaves, until they start to wilt, and season.

To serve the starter, add the spinach leaves and herbs to the bowl with the tomatoes and beetroot and toss everything together. Divide between your starter plates and serve immediately.

To serve the main course, place a large spoonful of the white bean mash on each serving plate, top with 2 pork skewers and drizzle over a little more oil.

To serve the cheese course, cut the bread into thin slivers. Transfer to a large serving plate or wooden board, take to the table and serve with the Gorgonzola on the side.

Baked Beetroot & Tomato Salad
6 medium raw beetroots (see page 24)
1 tablespoon maple syrup
1 tablespoon balsamic vinegar
1 teaspoon wholegrain mustard
3 tablespoons extra-virgin olive oil
1 teaspoon caraway seeds
300g baby leaf spinach
15g mint leaves
15g coriander leaves
6 tomatoes
sea salt and freshly ground black pepper

Pork & Fig Spiedini with Orange Spice Dressing & White Bean & Rocket Mash
3 x 400g tins butter beans (see page 8)
1 large orange
15g thyme leaves
½ teaspoon each ground cinnamon, nutmeg, allspice and clove
100ml olive oil, plus 3 tablespoons, plus extra for drizzling
2 x 500g pork fillets, trimmed of any sinew
6 figs
3 garlic cloves

50g Parmesan cheese, grated
100g rocket or other baby salad leaves
sea salt and freshly ground black pepper
12 wooden skewers

Schiacciata con L'uva (Grape Bread) with Gorgonzola Dolce
100g raisins
125ml red wine (or dessert wine)
500g white bread mix (suitable for hand baking)
sea salt
2 tablespoons olive oil, plus a little extra for greasing
250g small black seedless grapes
100g walnuts
½ teaspoon fennel seeds (optional)
400g Gorgonzola Dolce cheese, to serve

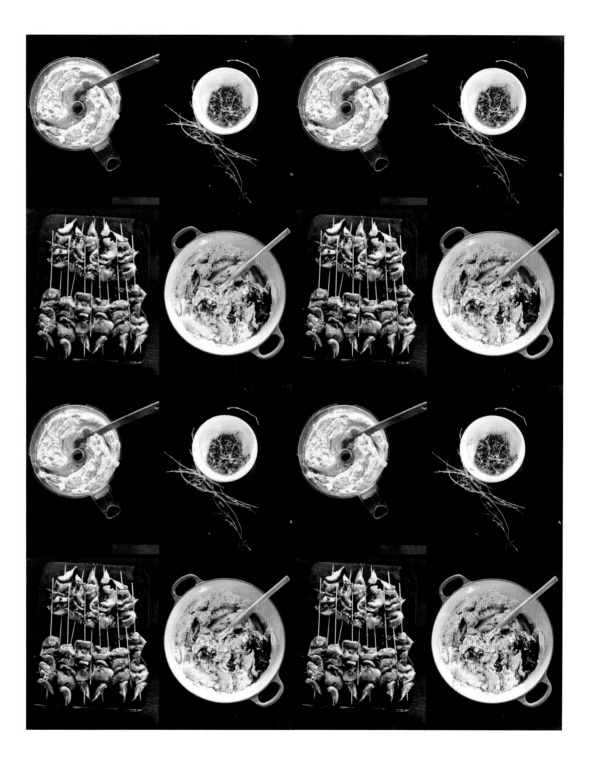

BAKED BEETROOT & TOMATO SALAD

A blue cheese such as Spanish Pico de Gallo or Italian Gorgonzola would work well with this salad, and perhaps a few little waxy potatoes to make it a bit more substantial. You could even add a handful of toasted pumpkin seeds... ad-lib at your leisure.

Preheat your oven to 200°C/gas mark 6.

Trim the beetroots, removing the stringy roots but leaving 5cm of stalk on top. Scrub really well, wrap in foil and bake in the oven for 30–40 minutes until tender.

In a large serving bowl, mix together the maple syrup, vinegar, mustard and oil. Crush the caraway seeds in a pestle and mortar and add to dressing with some salt and pepper.

Wash and dry the spinach. Remove the leaves from the herbs and chop roughly.

Chop the tomatoes into large chunks and add to the serving bowl.

Remove the cooked beetroots from the oven, cut each one into 6 wedges (no need to peel first) and add to the bowl.

To serve, toss all the ingredients together and divide between your starter plates.

6 medium raw beetroots (see page 24)
1 tablespoon maple syrup
1 tablespoon balsamic vinegar
1 teaspoon wholegrain mustard
3 tablespoons extra-virgin olive oil
1 teaspoon caraway seeds
300g baby leaf spinach
15g mint leaves
15g coriander leaves
6 tomatoes
sea salt and freshly ground black pepper

PORK & FIG SPIEDINI WITH ORANGE SPICE DRESSING & WHITE BEAN & ROCKET MASH

You could add a couple of tablespoons of cream to the mash if you wish.

Open the tins of beans, rinse and drain well. Finely grate the zest from the orange, squeeze the juice and add to a large bowl. Add the thyme to the bowl with the spices and 3 tablespoons olive oil.

Cut the pork fillets into rounds about 1cm thick. Cut each fig into 4 wedges. Add both to the bowl. Season with salt and pepper and toss well together. Set aside to marinate for 30 minutes. Meanwhile, soak 12 long wooden skewers in warm water.

Preheat the grill to high. Thread the slices of pork by weaving each piece onto a skewer. Add a couple of fig wedges to each one and place the skewers on a large baking tray. Drizzle over any of the remaining marinade and place under the grill for 5–8 minutes or until the meat is tender and cooked through.

Meanwhile, crush the garlic. Heat 100ml olive oil with the garlic in a medium pan over a low heat. Place the drained butter beans in a food processor and blend until smooth. Tip the blended beans into the garlic oil and stir well to combine. Cook over a low heat for 5 minutes, stirring occasionally, until fully heated through. Stir in the Parmesan and rocket or salad leaves, just so that they start to wilt, and season with salt and pepper.

To serve, place a large spoonful of the white bean mash on each serving plate, top with 2 pork skewers and drizzle with a little more olive oil.

3 x 400g tins butter beans (see page 8)
1 large orange
15g thyme leaves
½ teaspoon each ground cinnamon, nutmeg, allspice and clove
100ml olive oil, plus 3 tablespoons, plus extra for drizzling
2 x 500g pork fillets, trimmed of any sinew
6 figs
3 garlic cloves
50g Parmesan cheese, grated
100g rocket or other baby salad leaves
sea salt and freshly ground black pepper
12 wooden skewers

SCHIACCIATA CON L'UVA (GRAPE BREAD) WITH GORGONZOLA DOLCE

This is traditionally made during the grape harvest when there is an ambundance of fruit.

Tip the raisins into a small bowl, pour over the wine and set aside.

Place the bread mix in a large bowl and add a pinch of salt. Make a well in the centre and pour in the oil and 320ml lukewarm water (the amount of water will vary depending on the make of your mix, so refer to the packet instructions). Mix together with a fork until a dough starts to form, and then tip out onto your work surface and knead well for 5 minutes. Place the dough back in the bowl, cover with clingfilm and set aside to rest for 5 minutes.

Meanwhile, remove the grapes from their stalks, halve and tip into a large bowl. Crush the walnuts roughly using a rolling pin and add to the bowl with the grapes. Mix together. Crush the fennel seeds (if using) in a pestle and mortar and add to the bowl. Grease a large baking tray with a little oil.

Preheat your oven to 230°C/gas mark 8. Cut the dough in half and, using a rolling pin, roll out each half to form a 23cm circle. Place one circle of dough on of the baking tray. Drain the raisins and combine with the grape and walnut mixture. Spread half of this mixture evenly over the dough base. Top with the second circle of dough and scatter with the rest of the raisin, grape and walnut mixture. Cover loosely with clingfilm or a tea towel and leave for about 20–30 minutes until doubled in size.

Place the grape bread on the middle shelf of the oven and cook for about 30 minutes, or until the bread is golden brown and sounds hollow when tapped on the base.

Leave to cool, and then cut into thin slivers. Transfer to a large serving plate or wooden board, take to the table and serve with the Gorgonzola on the side.

100g raisins
125ml red wine
 (or dessert wine)
500g white bread mix
 (suitable for hand baking)
sea salt
2 tablespoons olive oil,
 plus a little extra
 for greasing
250g small seedless
 black grapes
100g walnuts
½ teaspoon fennel
 seeds (optional)
400g Gorgonzola
 Dolce cheese, to serve

POTAGE PARMENTIER WITH MINTED OIL.
LAMB FILLET WITH FENNEL SEED & THYME RUB WITH ROASTED SWEET & SOUR SQUASH.
MARZIPAN APPLES.

60 min Preheat your oven to 200°C/gas mark 6. Start with the soup. Chop the onion. Peel the potatoes and cut into 1.5cm cubes. Melt the butter in a large pan and stir in the potatoes and onion. Cover and cook over a low heat for 5–8 minutes until the onion is softened and translucent, stirring occasionally to prevent sticking.

50 min Add the bay leaves and milk, season with salt and pepper and bring to the boil. Reduce the heat and simmer for 15–20 minutes or until the potatoes are very tender.

Meanwhile, cut the squash in half lengthways and scoop out the seeds. Cut the flesh into 3.5cm pieces (no need to peel) and place in a large roasting tin. Remove the leaves from the sage, ripping any large leaves in half, and add to the tin with the olive oil and sugar. Season well and toss all together. Bake in the oven for 30–40 minutes, turning occasionally.

40 min Now for the dessert. Using an apple corer, remove the cores from the apples. Finely chop the orange peel. Knead the marzipan with the cinnamon and orange peel, divide into 6 pieces and roll into sausage shapes. Push each piece into the cavity of each apple. Rub the apples with the butter, place in a baking dish and bake in the oven for about 30–35 minutes until tender, basting occasionally.

30 min Back to the main course. To make the marinade for the lamb, place the garlic and lemon zest in a pestle and mortar with the thyme leaves, fennel seeds, chilli flakes (if using) and 2 tablespoons of the olive oil. Pound together to create a coarse paste. Place the lamb in a dish and rub the marinade all over each fillet. Set aside to marinate for at least 10 minutes.

The soup should now be ready. Remove it from the heat and leave to cool for about 10 minutes.

20 min To make the minted oil, remove the mint leaves from the stalks and chop roughly. Place in the bowl of a small food processor or spice grinder, along with two-thirds of the oil, and blitz until smooth. Scrape into a bowl, add the remaining oil and season.

Remove the squash from the oven, scatter the pecans over the top and return to the oven for a further 10 minutes.

10 min To cook the lamb, heat the remaining oil in an oven-proof frying pan. Season the fillets all over with salt and pepper and brown over a high heat for 2–3 minutes. Transfer to the oven to finish cooking for 8–10 minutes, or until tender but still pink in the middle. Transfer to a serving plate, cover with foil to keep warm and leave to rest.

To finish the soup, take out the bay leaves and purée in a blender until smooth. Pass through a fine sieve back into the pan. Reheat gently.

The squash should now be cooked. Remove it from the oven, place it directly on the hob and add the vinegar. Boil over a high heat until the pan is almost dry. Toss together and set aside.

To serve the starter, check the seasoning and ladle into soup bowls. Drizzle a few droplets of the minted oil over the surface.

To serve the main course, slice the lamb thinly and serve with the butternut squash.

To serve the dessert, place a baked apple on each plate and accompany with a dollop of the crème fraîche on the side.

Potage Parmentier with Minted Oil
1 large onion
600g floury potatoes
50g unsalted butter
2 fresh bay leaves
1.2 litres milk
25g mint
75ml extra-virgin olive oil
sea salt and freshly ground black pepper

Lamb Fillet with Fennel Seed & Thyme Rub
2 garlic cloves
finely grated zest of 1 lemon
15g thyme leaves
1 tablespoon fennel seeds
pinch of dried chilli flakes (optional)
3 tablespoons extra-virgin olive oil
900g whole lamb neck fillets
 (2–3 depending on size)
sea salt and freshly ground black pepper

Roasted Sweet & Sour Squash
1kg butternut squash
25g sage
75ml olive oil
25g golden caster sugar
50g pecan nuts
50ml sherry or red wine vinegar
sea salt and freshly ground black pepper

Marzipan Apples
6 apples
25g good-quality candied orange peel
100g natural undyed marzipan
pinch of ground cinnamon
50g butter, softened
200ml crème fraîche, to serve

POTAGE PARMENTIER WITH MINTED OIL

Named after the pioneer of nutritional chemistry, Antoine-Augustin Parmentier (1737–1813), a huge fan and promoter of the potato. This is a delicious and comfortably warming soup.

Chop the onion. Peel the potatoes and cut into 1.5cm cubes. Melt the butter in a large pan and stir in the potatoes and onion. Cover and cook over a low heat for 5–8 minutes until the onion is softened and translucent, stirring occasionally to stop everything from sticking. Add the bay leaves, milk, salt and pepper and bring to the boil. Reduce the heat and simmer for 15–20 minutes or until the potatoes are very tender.

Remove from the heat and leave to cool for about 10 minutes. Take out the bay leaves and purée the soup in a blender until smooth. Pass through a fine sieve back into the pan.

To make the minted oil, remove the mint leaves from the stalks and chop roughly. Place in the bowl of a small food processor or spice grinder, along with two-thirds of the oil, and blitz until smooth. Scrape into a bowl, add the remaining oil and season.

To serve, ladle the soup into soup bowls and drizzle droplets of the oil over the surface.

1 large onion
600g floury potatoes
50g unsalted butter
2 fresh bay leaves
1.2 litres milk
25g mint
75ml extra-virgin olive oil
sea salt and freshly
  ground black pepper

LAMB FILLET WITH FENNEL SEED & THYME RUB WITH ROASTED SWEET & SOUR SQUASH

Use other varieties of squash or pumpkin if available, you may need to remove the tough skin of some varieties.

Place the garlic and lemon zest in a pestle and mortar with the thyme leaves, fennel seeds, chilli flakes (if using) and 2 tablespoons of the olive oil. Pound together to create a coarse paste. Place the lamb in a dish and rub the marinade all over each fillet. Set aside to marinate for 30 minutes–1 hour.

Preheat your oven to 200°C/gas mark 6.

Cut the squash in half lengthways and scoop out the seeds. Cut the flesh into 3.5cm pieces (no need to peel) and place in a large roasting tin. Remove the leaves from the sage, ripping any large leaves in half, and add to the tin with the olive oil and sugar. Season well and toss all together.

Bake the squash in the oven for 30–40 minutes, turning occasionally. Scatter with the pecans for the last 10 minutes.

Heat the remaining oil for the lamb in an oven-proof frying pan. Season the fillets all over with salt and pepper and brown over a high heat for 2–3 minutes, turning occasionally. Transfer to the oven to finish cooking for 8–10 minutes. Remove from the oven and leave to rest for 5 minutes before slicing.

Remove the squash from the oven and place the tin directly on the hob. Add the vinegar and boil rapidly until the pan is almost dry. Remove from the heat, toss well together and tip into a large serving bowl.

To serve, cut the lamb into thin slices and serve with the butternut squash.

2 garlic cloves
finely grated zest
  of 1 lemon
15g thyme leaves
1 tablespoon fennel seeds
pinch of dried chilli flakes
  (optional)
3 tablespoons
  extra-virgin olive oil
900g whole lamb
  neck fillets, (2–3
  depending on size)
sea salt and freshly
  ground black pepper

For the Sweet & Sour
Squash
1kg butternut squash
25g fresh sage
75ml olive oil
25g golden caster sugar
50g pecan nuts
50ml sherry or red wine
  vinegar
sea salt and freshly
  ground black pepper

MARZIPAN APPLES

Avoid the very finely chopped candied orange peel if you can. It feels as though it has been kept for too long and is often bitter.

Preheat your oven to 200°C/gas mark 6.

Using an apple corer, remove the cores from the apples. Finely chop the orange peel. Knead the marzipan with the cinnamon and orange peel, divide into 6 pieces and roll each one into a sausage shape. Push one piece of the flavoured marzipan into the cavity of each apple.

Rub the apples all over with the butter, place in a baking dish and bake for about 30–35 minutes until tender, basting occasionally. Serve warm with a dollop of the crème fraîche on the side.

6 apples
25g good-quality
 candied orange peel
100g natural
 undyed marzipan
pinch of ground cinnamon
50g butter, softened
200ml crème fraîche,
 to serve

SWEET POTATO PAKORAS WITH COCONUT CHUTNEY.
BEETROOT & ORANGE RISOTTO WITH PRAWNS & WASABI MASCARPONE.
TREACLE NUT TART.

60 min   Preheat your oven to 190°C/gas mark 5. Trim the beetroots, removing any stringy roots and leaving 5cm of stalk on top. Wrap the beetroots in foil and bake for about 45 minutes or until tender.

To make the dessert, roll out the pastry thinly and use to line a 25cm tart tin. Cut a piece of parchment paper slightly bigger than the tin, place on the pastry lining and fill with baking beans. Bake in the oven for 10 minutes, then remove the paper and beans and cook for a further 5 minutes.

50 min   To make the chutney, finely chop the mint leaves. Finely grate the zest and squeeze the juice from the lime. Place the yogurt in a bowl, stir in the coconut, mint, lime zest and juice and season with salt and pepper.

To make the filling for the tart, cut the crusts off the bread and blitz in a food processor to make fine breadcrumbs – you need about 150g. Finely grate the zest and squeeze the juice from the lemon and mix together in a bowl with the breadcrumbs, syrup and the whole nuts. Remove the tart case from the oven, fill it with the breadcrumb mixture, level the top and return to the oven for 30–35 minutes or until lightly golden all over.

40 min   Now for the risotto. Finely chop the onion, fennel, celery and carrots and crush the garlic cloves. Heat the butter and oil together in a large, heavy-based saucepan, add the finely chopped vegetables and cook slowly over a moderate-to-low heat for 15 minutes without colouring, or until well softened.

30 min   To make the pakoras, thinly slice the sweet potatoes (no need to peel). Finely chop the red chilli. Mix together the gram flour, kalonji, turmeric, cinnamon and salt in a large bowl, add the chilli and then gradually whisk in 200–250ml water to make a fairly thick batter.

20 min   Back to the risotto. Remove the beetroots from the oven and leave them to cool slightly before peeling away the skins. Finely grate the zest from the orange and squeeze the juice.

The vegetables should now be soft. Chop the tomato and beetroot and add to the pan with the orange zest and thyme. Increase the heat and cook for 2 minutes, stirring. Meanwhile, place the stock in another pan and bring to just below boiling point; keep on the heat.

Add the rice to the vegetables and cook for about 2 minutes, stirring, or until the grains are slightly translucent. Add the vermouth (or wine) and orange juice and keep stirring until all of the liquid has been absorbed. Add a ladleful of the hot stock, stir in well and reduce the heat. Keep adding the stock, one ladleful at a time, stirring and making sure that each ladleful has been absorbed before adding the next. (You don't need to stir the risotto constantly – you can do other things – but you do need to stir it frequently to prevent it from sticking.)

10 min   While the rice is cooking, beat the mascarpone in a small bowl. Chop the dill finely and add half to the mascarpone with the wasabi and some salt and pepper to taste.

After about 15–20 minutes, check to see if the rice is cooked – the grains should be very slightly *al dente*. (If you feel the risotto needs a bit more liquid, you can always add a drop of boiling water if all your stock has been used up.) Once the risotto is cooked, remove the pan from the heat, check for seasoning, and then cover and leave to stand for 5 minutes.

Meanwhile, cook the pakoras. Heat the oil in a large, deep pan or wok. To check it is hot enough, drop in a cube of bread – it should turn golden brown in 40 seconds. Dip the

sweet potato slices into the batter a few pieces at a time and fry until golden. Drain on kitchen paper. To serve the starter, sprinkle the pakoras with sea salt flakes and serve hot with the chutney.

To serve the main course, spoon the risotto into soup bowls and top with a dollop of the wasabi mascarpone. Scatter with a few prawns and sprinkle with the remaining dill.

To serve the dessert, cut the treacle tart into wedges and accompany with the single cream.

Sweet Potato Pakoras
500g sweet potatoes
1 fresh red chilli
250g gram (chickpea) flour
2 teaspoons kalonji (black onion seeds)
½ teaspoon ground turmeric
1 teaspoon ground cinnamon
1 teaspoon salt
groundnut oil, for deep-frying
sea salt flakes, to serve

Coconut chutney
15g mint leaves
½ lime
400g natural yogurt
8 tablespoons unsweetened desiccated coconut
sea salt flakes and freshly ground black pepper

Beetroot & Orange Risotto with Prawns & Wasabi Mascarpone
1kg small raw beetroots
1 large onion
1 fennel bulb
4 celery sticks
2 carrots
2 garlic cloves

50g butter
2 tablespoons olive oil
1 orange
1 large tomato
2 sprigs of thyme
1.2 litres chicken or vegetable stock
400g risotto rice (such as Carnaroli or Arborio)
200ml dry white vermouth or white wine
250g mascarpone
10g dill
½–1 teaspoon wasabi paste, to taste
250g cooked peeled prawns
sea salt and freshly ground black pepper

Treacle Nut Tart
350g shortcrust or sweetcrust pastry
6 thick slices of white bread (see page 27)
½ lemon
250g golden syrup
200g mixed whole nuts
300ml single cream, to serve

SWEET POTATO PAKORAS WITH COCONUT CHUTNEY

If you're not keen on coconut, why not serve with mango chutney or sweet chilli sauce.

To make the chutney, remove the mint leaves from their stalks and chop finely. Finely grate the zest and squeeze the juice from the lime. Place the yogurt in a bowl, stir in the coconut, the lime zest and juice and the mint and season with salt and pepper.

To make the pakoras, thinly slice the sweet potatoes (no need to peel). Finely chop the red chilli. Mix together the gram flour, kalonji, turmeric, cinnamon and salt in a large bowl, add the chilli and then gradually whisk in 200–250ml water to make a fairly thick batter.

Heat the oil in a large, deep pan or wok. To check it is hot enough, drop in a cube of bread – it should turn golden brown in 40 seconds.

Dip the potato slices into the batter a few pieces at a time and fry until golden. Drain on kitchen paper, sprinkle with sea salt flakes and serve hot with the chutney.

500g sweet
 potatoes
1 fresh red chilli
250g gram (chickpea)
 flour
2 teaspoons kalonji
 (black onion seeds)
½ teaspoon ground
 turmeric
1 teaspoon ground
 cinnamon
1 teaspoon salt
groundnut oil,
 for deep-frying
sea salt flakes, to serve

For the coconut chutney
15g mint
½ lime
400g natural yogurt
8 tablespoons
 unsweetened
 desiccated coconut
sea salt and freshly
 ground black pepper

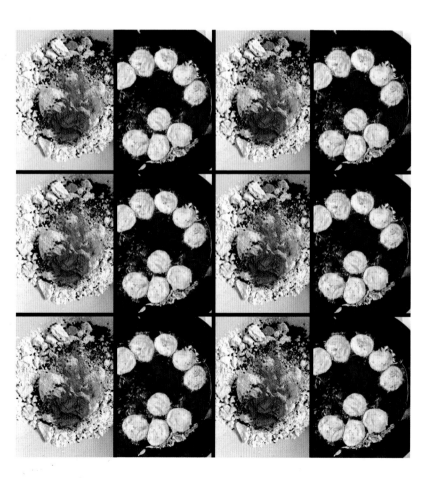

BEETROOT & ORANGE RISOTTO WITH PRAWNS & WASABI MASCARPONE

Stunningly beautiful risotto.

Preheat your oven to 190°C/gas mark 5.

Trim the beetroots, removing any stringy roots and leaving 5cm of stalk on top. Wrap the beetroots in foil and bake for about 45 minutes or until tender. Leave until cool enough to handle, and then peel. Finely chop the onion, fennel, celery and carrots and crush the garlic cloves.

Heat the butter and oil together in a large, heavy-based saucepan and add the onion, fennel, celery, carrots and garlic. Cook slowly over a low-to-moderate heat for 15 minutes without colouring until well softened.

Finely grate the zest from the orange and squeeze the juice. Chop the tomato and beetroots and add to the saucepan with the orange zest and thyme. Increase the heat and cook for 2 minutes, stirring. Meanwhile, place the stock in another pan and bring to just below boiling point; keep on the heat. Add the rice to the vegetables and stir for about 2 minutes, or until the grains are slightly translucent. Add the vermouth (or wine) and orange juice and keep stirring until all of the liquid has been absorbed. Add a ladleful of the hot stock, stir in well and reduce the heat. Keep adding ladlefuls of stock, stirring and making sure that each ladleful has been absorbed before adding the next. (You don't need to stir the risotto constantly – you can do other things – but you do need to stir it frequently to prevent it from sticking.)

After about 15–20 minutes, check to see if the rice is cooked: the grains should be very slightly *al dente*. If you feel it needs a little more time you can always add a drop of boiling water if all the stock has been used up. Once the risotto is cooked, remove the pan from the heat, check for seasoning, and then cover and leave to stand for 5 minutes.

Beat the mascarpone in a small bowl. Finely chop the dill and add half to to the mascarpone with the wasabi and some salt and pepper to taste.

To serve, spoon the risotto into soup bowls and top with a dollop of the wasabi mascarpone. Scatter over a few peeled prawns and sprinkle with the remaining dill.

1kg small raw beetroots
1 large onion
1 fennel bulb
4 celery sticks
2 carrots
2 garlic cloves
50g butter
2 tablespoons olive oil
1 orange
1 large tomato
2 sprigs of thyme
1.2 litres chicken
 or vegetable stock
400g risotto rice (such
 as Carnaroli or Arborio)
200ml dry white vermouth
 or white wine
250g mascarpone
10g fresh dill
½–1 teaspoon wasabi
 paste, to taste
250g cooked
 peeled prawns
sea salt and freshly
 ground black pepper

TREACLE NUT TART

A nutty and chewy twist on a classic.

Preheat your oven to 190°C/gas mark 5. Roll out the pastry thinly and use to line a 25cm tart tin. Cut a piece of parchment paper slightly bigger than the tin, place on the pastry lining and fill with baking beans. Place in the oven and bake for 10 minutes, and then remove the paper and beans and cook for a further 5 minutes (see page 35).

Cut the crusts off the bread and blitz in a food processor to make fine breadcrumbs – you need about 150g. Finely grate the zest and squeeze the juice from the lemon and mix together in a bowl with the breadcrumbs, syrup and the whole nuts. Fill the tart case, level the top and bake for 30–35 minutes or until lightly golden all over.

To serve, cut into wedges and accompany with the single cream.

350g shortcrust
 or sweetcrust pastry
6 thick slices of
 white bread
 (see page 27)
½ lemon
250g golden syrup
200g mixed whole nuts
300ml single cream,
 to serve

CHICKPEA & HAZELNUT HUMMUS WITH ROAST PARSNIP CHIPS.
SMOKED HADDOCK & LEEK CHOWDER WITH FAUX CAVIAR & CRACKERS.
HONEYED QUINCE & VANILLA TARTE TATIN.

60 min   Preheat your oven to 200°C/gas mark 6. Begin with the starter. Cut the parsnips into long, thin chips. Place in a roasting tin, drizzle with 5 tablespoons of the olive oil, season with salt, pepper and the paprika and toss well together. Place in the oven and cook for 45–50 minutes, turning occasionally, until golden all over and slightly crisp. Add the sesame seeds for the last 10 minutes.

Scatter the hazelnuts on a baking sheet and roast for 5–10 minutes or until golden. Tip onto a plate and leave to cool slightly.

50 min   Now for the dessert. Peel and core the quinces (or pears) and cut into large wedges. Place in a bowl, squeeze over the lemon juice and toss well together. Melt the butter and honey over a moderate heat in a 23cm oven-proof frying pan (or cake tin with a fixed base). Cut the vanilla pod in half lengthways and scrape the seeds into the butter and honey mixture. Drop in the pod too. Cook over a moderate heat for about 5–8 minutes, until the mixture starts to caramelise. Add the quince slices and cook gently until just starting to soften and turn amber-coloured. Remove from the heat.

40 min   Roll out the pastry so it is 2.5–5cm larger all round than the pan. Slide the pastry on top of the quinces and tuck in the edges inside the rim of the pan. Transfer to the oven for about 30–40 minutes until crisp and golden.

Meanwhile, get on with the main course. Place the haddock skin-side up in a shallow pan and pour over the milk and 500ml water to cover. Bring to just below boiling point, reduce the heat and poach gently for about 5–8 minutes or until just cooked.

Slice the leeks thinly and wash very well to remove any dirt, then drain. Cut the pancetta (or bacon) into little cubes and chop the onion.

30 min   Carefully lift the cooked fish onto a plate and set aside. Strain the poaching liquid through a fine sieve into a jug and reserve.

Melt the butter in a large pan over a low-to-moderate heat, add the pancetta and cook for about 5 minutes or until just starting to get crispy. Add the chopped onion and leeks and sauté gently for 5–10 minutes until softened.

Meanwhile, prepare the ingredients for the hummus. Crush the garlic. Drain and rinse the chickpeas, and then drain again. Chop the parsley. Squeeze the juice from the lemon.

20 min   The onions and leeks should now be soft. Add the flour to the pan and cook, stirring, for 1–2 minutes without colouring. Stir in a little of the reserved fish-poaching liquid and mix until smooth, then add the remainder. Cube the potatoes and add to the pot with the bay leaves. Simmer for 8–10 minutes until tender.

Gently scrape away the skin from the haddock and break the flesh into large flakes, removing any bones. Chop the parsley (reserve a couple of teaspoons) and roughly chop the watercress.

10 min   To make the hummus, roughly chop 2–3 tablespoons of the roasted hazelnuts and place in a small bowl. Add a handful of the chickpeas, 2 tablespoons of the olive oil, some salt and pepper and a pinch of smoked paprika. Mix well and set aside.

Place the remaining chickpeas and hazelnuts in a food processor with the tahini and blitz until smooth. With the motor running, gradually pour in the remaining olive oil in a thin stream until well incorporated. Tip out into a serving bowl, stir in half the parsley, season with salt and pepper and add lemon juice to taste. Spoon the reserved chickpea and hazelnut mixture over the top.

To serve the starter, sprinkle the hummus with the remaining parsley. Tip the hot parsnip chips into a large serving dish and accompany with the bowl of hummus for everyone to dip into.

To finish the main course, stir the chopped parsley (reserve a couple of tablespoons) and watercress into the soup, along with the cream. Bring to a simmer, carefully fold in the chunks of fish and remove from the heat. Season to taste with salt and pepper.

To serve the main course, ladle the chowder into large bowls, top with a couple of teaspoons of roe and sprinkle with the reserved chopped parsley. Serve with the crackers (flatbreads).

To finish the dessert, beat the mascarpone with the sugar and place in a small bowl. Invert the tarte tatin onto a large serving plate, cut into wedges and serve with a spoonful of the sweetened mascarpone.

Chickpea & Hazelnut Hummus with Roast Parsnip Chips
1kg parsnips
300ml extra-virgin olive oil (if soaking and cooking dried chickpeas you may need up to 500ml)
1 teaspoon smoked paprika, plus a pinch
2 tablespoons sesame seeds
100g hazelnuts
2 garlic cloves
2 x 400g tins cooked chickpeas (see page 8)
1 small bunch of flat-leaf parsley
1 lemon
2 tablespoons tahini paste
sea salt and freshly ground black pepper

Smoked Haddock & Leek Chowder with Faux Caviar &
Crackers
900g undyed smoked haddock
500ml milk
2 large leeks
100g sliced pancetta (or streaky bacon)
1 onion
50g butter
1 tablespoon plain flour
500g potatoes
2 bay leaves
1 small bunch of flat-leaf parsley
1 bunch of watercress
500ml single cream
1 x 100g jar of herring roe (Avruga, Arenkha)
 or lumpfish roe (see page 10)
sea salt and freshly ground black pepper
1 packet of crisp crackers
 (American flatbreads), to serve

Honeyed Quince & Vanilla Tarte Tatin
3 quinces (about 800g) or large pears
1 lemon
100g butter
100g runny honey
1 vanilla pod
200g puff pastry
250g mascarpone
1–2 tablespoons caster sugar

CHICKPEA & HAZELNUT HUMMUS WITH ROAST PARSNIP CHIPS

To tailor this recipe to your own taste, you can add extra lemon juice, tahini or garlic.

Preheat your oven to 200°C/gas mark 6. Cut the parsnips into long, thin chips. Place in a large roasting tin, drizzle with 5 tablespoons of the olive oil, season with salt, pepper and the smoked paprika and toss well together. Place in the oven and cook for 45–50 minutes, turning occasionally, until golden all over and slightly crisp. Add the sesame seeds for the last 10 minutes.

Scatter the hazelnuts on a baking sheet and roast for 5–10 minutes or until golden. Tip onto a plate and leave to cool slightly.

Crush the garlic. Drain and rinse the chickpeas, and then drain again. Chop the parsley. Squeeze the juice from the lemon.

Roughly chop 2–3 tablespoons of the roasted hazelnuts and place in a small bowl. Add a handful of the chickpeas, 2 tablespoons of the olive oil, some salt and pepper and a pinch of smoked paprika. Mix well and set aside.

Place the remaining chickpeas and hazelnuts in a food processor with the tahini and blitz until smooth. With the motor running, gradually pour in the remaining olive oil in a thin stream until well incorporated. Tip out into a serving bowl, stir in half of the parsley, season with salt and pepper and add lemon juice to taste. Spoon the reserved chickpea and hazelnut mixture on top, cover and set aside in the fridge until ready to serve.

To serve, sprinkle the hummus with the remaining parsley. Tip the hot parsnip chips into a large serving dish and accompany with the bowl of hummus for everyone to dip into.

1kg parsnips
300ml extra-virgin olive oil (if soaking and cooking dried chickpeas you may need up to 500ml)
1 teaspoon smoked paprika, plus a pinch
2 tablespoons sesame seeds
100g hazelnuts
2 garlic cloves
2 x 400g tins cooked chickpeas (see page 8)
1 small bunch of flat-leaf parsley
1 lemon
2 tablespoons tahini paste
sea salt and freshly ground black pepper

SMOKED HADDOCK & LEEK CHOWDER WITH FAUX CAVIAR & CRACKERS

Herring roe is a great substitute for caviar, and not as salty or dyed as lumpfish roe. It is lovely here stirred into the chowder – when you take a spoonful of the tiny little beads of roe they pop gently in your mouth.

Place the haddock skin-side up in a shallow pan and pour over the milk and 500ml water to cover. Bring to just below boiling point, reduce the heat and poach gently for about 5–8 minutes or until just cooked. Lift out the fish onto a plate and leave to cool slightly. Strain the poaching liquid through a fine sieve into a jug and reserve.

Slice the leeks thinly and wash very well to remove any dirt, then drain. Cut the pancetta (or bacon) into little cubes and chop the onion.

Melt the butter in a large pan over a low-to-moderate heat, add the pancetta and cook for about 5 minutes or until just starting to get crispy. Add the chopped onion and leeks and sauté gently for 5–10 minutes until softened. Add the flour and cook, stirring, for 1–2 minutes without colouring. Stir in a little of the reserved fish-poaching liquid and mix until smooth, then add the remainder.

Cube the potatoes and add to the pot with the bay leaves. Simmer for 8–10 minutes until tender. Remove the haddock from its skin and break the flesh into large flakes, removing any bones. Chop the parsley (reserve a couple of teaspoons), roughly chop the watercress and stir into the pan with the cream. Bring to a simmer, carefully fold in the chunks of fish and remove from the heat. Season to taste with salt and pepper.

To serve, ladle the chowder into bowls, top each one with a couple of teaspoons of the roe and sprinkle with the reserved chopped parsley. Serve with the crackers (American flatbreads).

900g undyed
 smoked haddock
500ml milk
2 large leeks
100g sliced pancetta
 (or streaky bacon)
1 onion
50g butter
1 tablespoon plain flour
500g potatoes
2 bay leaves
1 small bunch of flat-leaf
 parsley
1 bunch of watercress
500ml single cream
1 x 100g jar of herring roe
 (Avruga, Arenkha)
 or lumpfish roe (see
 page 10)
sea salt and freshly
 ground black pepper
1 packet of crisp crackers
 (American flatbreads),
 to serve

HONEYED QUINCE & VANILLA TARTE TATIN

Quinces have a unique, delicate perfumed flavour. Make the most of their short season in the autumn.

Preheat your oven to 200°C/gas mark 6. Peel and core the quinces (or pears) and cut into large wedges. Place in a bowl, squeeze over the lemon juice and toss well together. Melt the butter and honey over a moderate heat in a 23cm oven-proof frying pan (or cake tin with a fixed base).

Cut the vanilla pod in half lengthways and scrape the seeds into the butter and honey mixture. Drop in the pod too. Cook over a moderate heat for about 5–8 minutes, until the mixture starts to caramelise. Add the quince slices and cook gently until just starting to soften and turn amber-coloured. Remove from the heat.

Roll out the pastry so it is about 2.5–5cm larger all round than the pan. Slide the pastry on top of the quinces and tuck in the edges inside the rim of the pan. Transfer to the oven for about 30–40 minutes until the pastry is crisp and golden. Leave to cool for 5 minutes.

To serve, beat the mascarpone with sugar to taste and place in a small bowl. Invert the tarte tatin onto a large serving plate, cut into wedges and serve with a spoonful of the sweetened mascarpone.

3 quinces (about 800g)
 or large pears
1 lemon
100g butter
100g runny honey
1 vanilla pod
200g puff pastry
250g mascarpone
1–2 tablespoons caster
 sugar

CARROT & SAGE SOUP WITH SAGE CRISPS.
GOAT'S CHEESE & PRUNE STUFFED CHICKEN ON ROASTED BEETROOTS & POTATOES.
PEAR PIE WITH WALNUT CRUMBS.

60 min   Preheat your oven to 190°C/gas mark 5. To make the soup, chop the shallots, garlic, spring onions and celery. Chop the carrots into 1.5cm cubes. Melt the butter in a large pan and add the shallots, garlic, spring onions, celery and about 4 large sage leaves. Cook over a low-to-moderate heat without colouring for about 5–7 minutes or until soft, then add the carrots and stock or water to the pan and bring to the boil. Reduce the heat and simmer for about 15 minutes.

50 min   For the dessert, grind the walnuts in a food processor with 50g of the sugar until roughly ground. Squeeze the lemon into a large bowl. Peel, core and thinly slice the pears (see page 27), add to the bowl with the lemon juice and toss well to coat.

Roll out the pastry into a 38cm circle and transfer to a large baking sheet. Leaving a 5cm border, sprinkle the centre with three-quarters of the walnut mixture. Drain the pears and toss with the vanilla extract and the remaining sugar and arrange on top of the walnut mixture. Bring up the edges of the pastry almost to cover the pears, pinching as you go but leaving the centre open. Brush the pastry with milk and scatter over the remaining walnut mix. Bake in the middle of the oven for about 45 minutes, or until the pastry is well browned and the centre is bubbling.

40 min   Remove the soup from the heat and set aside to cool slightly, then purée until smooth. Strain through a sieve into a pan. Meanwhile, get on with the main course. Cut the potatoes and beetroots into 1.5cm cubes. Drop into a large roasting tin. Cut each red onion into 6 wedges and add to the tin with the whole (unpeeled) garlic cloves. Drizzle with 6 tablespoons of the olive oil. Rip the bay leaves into pieces and add to the tin. Season with salt and pepper. Toss well together, and then spread out in a single layer. Place in the top of the oven and roast for about 20 minutes.

30 min   Slice the goat's cheese into 6 pieces. Use a small knife to make a slit in the thickest part of each chicken breast to create a little pocket. Slide a piece of goat's cheese into the cavity, pop in a prune and insert a tiny piece of thyme. Season the inside, and then use a cocktail stick to secure.

Squeeze the juice from the lemon into a large bowl and add the leaves from the remaining thyme. Add the chilli flakes and the remaining olive oil and season well. Put in the chicken breasts, turn to coat and then set aside to marinate.

20 min   To make the sage crisps for the starter, brush a large baking tray liberally with some of the olive oil. Lay the remaining sage leaves in a single layer on the tray and brush with any remaining oil. Place in the bottom of the oven and bake for about 4–5 minutes until just crisp. Do not let them brown! Remove from the oven and set aside.

10 min   When the vegetables have roasted, remove them from the oven. Toss well together and spread out in a single layer. Arrange the chicken breasts on top, skin-side up, and return to the top of the oven for 20 minutes or until the chicken is tender and cooked through.

Reheat the soup, season well and ladle into soup bowls. Accompany with a few sage crisps on the side.

To finish the main course, remove the chicken breasts from the tin and place the vegetables over a moderate heat. Toss well together and then pour in the balsamic vinegar. Bring to the boil, stirring. To serve, divide the vegetables between each of 6 dinner plates (make sure everyone has a whole garlic clove so they can eat the sweet roasted flesh). Slice each chicken breast and arrange on top of the vegetables.

To serve the dessert, cut the pie into slices and accompany with custard on the side.

Carrot & Sage Soup with Sage Crisps
3 shallots
2 garlic cloves
6 spring onions
2 celery sticks (with a little leaf attached, if possible)
750g carrots
70g butter
about 30 fresh sage leaves
1.4 litres vegetable or chicken stock, or water
3 tablespoons olive oil
sea salt and freshly ground black pepper

Goat's Cheese & Prune Stuffed Chicken on Roasted Beetroots & Potatoes
12 small potatoes
6 large raw beetroots (see page 24)
2 red onions
6 garlic cloves
8 tablespoons olive oil
2 fresh bay leaves
100g goat's cheese
6 x 200g chicken breasts, skin on (choose breasts with the wing bone attached as this will keep the meat moister)
6 stoned ready-to-eat prunes
2 sprigs of thyme
1 lemon
pinch of dried red chilli flakes
2 tablespoons balsamic vinegar
sea salt and freshly ground black pepper

Pear Pie with Walnut Crumbs
100g walnuts
85g dark muscovado sugar
1 lemon
6 pears
500g shortcrust or sweetcrust pastry
1 teaspoon vanilla extract
a little milk, to glaze
good-quality custard, to serve

CARROT & SAGE SOUP WITH SAGE CRISPS

The sage crisps are very easy to make and add a lovely crunchy texture to the smooth soup.

Chop the shallots and garlic. Chop the spring onions and celery. Chop the carrots into 1.5cm cubes. Melt the butter in a large pan and add the shallots, garlic, spring onions, celery and about 4 large sage leaves. Cook over a low-to-moderate heat without colouring for about 5–7 minutes, or until soft.

Add the carrots and stock or water and bring to the boil. Reduce the heat and simmer for about 15 minutes, or until the carrots are tender. Remove from the heat and set aside to cool slightly, then purée in a blender until smooth. Strain through a sieve into a clean pan.

Preheat your oven to 190°C/gas mark 5. To make the sage crisps, brush a large baking tray liberally with some of the olive oil. Lay the remaining sage leaves in a single layer on the tray and brush with any remaining oil. Place in the oven and bake for about 4–5 minutes until just crisp. Do not let them brown! Remove from the oven and set aside to cool.

To serve, reheat the soup, season well and ladle into soup bowls. Accompany with a few sage crisps on the side.

3 shallots
2 garlic cloves
6 spring onions
2 celery sticks (with a little leaf attached, if possible)
750g carrots
70g butter
about 30 fresh sage leaves
1.4 litres vegetable or chicken stock, or water
3 tablespoons olive oil
sea salt and freshly ground black pepper

GOAT'S CHEESE & PRUNE STUFFED CHICKEN ON ROASTED BEETROOTS & POTATOES

Preheat your oven to 190°C/gas mark 5.

Cut the potatoes and beetroots into 1.5cm cubes. Drop into a large roasting tin. Cut each red onion into 6 wedges and add to the tin with the whole (unpeeled) garlic cloves. Drizzle with 6 tablespoons of the olive oil. Rip the bay leaves into pieces and add to the tin. Season with salt and pepper. Toss well together, and then spread out in a single layer. Place in the oven and roast for about 20 minutes.

Slice the goat's cheese into 6 pieces. Use a small knife to make a slit in the thickest part of each chicken breast to create a little pocket. Slide a piece of goat's cheese into the cavity, pop in a prune and insert a tiny piece of thyme. Season the inside, and then use a cocktail stick to secure.

Squeeze the juice from the lemon into a large bowl and add the leaves from the remaining thyme. Add the chilli flakes and the remaining olive oil and season well. Put in the chicken breasts, turn to coat and then set aside to marinate.

When the vegetables have roasted for 20 minutes, remove them from the oven. Toss well together and spread out in a single layer again. Arrange the chicken breasts on top, skin-side up, and return to the oven for 20 minutes or until the chicken is tender and cooked through. Remove from the oven, cover with foil to keep warm and set aside to rest.

When you are ready to serve, remove the chicken breasts from the tin and place the vegetables over a moderate heat. Stir until hot, and then pour in the balsamic vinegar. Bring to the boil, stirring.

To serve, divide the vegetables between each of 6 dinner plates (make sure everyone has a whole garlic clove so they can squeeze out the sweet roasted flesh). Cut each chicken breast into slices and arrange on top of the roasted vegetables.

12 small potatoes
6 large raw beetroots
 (see page 24)
2 red onions
6 garlic cloves
8 tablespoons olive oil
2 fresh bay leaves
100g goat's cheese
6 x 200g chicken breasts,
 skin on (if possible,
 choose breasts with
 the little wing bone still
 attached as this will keep
 the meat moister)
6 stoned ready-to-eat
 prunes
2 sprigs of thyme
1 lemon
pinch of dried red
 chilli flakes
2 tablespoons
 balsamic vinegar
salt and freshly ground
 black pepper

PEAR PIE WITH WALNUT CRUMBS

You could use pecans or hazelnuts instead of walnuts for this pie.

Preheat your oven to 190°C/gas mark 5. Grind the walnuts in a food processor with 50g of the sugar until roughly ground. Squeeze the lemon into a large bowl. Peel, core and thinly slice the pears (see page 27), add to the bowl with the lemon juice and toss well to coat.

Roll out the pastry to form a 38cm circle and transfer to a large baking sheet. Sprinkle the centre with three-quarters of the walnut mixture, leaving a 5cm border all the way round the outside. Drain the pears and toss with the vanilla extract and the remaining sugar.

Arrange the pears on top of the walnut mixture, and then bring up the edges of the pastry almost to cover the pears, pinching as you go but leaving the centre open.

Brush the pastry with milk and scatter the remaining walnut mix over the pastry and pears. Bake in the oven for about 45 minutes, or until the pastry is well browned and the centre is bubbling.

To serve, cut the pie into slices and accompany with the custard.

100g walnuts
85g dark muscovado
 sugar
1 lemon
6 ripe pears
500g shortcrust or
 sweetcrust pastry
1 teaspoon vanilla extract
a little milk, to glaze
good-quality custard,
 to serve

JERUSALEM ARTICHOKE & PORCINI SOUP.
PAN-FRIED CHICKEN LIVERS WITH PRUNE POLENTA WITH CHICORY SALAD.
TURKISH APPLE SNOW.

60 min   Begin with the starter. Place the dried porcini in a heatproof measuring jug and pour over 500ml boiling water to cover. Leave to soak for 20 minutes.

Now for the polenta. Pour the stock or water into a large pan and bring to the boil. Roughly chop the prunes. Once the stock or water is boiling rapidly, gradually pour in the polenta in a thin stream, beating all the time. Keep beating until the mixture thickens and starts to leave the sides of the pan. Remove from the heat and stir in the thyme leaves, prunes and a little salt – go easy on the salt as the stock may already be quite salty. Season with plenty of black pepper. Keep beating for about 3 minutes, then tip onto a chopping board in a neat, round heap. Leave to cool slightly.

50 min   To make the apple snow, squeeze the juice from the lemon. Peel, core and slice the apples and place in a medium saucepan with the lemon juice. Cook, covered, over a low heat until very soft, about 10–15 minutes.

Meanwhile, cut the Turkish Delight into small pieces and place in a small heatproof bowl with 3 tablespoons water and the orange flower water. Set over a pan of gently simmering water and stir gently to melt.

40 min   Back to the starter. Drain the porcini, reserving the soaking water, and finely chop the mushrooms. Chop the onion and celery and crush the garlic. Melt the butter in a large, heavy-based pan and add the onion, garlic, celery and thyme sprigs. Cook gently without colouring for 5 minutes. Add the chopped porcini and continue to cook for a further 10 minutes.

Meanwhile, make the chicory salad. Squeeze the juice from the orange and lemon and pour into a small bowl. Whisk in the olive oil and season well with salt and pepper. Trim a thin slice from the bottom of each chicory head, separate the leaves and place in a large serving bowl.

The apples should now be cooked. Tip them into a coarse sieve placed over a large bowl and push through the pulp with the back of a ladle. Set aside and leave to cool.

30 min   For the starter, slice the artichokes thickly and add to the pan with the stock and reserved mushroom water. Season, bring to the boil, reduce the heat and simmer for about 15 minutes until the artichokes are tender.

The polenta should have firmed up by now. Cut it into quarters across the middle, and then slice each quarter into 4–5 thick slices. Brush a large baking sheet with a little oil and lay the polenta slices out in a single layer. Preheat your oven to 200°C/gas mark 6.

20 min   Back to the main course. Finely chop the shallots and cut the pancetta into little lardons. Cut away any membranes from the chicken livers and season with salt and pepper.

The artichokes should now be tender. Remove the pan from the heat, add the milk and leave to cool for about 10 minutes.

To finish the apple snow, whisk the egg whites in a large bowl with an electric mixer until soft peaks form. Gradually spoon the warm, melted Turkish Delight into the beaten egg whites, beating constantly until thoroughly combined. Fold 1 large spoonful of the meringue into the apple purée, to loosen the mixture, then carefully fold in the rest. Spoon into pretty glasses and transfer to the fridge to chill.

10 min   To finish the starter, purée the soup in batches in a blender until smooth and strain through a fine sieve into a clean pan.

For the main course, heat 1 tablespoon olive oil in each of two large frying pans. Divide the chopped shallots between

the pans and cook for 2–3 minutes until just starting to soften. Add the pancetta pieces to the pans and cook for a further 5 minutes until just going crispy. Remove with a slotted spoon and set aside. Keep the pans. Place the tray of polenta in the oven and bake for about 20 minutes or until hot and slightly crispy. Finely chop the parsley.

Lightly whip the cream for the apple snow and place a spoonful in each glass. Finely chop the pistachios and set aside.

To serve the starter, reheat the soup, season to taste and ladle into soup bowls and sprinkle with Parmesan cheese.

Season the chicken livers with salt and pepper. Place the frying pans back on the hob over a moderate-to-high heat. Add ½ a tablespoon oil and half of the butter to each pan, let the butter melt and sizzle then add half of the livers to each. Cook the chicken livers for about 30 seconds–1 minute on each side so that they're nice and brown on the outside but still pink in the middle. (They need to cook in a single layer over quite a high heat so that they caramelise slightly, rather than boil.)

Raise the heat on the pans again and return half of the cooked shallots and bacon to each. Add the vinegar and boil rapidly. Place about 3 slices of polenta on to each of 6 dinner plates and divide the chicken liver mixture between them. Scatter with the chopped parsley and serve immediately.

To serve the dessert, sprinkle over the chopped pistachios and serve with the sponge fingers on the side.

Jerusalem Artichoke & Porcini Soup
15g dried porcini mushrooms
1 onion
1 celery stick
1 garlic clove

50g butter
a few sprigs of lemon thyme (or normal thyme and a sliver
 of lemon zest)
600g Jerusalem artichokes
700ml vegetable or chicken stock
300ml milk
sea salt and freshly ground black pepper
3 tablespoons finely grated Parmesan cheese, to serve

<u>Pan-fried Chicken Livers with Prune Polenta</u>
1.2 litres vegetable or chicken stock, or water
250g stoned ready-to-eat prunes
300g 'quick cook' polenta
1 small bunch of thyme, leaves removed
3 tablespoons olive oil, plus a little extra
 for brushing baking sheet
4 shallots
150g pancetta, sliced or streaky bacon
800g chicken livers
50g butter
25g flat-leaf parsley
4 tablespoons red wine vinegar
sea salt and freshly ground black pepper

<u>Chicory Salad</u>
½ orange
½ lemon
4 tablespoons extra-virgin olive oil
2 heads of chicory
sea salt and freshly ground black pepper

<u>Turkish Apple Snow</u>
½ lemon
500g apples
150g Turkish Delight
¼ teaspoon orange flower water
2 egg whites
25g pistachios
150ml double cream
12 sponge fingers

JERUSALEM ARTICHOKE & PORCINI SOUP

Although similar in taste and smell to the globe artichoke, this knobbly root has a more nutty flavour that goes well with the porcini mushrooms.

Place the dried porcini in a heatproof measuring jug and pour over 500ml boiling water to cover. Leave to soak for 20 minutes and then drain, reserving the soaking liquor. Finely chop the mushrooms.

Chop the onion and celery and crush the garlic. Melt the butter in a large, heavy-based pan and add the onion, garlic, celery and thyme sprigs. Cook gently without colouring for 5 minutes, and then add the chopped porcini. Continue to cook for a further 10 minutes.

Slice the artichokes thickly and add to the pan with the stock and reserved mushroom liquor. Season, bring to the boil, reduce the heat and simmer for about 15 minutes until the artichokes are tender. Remove from the heat, add the milk and leave to cool for about 10 minutes.

Purée the soup in batches in a blender until smooth, and then strain through a fine sieve. Season to taste.

To serve, reheat the soup, ladle into soup bowls and sprinkle with a little Parmesan cheese.

15g dried porcini
 mushrooms
1 onion
1 celery stick
1 garlic clove
50g butter
a few sprigs of lemon
 thyme (or normal
 thyme and a sliver
 of lemon zest)
600g Jerusalem
 artichokes, scrubbed
700ml vegetable
 or chicken stock
300ml milk
sea salt and freshly
 ground black pepper
3 tablespoons finely
 grated Parmesan cheese,
 to serve

PAN-FRIED CHICKEN LIVERS WITH PRUNE POLENTA WITH CHICORY SALAD

Preheat your oven to 200°C/gas mark 6. Pour the stock or water into a large pan and bring to the boil. Roughly chop the prunes. Once the stock or water is boiling rapidly, slowly pour in the polenta, beating all the time. Beat until the mixture thickens and starts to leave the sides of the pan. Remove from the heat and stir in the thyme leaves, prunes and a little salt. Season with plenty of pepper. Beat for about 3 minutes, then tip out onto a chopping board in a neat round heap. Leave to cool slightly. When the polenta has firmed up, cut it into quarters, and slice each quarter into 4–5 slices. Brush a large baking sheet with a little oil and lay the polenta slices out in a single layer. Bake for about 20 minutes or until hot and slightly crisp.

Finely chop the shallots. Heat 1 tablespoon of the olive oil in a large frying pan. Add the shallots and cook for 2–3 minutes until just starting to soften. Cut the pancetta into little pieces and add to the pan. Cook for a further 5 minutes until the pancetta is just going crisp. Remove with a slotted spoon and set aside. Keep the pan for later.

Remove any membranes from the chicken livers and season. You will need to cook the livers in 2–3 batches to avoid overcrowding the pan (otherwise they will boil rather than fry). Return the pan to a moderate-to-high heat and add a little of the remaining oil and one-third of the butter. Allow it to sizzle, then add a handful of the livers. Cook for about 30 seconds on each side so that they are brown on the outside but still pink in the middle. Remove with a slotted spoon, place on a baking tray and keep warm in the oven while you fry the rest of the livers, adding more butter and olive oil as needed. Finely chop the parsley. Once the livers are cooked, raise the heat and return the shallots and pancetta to the pan. Add the cooked chicken livers, pour in the vinegar and boil rapidly. To serve, place 3 slices of polenta on each plate, spoon the chicken livers over the top and scatter with the parsley.

For the salad, squeeze the juice from the orange and lemon and pour into a small bowl. Whisk in the olive oil and season well with salt and pepper. Trim a thin slice from the bottom of each chicory head and separate the leaves. Place the leaves in a large serving bowl, pour over the dressing, toss well together and serve with the chicken livers.

1.2 litres vegetable or chicken stock, or water
250g stoned ready-to-eat prunes
300g 'quick cook' polenta
1 small bunch of thyme, leaves removed
3 tablespoons olive oil, plus a little extra for brushing baking sheet
4 shallots
150g pancetta, sliced or streaky bacon
800g chicken livers
50g butter
25g flat-leaf parsley
4 tablespoons red wine vinegar
sea salt and freshly ground black pepper

Chicory Salad
½ orange
½ lemon
4 tablespoons extra-virgin olive oil
salt and freshly ground black pepper
2 heads of chicory

TURKISH APPLE SNOW

A light and fluffy perfumed pudding.

Squeeze the juice from the lemon. Peel, core and slice the apples and place in a medium saucepan with the lemon juice. Cook, covered, over a low heat until very soft, about 10–15 minutes. Tip into a coarse sieve placed over a large bowl and push through the pulp with the back of a ladle. Leave to cool.

Cut the Turkish Delight into small pieces and place in a small heatproof bowl with 3 tablespoons water and the orange flower water. Set over a pan of gently simmering water and stir gently to melt.

Whisk the egg whites in a large bowl with an electric mixer until soft peaks form. Gradually spoon the warm, melted Turkish Delight into the beaten egg whites, beating constantly until thoroughly combined. Fold 1 large spoonful of the meringue into the apple purée, to loosen the mixture, then carefully fold in the rest. Spoon into pretty glasses and transfer to the fridge to chill. Meanwhile, finely chop the pistachios and lightly whip the cream.

To serve, add a spoonful of whipped cream to each glass and sprinkle over the chopped pistachios. Serve with the sponge fingers on the side.

½ lemon
500g apples
150g Turkish Delight
¼ teaspoon orange flower water
2 egg whites
25g pistachios
150ml double cream
12 sponge fingers

MUSHROOMS À LA CRÈME ON TOASTED BRIOCHE.
SAGE CHICKEN WITH ROASTED LEEKS & BUTTERNUT SQUASH.
CHILLI CHOCOLATE MOUSSE.

60 min Preheat your oven to 200°C/gas mark 6. Begin with the dessert. Bring a small pan of water to the boil, and then reduce the heat to barely simmering. Finely chop the chocolate and place in a heatproof bowl. Add the chilli powder and smoked paprika (if using) and set the bowl over the pan of water. Remove the pan from the heat immediately and allow the chocolate to melt, stirring occasionally.

50 min Once the chocolate has melted, beat in the crème fraîche and icing sugar and blend until smooth. Spoon the chocolate mixture into 6 little glasses and place in the fridge to set.

Peel the clementines (or satsumas) and, using a small sharp knife, cut in between each piece of membrane to remove the little skinless segments. Set aside.

40 min Now for the main course. Trim and slice the leeks and wash well to remove any grit. Drain. Peel the squash, scoop out the seeds and cut the flesh into 5cm cubes. Place in a large roasting tin with the olive oil, 3 of the sage leaves, some salt and pepper and the sliced leeks. Toss well together and then roast in the oven for 10 minutes.

30 min Meanwhile, cut the Parmesan into 6 equal-sized pieces. Using a small knife, make a slit in the side of each chicken breast and pop a piece of Parmesan and a sage leaf into the cavity. Season inside with salt and pepper, and then press the open chicken edges together to close.

20 min Remove the roasted squash and leeks from the oven, toss well together and spread out in a single layer again. Arrange the chicken breasts on top, skin-side up, and return to the oven for a further 10–15 minutes until the chicken is tender and cooked through.

10 min Now for the starter. Finely chop the onion. Melt the butter in a medium pan, add the chopped onion and pull the leaves from the thyme into the pan. Cook over a low heat for 5 minutes, without colouring, until the onion is soft.

Slice the mushrooms and stir into the pan with some salt and pepper. Cook for a further 5 minutes, or until the mushrooms are tender. Stir in the cream and let it bubble for a minute or two to thicken slightly. Remove from the heat and check for seasoning. Chop the parsley and stir two-thirds into the mushrooms.

When the chicken is cooked, remove it from the oven and transfer to a serving plate. Cover with foil to keep warm.

To serve the starter, slice the mini brioche in half across the middle and toast on both sides. Place 2 halves of warm toasted brioche on each of 6 plates. Spoon the mushrooms over the top and sprinkle with the remaining parsley. Serve immediately.

To finish the main course, place the tin of roasted vegetables over a high heat, pour in the vinegar and toss well to coat. Divide the vegetables between each of 6 dinner plates and top with a chicken breast to serve.

To serve the dessert, top each chocolate mousse with a few clementine segments.

Mushrooms à la Crème on Toasted Brioche
1 small onion
25g butter
2 sprigs of thyme
250g field or portobello mushrooms, cleaned (see page 23)
200ml double cream
10g flat-leaf parsley leaves
sea salt and freshly ground black pepper
6 mini brioche, to serve

Sage Chicken with Roasted
Leeks & Butternut Squash
3 leeks
1 large butternut squash
6 tablespoons olive oil
9 sage leaves
90g piece of Parmesan cheese
6 x 200g chicken breasts, skin on
1 tablespoon balsamic or sherry vinegar
sea salt and freshly ground black pepper

Chilli Chocolate Mousse
150g good-quality dark chocolate
 (50–70 per cent cocoa solids)
¼ teaspoon chilli powder
¼ teaspoon sweet smoked paprika (optional)
250g crème fraîche
1 tablespoon icing sugar
3 clementines or satsumas

MUSHROOMS À LA CRÈME ON TOASTED BRIOCHE

If you can't find mini brioche, use a brioche loaf and cut into slices.

Finely chop the onion. Melt the butter in a medium pan, add the chopped onion and pull the leaves from the thyme into the pan. Cook over a low heat for 5 minutes without colouring until the onion is soft.

Slice the mushrooms and stir into the pan with some salt and pepper. Cook for a further 5 minutes, or until the mushrooms are tender. Stir in the cream and let it bubble for a minute or two to thicken slightly.

Remove from the heat and check the seasoning. Chop the parsley and stir two-thirds into the mushrooms.

Slice the mini brioche in half across the middle and toast on both sides. Place 2 halves of warm toasted brioche on each of 6 plates. Spoon the mushrooms over the top and sprinkle with the remaining parsley. Serve immediately.

1 small onion
25g butter
2 sprigs of thyme
250g field or
  portobello mushrooms,
  cleaned (see page 23)
200ml double cream
10g flat-leaf parsley
  leaves
sea salt and freshly
  ground black pepper
6 mini brioche, to serve

SAGE CHICKEN WITH ROASTED LEEKS & BUTTERNUT SQUASH

As an alternative use thyme instead of sage. Pull off its little leaves and sprinkle them inside the chicken breasts.

Preheat your oven to 200°C/gas mark 6.

Trim and slice the leeks and wash well to remove any grit. Drain. Peel the squash, scoop out the seeds with a spoon and cut the flesh into 5cm cubes. Place in a large roasting tin with the olive oil, 3 of the sage leaves, some salt and pepper and the sliced leeks. Toss well together and then roast in the oven for 10 minutes.

Meanwhile, cut the Parmesan into 6 equal-sized pieces. Using a small knife, make a slit in the side of each chicken breast and pop a piece of Parmesan and a sage leaf into the cavity. Season inside with salt and pepper, and then press the open chicken edges together to close.

Remove the roasted squash and leeks from the oven, toss well together and spread out in a single layer again. Arrange the chicken breasts on top, skin-side up, and return to the oven for a further 10–15 minutes until the chicken is tender and cooked through.

Remove the tin from the oven and transfer the chicken breasts to a plate. Place the tin of vegetables over a high heat, pour in the vinegar and toss well.

To serve, divide the vegetables between the dinner plates and top with a chicken breast.

3 leeks
1 large butternut squash
6 tablespoons olive oil
9 sage leaves
90g piece of Parmesan
  cheese
6 x 200g chicken
  breasts, skin on
1 tablespoon balsamic
  or sherry vinegar
sea salt and freshly
  ground black pepper

CHILLI CHOCOLATE MOUSSE

Rich, dark and firey.

Bring a small pan of water to the boil, and then reduce the heat to barely simmering. Finely chop the chocolate and place in a heatproof bowl. Add the chilli powder and smoked paprika (if using) and set the bowl over the pan of water. Remove the pan from the heat immediately and allow the chocolate to melt, stirring occasionally.

Once the chocolate has melted, beat in the crème fraîche and icing sugar and blend until smooth.

Spoon the chocolate mixture into 6 little glasses and place in the fridge to set.

Peel the clementines (or satsumas) and, using a small, sharp knife, cut in between each piece of membrane to remove the little skinless segments. Set aside.

To serve, top each chocolate mousse with a few clementine segments.

150g good-quality dark
 chocolate (50–70
 per cent cocoa solids)
¼ teaspoon chilli powder
¼ teaspoon sweet
 smoked paprika (optional)
250g crème fraîche
1 tablespoon
 icing sugar
3 clementines or satsumas

WINTER

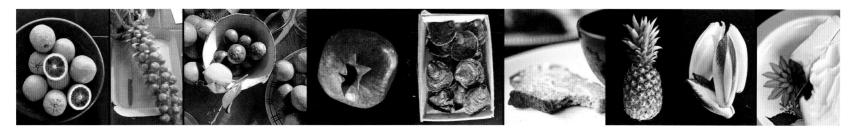

WILD MUSHROOM CAVIAR.

CHICKEN STUFFED WITH BLACK PUDDING ON CAULIFLOWER PURÉE.

APPLE TARTS WITH MINCEMEAT ICE CREAM.

60 min   Remove the ice cream from the freezer to soften it for about 20 minutes.

Meanwhile, get on with the mushroom caviar. Roughly chop the mushrooms. Tip into the bowl of a food processor (you may need to do this in batches) and chop finely. Crush the garlic and finely chop the spring onions. Heat the oil in a large frying pan, add the spring onions and garlic and cook for about 2 minutes until soft. Add the chopped mushrooms and cook over a moderate heat for 10–12 minutes. Water will come out of the mushrooms at first, but carry on cooking until all the liquid has evaporated, stirring frequently, until the mushrooms are dark and rich in colour. Set aside to cool.

50 min   To make the apple tarts, roll out the pastry on a lightly floured surface to form a rectangle about 42 x 28cm. Using a 14cm cutter, or a saucer, cut out 6 rounds of pastry. Set on a baking sheet and chill in the fridge. Squeeze the lemon juice into a bowl. Peel and core the apples, and then slice each one into 16 slices. Place in a bowl with the lemon juice and toss well together. Melt the butter and sugar in a large frying pan over a moderate heat. Add the apple slices and toss gently to coat. Cook for 2–3 minutes, carefully turning once again, until just soft. Remove from the heat and leave to cool. Meanwhile, scrape the ice cream into a bowl, stir in the mincemeat or ground cinnamon and return to the freezer.

40 min   Now for the chicken. Slice the black pudding or sausage into 18 slices. Push your fingers under the skin of each chicken breast to create a pocket. Slide in 3 slices of black pudding and pull the skin back over to cover it. Season each piece of chicken all over and wrap in a rasher of bacon, securing with a cocktail stick. Preheat your oven to 220°C/gas mark 7.

30 min   Back to the apple tarts. Remove the pastry from the fridge and arrange the apple slices onto the pastry bases, leaving a 1.5cm rim around the edge. Bake in the oven for 15–20 minutes until the pastry is well risen and golden brown. Once the tarts are cooked, reduce the oven temperature to 200°C/gas mark 6.

Meanwhile, get on with the cauliflower purée. Cut the cauliflower into small florets and place in a large saucepan with a pinch of salt. Pour in the hot vegetable stock and bring to the boil. Reduce the heat and simmer for 5–8 minutes or until very tender.

20 min   To cook the chicken, heat the butter and oil in a large oven-proof frying pan over a moderate heat. Add the chicken breasts and cook for a minute or two on each side, to colour them slightly. Turn the chicken breasts skin-side up and finish off in the oven for 15–20 minutes, or until tender and cooked through. Remove the chicken breasts from the pan and keep warm on a plate. Place the pan to one side, ready for the sauce.

10 min   Drain the cauliflower thoroughly and tip into the bowl of a food processor. Blitz until smooth, and then return to the pan. Finely chop the olives for the mushroom caviar, squeeze the juice from the lemon and chop the dill. Stir the olives and two-thirds of the dill into the cooled mushroom mixture and season with lemon juice, paprika, nutmeg and salt and pepper – go easy on the salt because the olives will be quite salty already.

To serve the starter, stack the warmed blinis or pieces of pumpernickel bread on a large serving plate and accompany with a bowl of crème fraîche or soured cream and the mushroom caviar for everyone to help themselves. Alternatively, spoon the caviar onto the blinis or small pieces of the bread, top with a little soured cream or crème fraîche and garnish with dill.

Just before you are ready to serve the main course, add the cream to the cauliflower purée, season well and reheat. To make the sauce, pour off any excess fat from the pan you used to cook the chicken and place over a high heat. Add the Marsala, scraping the bottom of the pan with a wooden spoon, and then add the chicken stock. Bring to the boil and cook until slightly reduced. Season to taste. To serve, place a couple of spoonfuls of the cauliflower purée onto your warmed dinner plates. Top each one with a chicken breast and drizzle the sauce around.

To serve the dessert, return the apple tarts to the oven for about 5 minutes to warm them through if necessary. Serve them with a scoop of the ice cream.

Wild Mushroom Caviar
650g mixture of wild, field and chestnut
 mushrooms, cleaned (see page 23)
1 large garlic clove
8 spring onions
4 tablespoons olive oil
70g pitted dry black olives
½ lemon
10g fresh dill
pinch of paprika
large pinch of grated nutmeg
sea salt and freshly ground black pepper
pumpernickel bread or warmed blinis, to serve
200ml crème fraîche or soured cream, to serve

Chicken Stuffed with Black Pudding on Cauliflower Purée
125g black pudding, chorizo or other sausage
6 x 200g chicken breasts, with skin on
6 smoked bacon rashers
15g butter
1 tablespoon olive oil
1 large cauliflower (about 1kg)
1 litre hot vegetable stock
100ml double cream
100ml Marsala
200ml chicken stock
sea salt and freshly ground black pepper

Apple Tarts with Mincemeat Ice Cream
500ml vanilla ice cream
6 tablespoons mincemeat (or ½ teaspoon
 ground cinnamon)
500g puff pastry
1 lemon
6 apples
50g butter
25g golden caster sugar

WILD MUSHROOM CAVIAR

Originally from Russia, I like to imagine this being served in the palaces of the Tsars. Who would have thought that mushrooms could taste this luxurious?!

Roughly chop the mushrooms. Tip into the bowl of a food processor (you may need to do this in batches) and finely chop. Crush the garlic and finely chop the spring onions.

Heat the oil in a large frying pan, add the spring onions and garlic and cook for about 2 minutes until soft. Tip in the chopped mushrooms and cook over a moderate heat for 10–12 minutes. Water will come out of the mushrooms at first, but carry on cooking until all the liquid has evaporated, stirring frequently, until the mushrooms are dark and rich in colour. Set aside to cool.

Finely chop the olives, squeeze the juice from the lemon and chop the dill. Stir the olives and dill into the cooled mushroom mixture and season to taste with lemon juice, paprika, nutmeg, salt and pepper – go easy on the salt because the olives will be quite salty already. Spoon into a serving bowl.

To serve, stack the warmed blinis or pieces of pumpernickel bread on a large serving plate and accompany with a bowl of crème fraîche or soured cream and the mushroom caviar for everyone to help themselves.

650g mixture of wild, field and chestnut mushrooms
1 large garlic clove
8 spring onions
4 tablespoons olive oil
70g pitted dry black olives
½ lemon
10g fresh dill
pinch of paprika
large pinch of grated nutmeg
sea salt and freshly ground black pepper
pumpernickel bread or warmed blinis, to serve
200ml crème fraîche or soured cream, to serve

CHICKEN STUFFED WITH BLACK PUDDING ON CAULIFLOWER PURÉE

Preheat your oven to 200°C/gas mark 6.

Slice the black pudding or sausage into 18 slices. Push your fingers under the skin of each chicken breast to create a pocket. Slide in 3 slices of black pudding and pull the skin back over to cover it. Season well and wrap each breast with a rasher of bacon, securing with a cocktail stick.

Heat the butter and oil in a large, oven-proof frying pan over a moderate heat. Add the chicken breasts and cook for a minute or two on each side to colour them slightly. Turn them all skin-side up and finish off in the oven for 15–20 minutes or until tender and cooked through. Remove the chicken breasts from the pan and keep warm. Keep the pan to one side for later.

Cut the cauliflower into small florets and place in a large saucepan with a pinch of salt. Pour in the vegetable stock and bring to the boil. Reduce the heat and simmer for 5–8 minutes, or until very tender. Drain well and tip the cooked cauliflower into the bowl of a food processor. Blitz until smooth, and then return to the pan. Beat in the cream, season well and reheat gently.

To make the sauce, pour off any excess fat from the pan you used to cook the chicken and place over a high heat. Add the Marsala, scraping the bottom of the pan with a wooden spoon, and then add the chicken stock. Bring to the boil and cook until slightly reduced. Season to taste.

To serve, place a couple of spoonfuls of the cauliflower purée onto your warmed dinner plates, top with a chicken breast and drizzle the sauce around.

125g black pudding, chorizo or other sausage
6 x 200g chicken breasts, with skin on
6 smoked bacon rashers
15g butter
1 tablespoon olive oil
1 large cauliflower, (about 1kg)
1 litre hot vegetable stock
100ml double cream
100ml Marsala
200ml chicken stock
salt and freshly ground black pepper

APPLE TARTS WITH MINCEMEAT ICE CREAM

Remove the ice cream from the freezer to soften it for about 20 minutes. Scrape the softened ice cream into a bowl, stir in the mincemeat (or ground cinnamon) and return to the freezer until needed.

Roll out the pastry on a lightly floured surface to form a rectangle about 42 x 28cm. Using a 14cm cutter, or a saucer, cut out 6 rounds of pastry. Set on a baking sheet and chill in the fridge until needed.

Squeeze the lemon juice into a bowl. Peel and core the apples, and then slice each one into 16 slices. Place in a bowl with the lemon juice and toss well together.

Melt the butter and sugar in a large frying pan over a moderate heat. Add the apple slices and toss gently to coat. Cook for 2–3 minutes, carefully turning once again, until just soft. Remove from the heat and leave to cool.

Preheat your oven to 220°C/gas mark 7. Remove the pastry from the fridge and arrange the apple slices on the pastry bases, leaving a 1.5cm rim around the edge. Bake in the oven for 15–20 minutes until the pastry is well risen and golden brown.

Serve warm with a scoop of the ice cream.

500ml vanilla ice cream
6 tablespoons mincemeat (or ½ teaspoon ground cinnamon)
500g puff pastry
1 lemon
6 apples
50g butter
25g golden caster sugar

SWEDE SOUP WITH BLACK OLIVE TAPENADE.
DUCK & PEAR PITHIVIER WITH FRESH PINEAPPLE CHUTNEY.
GIANT CHOCOLATE & GINGER BUTTONS WITH CHOCOLATE CREAM.

60 min Preheat your oven to 220°C/gas mark 7. Prick the skin of the duck breasts all over and season. Heat a small oven-proof frying pan over a moderate heat and add the breasts, skin-side down. Cook for 3 minutes on each side. Transfer to the oven to finish cooking for a further 12 minutes, or until tender but still pink. (Alternatively, place the duck legs on a roasting tray and place in the oven for 30 minutes, or until tender.) Remove from the oven and leave to cool.

Meanwhile, scatter the pine nuts for the dessert on a baking tray and toast in the bottom of the oven for 5–6 minutes until golden brown (make sure they don't burn). Remove from the oven and spread on a plate to cool.

50 min To make the chocolate buttons, bring a small pan of water to the boil, reduce the heat until barely simmering and set an oven-proof bowl on top. Finely chop the chocolate and place in the bowl. Remove the pan from the heat and stir occasionally until the chocolate has melted – do not let the pan get too hot. Line 2 baking trays with parchment paper. Finely chop the ginger.

Now for the soup. Roughly chop the swede and potato. Chop the onion and celery and crush the garlic.

40 min Heat the olive oil for the soup in a large pan. Add the onion, celery and garlic and cook without colouring for 5–10 minutes, or until soft. Add the potato, swede and stock, bring to the boil and simmer for 15–20 minutes, or until the swede and potato are tender. Set aside to cool.

To make the pineapple chutney, peel, core and finely dice the pineapple (see page 27). Crush the garlic, peel and finely grate the ginger, and finely chop the red onion. Squeeze the juice from the limes into a bowl. Deseed and finely chop the red chilli. Place all the ingredients in a bowl, season and stir in the sugar.

30 min Back to the dessert. Reserve one-third of the melted chocolate for the chocolate cream. To make the buttons, place 12 spoonfuls of the remaining melted chocolate onto the prepared baking trays, spreading them out into rounds about 10cm in diameter. Scatter evenly with crystallised ginger and pine nuts and place in the fridge to harden.

20 min To make the duck filling for the main course, remove the skin from the duck and finely dice the flesh to create a coarse mince. Place in a small bowl. Peel the ginger and finely chop with the garlic for the marinade. Combine with the other marinade ingredients in a bowl, and then pour over the minced duck. Finely slice the spring onions. Peel and core the pear and chop finely. Add the onions and pear to the duck mixture and combine well.

10 min Roll out the pastry thinly and cut into 12 discs, about 15cm in diameter. Separate the egg, placing the yolk and white in separate little bowls. Add a pinch of salt to each and beat well with a fork. Arrange 6 of the discs on a baking sheet and place a spoonful of the duck mixture in the centre of each. Roll out the remaining 6 discs of pastry to make them about 1cm larger all round than the bases. Brush the edges of the pastry bases with a little beaten egg white and lay the other discs of pastry on top. Press the edges to seal. Brush the tops with beaten egg yolk and use the blunt side of a knife to make little scores from the centre to the edge. Chill in the fridge until ready to cook.

To finish the starter, blend the soup until smooth and pass through a fine sieve into a clean pan. Reheat and season to taste. Ladle into bowls, place a spoonful of the tapenade in each and serve with the toasted sourdough on the side.

To finish the main course, place the pithiviers in the oven while you have the starter and bake for 15–20 minutes

until the pastry is golden and has risen well. Serve hot with the pineapple chutney on the side.

To finish the dessert, beat the mascarpone in a small bowl with the crème fraîche, and then beat in the reserved melted chocolate. (If it has hardened, reheat over hot water.) Gently pull the chocolate buttons away from the parchment paper and place one on each of your 6 dessert plates. To serve, place a spoonful of the chocolate cream on each one, dust with a little cocoa and top with another button slightly on the squiff.

Swede Soup with Black Olive Tapenade
1 large swede
1 large potato
1 large onion
1 celery stick
2 garlic cloves
2 tablespoons olive oil
1.7 litres vegetable or chicken stock
50g black olive tapenade
sea salt and freshly ground black pepper
thinly sliced toasted sourdough, to serve

Duck & Pear Pithivier
2 x 200g duck breasts (or 2 x 350g duck legs)
6 spring onions
1 large ripe pear (about 200g)
700g puff pastry
1 large egg
sea salt and freshly ground black pepper

Marinade
5cm piece of fresh root ginger
3 garlic cloves
1 tablespoon Shaohsing or Chinese cooking wine
1 tablespoon dark soy sauce

2 teaspoons Chinese five-spice powder
2 tablespoons honey
6 tablespoons hoisin sauce
1 tablespoon sesame oil

Pineapple Chutney
½ ripe fresh pineapple (about 800g)
1 garlic clove
5cm piece of fresh root ginger
½ red onion
1½ limes
1 red chilli
1 teaspoon brown sugar
sea salt and freshly ground black pepper

Giant Chocolate & Ginger Buttons with Chocolate Cream
50g pine nuts
300g good-quality dark chocolate
50g crystallised ginger
250g mascarpone
200g crème fraîche
cocoa powder, to dust

SWEDE SOUP WITH BLACK OLIVE TAPENADE

I have my friend, the food writer Rosie Stark, to thank for this inspirational combination of swede and tapenade.

Roughly chop the swede and potato. Chop the onion and celery and crush the garlic.

Heat the olive oil in a large pan. Add the onion, celery and garlic and cook without colouring for 5–10 minutes, or until soft.

Add the swede, potato and stock, bring to the boil and simmer for 15–20 minutes, or until the swede and potato are tender. Leave the soup to cool slightly, and then blend until smooth. Pass through a fine sieve and return to the pan.

Season to taste with salt and pepper. Reheat and serve with a spoonful of the tapenade dolloped in the centre and the toasted sourdough on the side.

1 large swede
1 large potato
1 large onion
1 celery stick
2 garlic cloves
2 tablespoons olive oil
1.7 litres vegetable or
 chicken stock
50g black olive tapenade
sea salt and freshly
 ground black pepper
thinly sliced toasted
 sourdough, to serve

DUCK & PEAR PITHIVIER WITH FRESH PINEAPPLE CHUTNEY

Pithivier is a French style of pie which has little 'humps' of filling sandwiched between two layers of buttery puff pastry.

Preheat your oven to 220°C/ gas mark 7.

Prick the skin of the duck breasts all over and season. Heat a small oven-proof frying pan over a moderate heat and add the breasts, skin-side down. Cook for 3 minutes before turning the breasts over and cooking for a further 3 minutes on the other side. Transfer to the oven and cook for about 12 minutes, or until tender but still pink. (Alternatively, place the duck legs on a roasting tray and place in the oven for 30 minutes, or until tender.) Remove from the oven and leave to cool.

Remove the skin from the duck, and then dice the flesh very finely to create a coarse mince. Place in a small bowl.

Peel the ginger and finely chop with the garlic for the marinade. Combine with the other marinade ingredients in a bowl, and then pour over the minced duck. Finely slice the spring onions. Peel and core the pear and chop finely. Add the onions and pear to the duck mixture and combine well.

Roll out the pastry thinly and cut into 12 discs, about 15cm in diameter. Separate the egg, placing the yolk and white in separate little bowls. Add a pinch of salt to each and beat well with a fork. Arrange 6 of the pastry discs on a baking sheet and place a spoonful of the duck mixture in the centre of each. Roll out the remaining 6 discs of pastry to make them about 1cm larger all round than the bases. Brush the edges of the pastry bases with a little beaten egg white and lay the other discs of pastry on top. Press the edges to seal.

Brush the tops with beaten egg yolk and, using the blunt side of a knife, make little scores from the centre to the edge. Chill in the fridge until ready to cook, and then bake in the oven for 15–20 minutes until the pastry is golden and has risen well.

To make the chutney, peel, core and finely dice the pineapple (see page 27). Crush the garlic, peel and finely grate the ginger and finely chop the red onion. Squeeze the juice from the limes into a bowl. Deseed and finely chop the red chilli. Place all the ingredients in a bowl, stir in the sugar and season.

2 x 200g duck breasts (or 2 x 350g duck legs)
6 spring onions
1 large ripe pear (about 200g)
700g puff pastry
1 large egg

For the marinade
5cm piece of fresh root ginger
3 garlic cloves
1 tablespoon Shaohsing or Chinese cooking wine
1 tablespoon dark soy sauce
2 teaspoons Chinese five-spice powder
2 tablespoons honey
6 tablespoons hoisin sauce
1 tablespoon sesame oil
sea salt and freshly ground black pepper

For the Pineapple Chutney
½ ripe fresh pineapple, (about 800g)
1 garlic clove
5cm piece of fresh root ginger
½ red onion
1½ limes
1 red chilli
1 teaspoon brown sugar

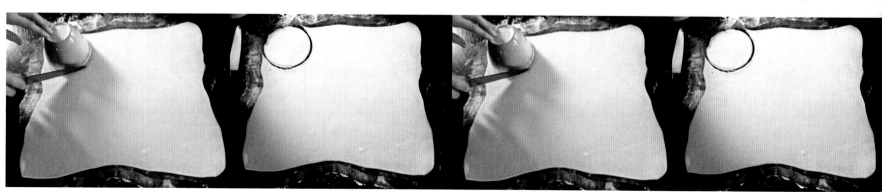

GIANT CHOCOLATE & GINGER BUTTONS WITH CHOCOLATE CREAM

300g good-quality
 dark chocolate
50g pine nuts
50g crystallised ginger
250g mascarpone
200g crème fraîche
cocoa powder, to dust

You could experiment with milk chocolate if dark chocolate isn't your thing.

Preheat your oven to 180°C/gas mark 4.

Bring a small pan of water to the boil, and then reduce the heat until barely simmering. Finely chop the chocolate, place in a small heatproof bowl and set over the water. Remove the pan from the heat and stir occasionally until melted and smooth.

Scatter the pine nuts on a baking tray and toast in the oven for 5–10 minutes until golden brown. Remove from the oven and spread on a plate to cool. Line 2 baking trays with parchment paper. Finely chop the ginger.

Reserve one-third of the melted chocolate for the chocolate cream. To make the buttons, place 12 spoonfuls of the remaining melted chocolate onto the prepared baking trays, spreading them out into rounds about 10cm in diameter. Scatter evenly with crystallised ginger and pine nuts and place in the fridge to harden.

Beat the mascarpone in a small bowl with the crème fraîche, and then beat in the reserved melted chocolate.

To serve, gently pull the chocolate buttons away from the parchment paper and place one on each of your 6 dessert plates. Place a spoonful of the chocolate cream on each one, dust with a little cocoa and top with another button slightly on the squiff – like a Philip Treacy fascinator!

BEETROOT MISO.

TEA-SMOKED SALMON WITH SATSUMA & POMEGRANATE SALAD.

ROSEWATER ZABAGLIONE.

60 min   Start with the zabaglione. Chop the pistachios finely and set aside. Place the egg yolks, sugar, wine and rosewater in a large, heatproof bowl. Add 3 tablespoons boiling water and set over a pan of gently simmering water.

50 min   Using an electric whisk, beat the mixture until it thickens and becomes pale, light and fluffy (don't let it get too hot or you will end up with scrambled eggs!). To check if it is ready, drag the whisk across the surface – the zabaglione should leave a ribbon-like trail that sits there for a few moments before sinking in. Spoon into 6 small, pretty glasses and set aside at room temperature.

40 min   Now for the main course. Combine the sugar, rice and tea leaves in a bowl. Line the base of a wok (or deep roasting tin) with a double sheet of foil and tip in the rice mixture. Place a trivet on top. Season the salmon fillets, lay each one on an individual square of parchment paper and place in a single layer on the trivet. Cover very tightly with a lid or a tent of foil and set aside.

30 min   To make the salad, peel the satsumas or clementines and slice thinly. Lay the slices on a large serving platter. Remove the pomegranate seeds from the shell (see page 27), discarding all the bitter white pith, and scatter over the satsuma slices. To make the dressing, mix all the remaining ingredients for the salad together in a bowl, season and pour over the fruit. Cover and set aside.

20 min   To smoke the salmon, set the wok or roasting tin over a moderate heat. The tea will start to smoulder after only a couple of minutes. If you are unsure if this is happening, then lift the lid slightly and check. Reseal and continue. Once it is smoking, reduce the heat to low and leave to smoke gently for 15 minutes. Meanwhile, cook the jasmine rice according to the packet instructions. Remove

the salmon from the heat and leave to stand for a further 5 minutes before removing the lid.

To make the soup, shred the beetroot into large matchsticks, slice the ginger (no need to peel), thinly slice the spring onions and chop the mint.

10 min   Bring 1.2 litres water to the boil with the ginger. Add the beetroot matchsticks, reduce the heat and simmer for a minute or two. Stir in the miso paste, mint, spring onions and beansprouts and cook for a minute more. Check for seasoning – you may not need any salt because the miso is quite salty.

To serve, ladle the soup into small bowls and accompany with a little wasabi paste (if using) on the side for guests to whisk into their bowl if they wish.

To serve the main course, drain the rice and place a small pile on each dinner plate. Top with a piece of salmon and serve immediately with the salad on the side.

Just before you serve the zabaglione, scatter the tops with chopped pistachios and place a couple of sponge fingers on the side.

Beetroot Miso
250g cooked beetroot (not in vinegar)
 – see page 24
5cm piece of fresh root ginger
6 spring onions
a few mint leaves
4 tablespoons yellow, red or white miso paste
100g beansprouts
sea salt and freshly ground black pepper
wasabi paste, to serve (optional)

Tea-smoked Salmon with Satsuma &
Pomegranate Salad
100g dark muscovado sugar
100g rice (any kind)
100g tea leaves of your choice (I use jasmine tea)
6 x 150g salmon fillets, skin on
sea salt and freshly ground black pepper
350g jasmine rice, to serve

Satsuma and Pomegranate Salad
6 satsumas or clementines
½ pomegranate
2 tablespoons rice vinegar
pinch of Chinese five-spice powder
1 tablespoon sesame oil
2 tablespoons sesame seeds (optional)
2 tablespoons groundnut oil
sea salt and freshly ground black pepper

Rosewater Zabaglione
15g pistachios
6 large egg yolks
100g caster sugar
100ml dessert wine
2 teaspoons rosewater
12 sponge fingers, to serve

BEETROOT MISO

I would recommend reading the tips about miso on page 8.

Shred the beetroot into large matchsticks. Slice the ginger (no need to peel), thinly slice the spring onions and chop the mint.

Bring 1.2 litres water to the boil with the ginger. Add the beetroot, reduce the heat and simmer for a minute or two.

Stir in the miso paste, mint, spring onions and beansprouts and cook for a minute more. Check for seasoning — you may not need any salt because the miso is quite salty.

Ladle into small bowls and serve with a little wasabi paste (if using) on the side for guests to whisk into their bowls if they wish.

250g cooked beetroot
 (not in vinegar) — see
 page 24
5cm piece of fresh
 root ginger
6 spring onions
a few mint leaves
4 tablespoons yellow,
 red or white
 miso paste
100g beansprouts
sea salt and freshly
 ground black pepper
wasabi paste, to serve
 (optional)

TEA-SMOKED SALMON WITH SATSUMA & POMEGRANATE SALAD

Tea smoking imparts a beautifully delicate smokey flavour to the salmon.

To make the salad, peel the satsumas or clementines and slice thinly. Lay the slices on a large serving platter. Remove the pomegranate seeds from the shell (see page 27), discarding all the bitter white pith, and scatter over the satsuma slices. To make the dressing, mix all the remaining ingredients for the salad together in a small bowl and season. Pour over the fruit, cover and set aside until needed.

Combine the sugar, rice and tea leaves in a bowl. Line the base of a wok (or deep roasting tin) with a double sheet of foil and tip in the rice mixture. Place a trivet on top.

Season the salmon fillets, lay each one on an individual square of parchment paper and place in a single layer on the trivet. Cover very tightly with a lid or a tent of foil. Place the wok or roasting tin over a moderate heat. The tea will start to smoulder after only a couple of minutes. If you are unsure if this is happening, lift the lid slightly and check. Reseal and continue. When you are satisfied that the tea is smouldering, reduce the heat to low and leave to smoke gently for 15 minutes.

Meanwhile, cook the jasmine rice according to the packet instructions.

Once the salmon has finished smoking, remove it from the heat and leave to stand for a further 5 minutes before removing the lid. Serve immediately with the jasmine rice and salad.

CAUTION: IT'S POSSIBLE THAT A LOT OF SMOKE CAN BE PRODUCED, SO MAKE SURE YOUR KITCHEN IS WELL VENTILATED.

100g dark muscovado sugar
100g rice (any kind)
100g tea leaves of your choice (I use jasmine tea)
6 x 150g salmon fillets, skin on
sea salt and freshly ground black pepper
350g jasmine rice, to serve

For the salad
6 satsumas or clementines
½ pomegranate
2 tablespoons rice vinegar
pinch of Chinese five-spice powder
1 tablespoon sesame oil
2 tablespoons sesame seeds (optional)
2 tablespoons groundnut oil
sea salt and freshly ground black pepper

ROSEWATER ZABAGLIONE

Rosewaters can be quite potent as they do vary in strength and also their flavour will fade if they are kept for a length of time. Add a very little, then add more to taste.

Chop the pistachios finely.

Place the egg yolks, sugar, wine, rosewater and 3 tablespoons boiling water in a large, heatproof bowl and set over a pan of gently simmering water. Using an electric whisk, beat the mixture until it thickens and becomes pale, light and fluffy (don't let it get too hot or you will end up with scrambled eggs!). To check if it is ready, drag the whisk across the surface – the zabaglione should leave a ribbon-like trail that sits there for a few moments before sinking in.

Spoon into 6 small, pretty glasses, sprinkle with chopped pistachios and serve the sponge fingers on the side.

15g pistachios
6 large egg yolks
100g caster sugar
100ml dessert wine
2 teaspoons rosewater
12 sponge fingers, to serve

KIPPER & CAPER PÂTÉ WITH PARSLEY SALAD.
ROAST WOOD PIGEON WITH BLACK OLIVES & ROAST GARLIC ROSEMARY POTATOES.
BRANDY SNAP CANNOLI.

60 min   Preheat your oven to 220°C/gas mark 7. Fill a kettle and bring to the boil. Place the kippers in a deep heatproof bowl and pour over boiling water to submerge completely. Leave for 20 minutes. (This will cook the kippers thoroughly.)

Now for the dessert. To make the filling for the cannoli, finely chop the candied fruit and chocolate. Place the ricotta in a bowl with the candied fruit, chocolate, caster sugar, cinnamon and a few drops of orange flower water. Beat well together, cover with clingfilm and chill until needed.

50 min   Carefully drain the kippers and remove any skin and bones. Place the flesh in a food processor. Finely grate the zest and squeeze the juice from the lemon. Melt the butter, add to the food processor and blend until smooth. Add the capers and blend briefly again. Scrape out the mixture into a bowl and stir in half of the lemon juice, the lemon zest, cream, mace and cayenne. Season to taste with salt and pepper, adding more lemon juice if required. Spoon into a small serving bowl, cover and chill until needed.

40 min   For the main course, slice the potatoes very thinly and arrange on 2 large baking trays. Pull 6 of the rosemary sprigs along their length to remove the leaves and scatter over the potatoes. Drizzle with oil and season well with salt and pepper. Break the garlic bulb apart and scatter a few whole, unpeeled cloves over each tray. Mix everything together with your hands and spread out in a single layer. Place the trays on the top and middle shelves of the oven and cook for 35–40 minutes. Remove the potatoes from the oven occasionally and use a fish slice to turn them over, spreading them out in a single layer again – don't worry if some of the slices break up slightly. When you return the trays to the oven, swap them around so the tray that was on the middle shelf is now on the top and vice versa.

30 min   Back to the starter. For the parsley salad, slice the onion very finely and place with the parsley in a serving bowl. To make the dressing, finely grate the zest and squeeze the juice from the lemon. Place in a small bowl with the mustard, whisk in the olive oil and season with salt and pepper.

20 min   Season the pigeons inside and out and put a sprig of rosemary, a knob of butter and about 5 olives in the cavity of each bird. Melt the remaining butter in a roasting tray or oven-proof pan on the hob. When it is sizzling, put in the pigeons and quickly brown them all over.

10 min   Place the pigeons breast-side up and roast on the bottom shelf of the oven for 10–12 minutes. Remove from the oven, turn the pigeons upside down in the tray and cover with foil to keep warm while you eat the starter.

To serve the starter, combine the parsley leaves with the dressing and place in a serving bowl. Place the kipper pâté on the table and accompany with some thinly sliced rye or pumpernickel bread.

To serve the main course, make a little nest of potatoes on 6 dinner plates and top each one with a pigeon. Pour over any of the juices from the pan and garnish with fresh watercress.

To finish the dessert, just before serving pipe the filling into the brandy snap shells with a piping bag – or use a small teaspoon instead. Place a piece of candied fruit on each end of the brandy snaps to decorate.

Kipper & Caper Pâté
2 whole kippers
1 lemon
100g butter
2 tablespoons capers
100ml double cream
¼ teaspoon ground mace
¼ teaspoon cayenne
sea salt and freshly ground black pepper
rye or pumpernickel bread, to serve

Parsley Salad
½ red onion
100g flat-leaf parsley leaves
1 lemon
2 teaspoons wholegrain mustard
2 tablespoons olive oil
sea salt and freshly ground black pepper

Roast Wood Pigeon with Black Olives & Roast Garlic Rosemary Potatoes
800g potatoes
12 long sprigs of rosemary
100ml olive oil
1 whole garlic bulb
6 wood pigeons
100g butter
30 dry black or Kalamata olives
sea salt and freshly ground black pepper
watercress, to serve

Brandy Snap Cannoli
40g good-quality candied fruit, plus extra
  pieces to decorate
50g good-quality dark chocolate
375g ricotta
40g caster sugar
pinch of ground cinnamon (optional)
few drops of orange flower water
12 brandy snaps

KIPPER & CAPER PÂTÉ WITH PARSLEY SALAD

Don't worry about removing the very fine, hair-like bones from the kippers, as they will be whizzed smooth in the food processor.

Fill a kettle and bring to the boil. Place the kippers in a deep heatproof bowl and pour over boiling water to submerge completely. Leave for 20 minutes. (This will cook the kippers thoroughly.) Carefully drain, remove the skin and bones and place the flesh in the bowl of a food processor. Finely grate the zest and squeeze the juice from the lemon.

Melt the butter, add to the food processor with the kipper flesh and blend until smooth. Add the capers and blend briefly again. Scrape out the mixture into a bowl and stir in half of the lemon juice, the lemon zest, cream, mace and cayenne. Season to taste with salt and pepper, adding more lemon juice if required. Cover and chill until needed.

To make the parsley salad, slice the onion very finely and place in a serving bowl with the parsley leaves. To make the dressing, finely grate the zest and squeeze the juice from the lemon. Place in a small bowl with the mustard, whisk in the olive oil and season with salt and pepper. Just before you are ready to serve, add the dressing to the sliced onion and parsley leaves and mix well together.

Serve the pâté with the parsley salad and some thinly sliced rye or pumpernickel bread.

2 whole kippers
1 lemon
100g butter
2 tablespoons capers
100ml double cream
¼ teaspoon ground mace
¼ teaspoon cayenne
sea salt and freshly
 ground black pepper
rye or pumpernickel
 bread, to serve

For the Parsley Salad
½ red onion
100g flat-leaf parsley
 leaves 1 lemon
2 teaspoons wholegrain
 mustard
2 tablespoons olive oil
sea salt and freshly
 ground black pepper

ROAST WOOD PIGEON WITH BLACK OLIVES & ROAST GARLIC ROSEMARY POTATOES

Quail or partridge can both be used as alternatives to wood pigeon.

Preheat your oven to 220°C/gas mark 7.

Keeping the skins on, slice the potatoes very thinly (a mandolin is good for this) and divide between 2 large baking trays. Pull 6 of the rosemary sprigs along their length to remove the leaves and scatter over the potatoes, discarding the stalks. Drizzle with the oil and season well with salt and pepper. Break the garlic bulb apart and scatter a few whole, unpeeled cloves over each tray. Mix everything together with your hands and spread out in a single layer.

Place the trays on the top and middle shelves of the oven and cook for 35–40 minutes. Remove the potatoes from the oven occasionally and use a fish slice to turn them over, spreading them out again in a single layer – don't worry if some of the slices break up slightly. When you return the trays to the oven, swap them around so the tray that was on the middle shelf is now on the top and viceversa. You should end up with some lovely crispy potatoes and some soft ones.

Meanwhile, season the pigeons inside and out and put a sprig of rosemary, a knob of the butter and about 5 olives in the cavity of each bird.

Melt the remaining butter in a roasting tray or an oven-proof pan on the hob. When it is sizzling, put in the pigeons and brown them quickly all over. Place the birds, breast-side up, on the bottom shelf of the oven for 10–12 minutes.

Once the pigeons are cooked, remove them from the oven and turn the birds upside down in the tray. Cover loosely with foil to keep warm while the potatoes finish cooking.

To serve, make a little nest of potatoes on 6 dinner plates and top each one with a pigeon. Pour over any juices from the pan and garnish with fresh watercress.

800g potatoes
12 long sprigs of
 rosemary
100ml olive oil
1 whole garlic bulb
6 wood pigeons
100g butter
30 dry black or
 Kalamata olives
sea salt and freshly
 ground black pepper
watercress, to serve

BRANDY SNAP CANNOLI

Cannoli are Sicilian pastries of Arab origin, deep-fried pastry shells filled with sweetened ricotta filling. Here I have used crispy brandy snaps as an alternative, but you could always just sandwich the filling between fine biscuits or waffle biscuits. Get good-quality candied fruit if you can, with pieces you can chop yourself.

Finely chop the candied fruit and chocolate. Place the ricotta in a bowl with the candied fruit, chocolate, caster sugar, cinnamon if using and a few drops of orange flower water. Beat together well.

Before serving, use a piping bag to pipe the mixture into the brandy snap shells – or use a small teaspoon. Place a piece of candied fruit on each end of the brandy snaps to decorate.

Serve 2 brandy snap cannoli per diner.

40g good-quality
 candied fruit, plus extra
 pieces to decorate
50g good-quality
 dark chocolate
375g ricotta
40g caster sugar
pinch of ground cinnamon
 (optional)
few drops of orange
 flower water
12 brandy snaps

VENETIAN LEMON & MINT SGROPPINO.
DUCK & DATE CAKES WITH SARLADAISE POTATOES & BEETROOT CHICORY SALAD.
MARBLED BLACK FOREST ALASKA.

60 min   Start with the main course. Preheat your oven to 200°C/gas mark 6. Place the dates in a small pan with just enough water to cover and sprinkle in the cinnamon. Bring to the boil, reduce the heat and simmer for 10 minutes or until the dates are soft. Drain and leave to cool slightly. Place the pine nuts on a baking sheet and toast in the oven for 5–8 minutes or until golden.

50 min   Remove the meat pieces from the jar of confit and scrape most of the fat off (reserve the fat). Pull the flesh from the bones and place it in the bowl of a food processor. Slice the potatoes. Remove the leaves from the thyme sprigs and finely chop one of the garlic cloves.

40 min   Spoon 6 tablespoons of the fat from the confit jar into a roasting tin and set over a moderate heat. Add the potato slices, thyme leaves and chopped garlic. Season well with salt and pepper and stir for a minute or two over the heat. Place in the oven for 35–40 minutes until the potatoes are tender and golden brown.

30 min   Take the ice cream out of the freezer and leave to soften for about 20 minutes. Meanwhile, get on with the duck cakes. Peel and finely grate the ginger and crush the remaining garlic. Remove the leaves from the parsley and finely chop. Cut the preserved lemons in half and remove the seeds, then roughly chop. Add the ginger, garlic and lemon to the food processor, along with the dates, the remaining spices and the honey. Pulse 3 or 4 times until well combined, but not to a paste. Scrape the duck and date mixture into a bowl and stir in the toasted pine nuts and chopped parsley. Season well with salt and pepper. Divide the mixture into 6 equal patties and place on a plate or tray in the fridge until needed. Wash out the food processor.

20 min   Now for the baked Alaska. Lay the brownies (or chocolate cake) in a square on a baking sheet, butting the pieces up tightly so there are no gaps in between. Drain the cherries and spoon on top. Scrape the contents of the ice-cream container into the centre, allowing a 5cm rim all around. Place this back in the freezer until you are ready to serve.

To make the salad, separate the chicory leaves and place in a large serving bowl. Chop the cooked beetroot into 2.5cm cubes and tumble into the bowl. Prepare the mint for the starter by removing the leaves from the stalks (set aside a few leaves for the garnish).

10 min   Back to the dessert. Bring a small pan of water to the boil, reduce the heat to barely simmering and set a heatproof bowl on top. Finely chop the chocolate and place in the bowl. Remove the pan from the heat and stir occasionally until the chocolate has melted.

Meanwhile, heat a dry, non-stick pan for the duck cakes. Fry the duck cakes for 2–3 minutes on each side and keep warm while you make the sgroppino.

To make the starter, scrape the lemon sorbet into the bowl of a food processor. Add the mint and, with the motor running, pour in the vodka through the funnel. Quickly pour in the sparkling wine and blitz for a couple of seconds until just combined – don't overdo it. Pour the frozen slush into 6 pretty glasses, sprinkle with the reserved mint leaves and serve immediately.

To serve the main course, place a duck cake and a spoonful of potatoes on each of 6 dinner plates. Season the chicory and beetroot salad with salt and pepper and drizzle with balsamic vinegar. Toss well together and pile a little mound onto each plate.

To finish the dessert, whisk the egg whites and salt together in a large bowl until stiff. Gradually add the caster sugar, a spoonful at a time, making sure it is mixed in well after each addition. Keep whisking until the mixture is thick and glossy.

Drizzle a spoonful of the melted chocolate over the meringue in the bowl and scoop out large spoonfuls of the marbled meringue mixture onto the sponge and ice cream. Drizzle in a little more chocolate each time you take out a spoonful of meringue. Keep piling on the meringue mixture, making sure there are no gaps, so the ice cream is completely sealed beneath the meringue. Place in the oven and bake for about 10 minutes, or until the meringue is starting to brown around the edges. Remove from the oven and serve immediately.

Venetian Lemon & Mint Sgroppino
couple of springs fresh mint
500ml lemon sorbet
2 shots of vodka
¼ bottle Prosecco, Cava
 or other sparkling wine
6 cocktail umbrellas,
 to serve (optional)

Duck & Date Cakes with Sarladaise Potatoes
& Beetroot Chicory Salad
200g pitted dates
½ teaspoon ground cinnamon
50g pine nuts
750g duck confit in fat
6 medium potatoes
15g fresh thyme
3 garlic cloves
5cm piece of fresh root ginger
25g flat-leaf parsley
100g preserved lemons
1½ teaspoons ground cardamom

1 teaspoon ground allspice
2 tablespoons honey
3 heads of chicory
4 cooked, peeled beetroots
 (not in vinegar) – see page 24
1 tablespoon balsamic vinegar
sea salt and freshly ground black pepper

Marbled Black Forest Alaska
1 x 500ml tub chocolate ice cream
enough chocolate brownies (or chocolate
 sponge cake) to create a 20cm square
1 x 425g tin/jar black
 cherries in syrup
50g dark chocolate
3 egg whites
pinch of salt
175g caster sugar

VENETIAN LEMON & MINT SGROPPINO

An unusual starter of a fizzy, frozen, zingy slush that freshens and wakes up your palate. Something light before the rich duck main course.

Pull the mint leaves from the stalks and set aside a few leaves for the garnish. Scrape the lemon sorbet into the bowl of a food processor and add the rest of the mint leaves. With the motor running, pour in the vodka through the funnel.

Quickly pour in the sparkling wine and blitz for a couple of seconds until just combined – don't overdo it or you will melt the sorbet completely. Pour the frozen slush into 6 pretty glasses, sprinkle with the reserved mint leaves, add a cocktail umbrella for fun and serve immediately.

couple of sprigs
 of fresh mint
500ml lemon sorbet
2 shots of vodka
¼ bottle Prosecco, Cava
 or other sparkling wine
6 cocktail umbrellas,
 to serve, if you wish

DUCK & DATE CAKES WITH SARLADAISE POTATOES & BEETROOT CHICORY SALAD

Preheat your oven to 200°C/gas mark 6.

Place the dates in a small pan with just enough water to cover and sprinkle in the cinnamon. Bring to the boil, reduce the heat and simmer for 10 minutes or until the dates are soft. Drain and leave to cool slightly. Place the pine nuts on a baking sheet and toast in the oven for 5–8 minutes or until golden.

Remove the meat pieces from the jar of confit and scrape most of the fat off (reserve the fat). Pull the flesh from the bones and place it in the bowl of a food processor. Slice the potatoes. Remove the leaves from the thyme sprigs and finely chop one of the garlic cloves.

Spoon 6 tablespoons of the fat from the confit jar into a roasting tin and set over a moderate heat. Add the potato slices, thyme leaves and chopped garlic. Season well with salt and pepper and stir for a minute or two over the heat. Place in the oven for 35–40 minutes until the potatoes are tender and golden brown.

Peel and finely grate the ginger and crush the remaining garlic. Remove the leaves from the parsley and finely chop. Cut the preserved lemons in half and remove the seeds, then roughly chop. Add the ginger, garlic and lemon to the food processor, along with the dates, the remaining spices and the honey. Pulse 3 or 4 times until well combined, but not to a paste.

Scrape the duck and date mixture into a mixing bowl and stir in the toasted pine nuts and chopped parsley. Season well with salt and pepper. Divide the mixture into 6 equal patties and place on a plate or tray in the fridge until needed.

Heat a dry, non-stick frying pan over a moderate heat and fry the duck cakes for 2–3 minutes on each side. Keep warm.

To make the salad, separate the chicory leaves and place in a large bowl. Chop the cooked beetroot into 2.5cm cubes and tumble into the bowl. Season well with salt and pepper, drizzle with the balsamic vinegar and toss together. Serve with the potatoes and salad on the side.

200g pitted dates
½ teaspoon
 ground cinnamon
50g pine nuts
750g duck confit in fat
6 medium potatoes
15g fresh thyme
3 garlic cloves
5cm piece of fresh
 root ginger
25g flat-leaf parsley
100g preserved lemons
1½ teaspoons
 ground cardamom
1 teaspoon
 ground allspice
2 tablespoons honey
3 heads of chicory
4 cooked, peeled
 beetroots (not in
 vinegar) – see page 24
1 tablespoon
 balsamic vinegar
sea salt and freshly
 ground black pepper

MARBLED BLACK FOREST ALASKA

A celebratory baked Alaska. To make this even more special you could add a dusting of edible gold leaf or sparklers for a bit of glitz — one sheet of edible gold leaf (available from good art or cake-making suppliers) should be enough. And don't forget to clear a space in your freezer so the baking tray lays flat.

1 x 500ml tub
  chocolate ice cream
enough chocolate
  brownies (or chocolate
  sponge cake) to create a
  20cm square
1 x 425g tin/jar black
  cherries in syrup
50g dark chocolate
3 egg whites
pinch of salt
175g caster sugar

Take the ice cream out of the freezer and leave to soften for about 20 minutes. Lay the brownies (or chocolate cake) in a square on a baking sheet, butting them up tightly. Drain the cherries and spoon on top. Scrape the contents of the ice-cream container into the centre, allowing a 5cm rim all around. Place this back in the freezer until you are ready to serve.

Bring a small pan of water to the boil, reduce the heat to barely simmering and set a small heatproof bowl on top. Finely chop the chocolate and place in the bowl over the water. Remove the pan from the heat immediately and stir the chocolate from time to time until it has melted.

Preheat your oven to 200°C/gas mark 6. Whisk the egg whites and salt together in a large bowl until stiff. Gradually add the caster sugar, a spoonful at a time, making sure it is mixed in well after each addition. Keep whisking until the mixture is thick and glossy.

Drizzle a spoonful of the melted chocolate over the meringue in the bowl and scoop out large spoonfuls of the marbled meringue mixture onto the ice cream and sponge. Drizzle in a little more chocolate each time you take out a spoonful of meringue. Keep piling on the meringue mixture, making sure there are no gaps, so the ice cream is completely sealed beneath the meringue.

Place in the oven and bake for about 10 minutes, or until the meringue is starting to brown around the edges. Remove from the oven and serve immediately.

GIN & JUNIPER MARINATED SALMON WITH PINK GRAPEFRUIT.
TURKEY SALTIMBOCCA WITH ANCHOVY BUTTER & CRUSHED RED WINE POTATOES.
CARAMELISED CLEMENTINES & POMEGRANATE WITH VANILLA ICE CREAM.

60 min Begin with the dessert. Peel the clementines and remove all of the white pith. Slice 6 of the fruit into 3 slices across the middle and lay in a serving dish. Cut the pomegranate into quarters and turn the skin inside out to pop out all the seeds (see page 27). Make sure that none of the bitter white pith is attached. Scatter the pomegranate seeds over the clementines in the dish. Squeeze the juice from the 2 remaining clementines into a jug and set aside.

50 min Place the sugar in a saucepan with 175ml water and bring to the boil, stirring to dissolve. Simmer over a moderate heat for about 10 minutes, or until the syrup starts to take on a caramel colour. Boil a kettle of water. Remove the hot caramel from the heat and, covering your hand with a tea towel (because the caramel will spit and splutter), very carefully pour in 175ml boiling water along with the reserved clementine juice. Stir to mix. If the sugar starts to set slightly, return the pan to the heat for a minute or two to melt it again. Pour the caramel liquid over the sliced clementines, cover and leave to cool.

40 min Now for the starter. Slice the salmon as thinly as possible and lay in a single layer in a non-metallic dish. Cut a thin slice from the top and bottom of each grapefruit so they stand upright on the board. Use a knife to peel the grapefruits from top to bottom, removing all the pith. Holding the fruit over a dish to catch the juice, cut the grapefruits into segments by cutting down on either side of the membrane and removing the flesh (see page 26). Place the segments in a dish and squeeze over any remaining juice from the pulp. Slice the red onion very thinly and chop the cucumber into small cubes. Place the juniper berries and peppercorns in a pestle and mortar and crush well – or use a rolling pin. Sprinkle the mixture over the salmon and add the red onion, gin, vinegar, salt and walnut oil. Mix together and then spread the salmon out in a single layer. Cover and leave to marinate at room temperature for about 30 minutes, or until the salmon starts to turn opaque.

30 min Now prepare the potatoes for the main course. Put the (unpeeled) potatoes in a clean cloth and, using a wooden mallet or rolling pin, gently thump them to crack them open but not in half. Crush the peppercorns in a pestle and mortar. Heat the oil over a medium-to-high heat in a pan large enough to hold the potatoes in a single layer. Add the potatoes, crushed peppercorns and some salt and cook for 4–5 minutes until golden brown, turning occasionally. Then add the wine, bring to the boil and reduce the heat. Add the sprigs of thyme, cover with a lid and simmer gently for 25–30 minutes, shaking the pan and turning the potatoes occasionally, until tender.

20 min To make the anchovy butter, place the butter in a bowl and beat until soft. Rinse the capers in warm water, drain and roughly chop. Crush the garlic. Squeeze the juice from the lemon. Drain the anchovies and finely crush them on a board with the back of a knife. Add the crushed anchovies, garlic, capers and lemon juice to the butter, season with black pepper and mix well.

10 min Season the turkey breast steaks (or fillets) on both sides with salt and pepper. Place a few sage leaves on each turkey breast and lay a slice of Parma ham on top, pleating it in the middle to fit. Attach with a wooden cocktail stick or two. Cut the cabbage into large wedges.

To serve the starter, turn the salmon over in the serving dish and place the dish on the table. Accompany with plenty of crusty country bread to mop up the gorgeous juices.

To cook the cabbage for the main course, bring a large pan of salted water to the boil, add the cabbage and boil for 3–4 minutes until just tender. Drain well, season with lots of black pepper and keep warm while you cook the saltimbocca. Divide the oil and butter between 2 frying pans over a high heat, and add the saltimbocca, Parma-ham-side down. Fry for 1–2 minutes on the first side, adding a few more sage

leaves to the pan as you cook, and then turn over and cook for a further 1–2 minutes on the other side or until cooked through. Spoon the hot butter over the saltimbocca as they cook, and then transfer them to a serving plate. Scoop a spoonful of the anchovy butter onto each saltimbocca, add cooking juices from the pan and serve with the potatoes and cabbage.

To serve the dessert, place the dish of clementines on the table for everyone to help themselves. Accompany with the vanilla ice cream.

Gin & Juniper Marinated Salmon with Pink Grapefruit
600g really fresh salmon
3 pink grapefruits
1 small red onion
½ cucumber
1 tablespoon juniper berries
½ teaspoon white or black peppercorns
4 tablespoons good-quality gin
1 tablespoon balsamic vinegar
½ teaspoon sea salt flakes
2 tablespoons walnut oil
crusty country bread, to serve

Turkey Saltimbocca
6 x 150g turkey breast steaks or fillets
15g sage leaves
6 slices of Parma ham
1 tablespoon olive oil
25g butter
1 savoy cabbage
sea salt and freshly ground black pepper

Anchovy Butter
100g unsalted butter
½ tablespoon capers
1 large garlic clove

juice of ½ lemon
8 anchovies in oil

Crushed Red Wine Potatoes
1kg new potatoes
½ tablespoon whole black peppercorns
4 tablespoons olive oil
300ml red wine
15g fresh thyme
sea salt and freshly ground black pepper

Caramelised Clementines &
Pomegranate with Vanilla Ice Cream
8 clementines
1 pomegranate
100g golden caster sugar
vanilla ice cream, to serve

GIN & JUNIPER MARINATED SALMON WITH PINK GRAPEFRUIT

This is a version of ceviche where fish (in this case salmon) is very lightly cured. It 'cold cooks' in the juices. Leave it for 30 minutes, though you can leave it longer. You could get your fishmonger to slice it thinly for you.

Slice the salmon as thinly as possible and lay in a single layer in a non-metallic dish.

Cut a thin slice from the top and bottom of each grapefruit so they stand upright on the board. Holding each one the right way up, use a knife to peel the grapefruits from top to bottom, removing all the pith. Holding the fruit over a dish to catch the juices, cut the grapefruits into segments by cutting down on either side of the membrane and removing the flesh (see page 26). Place the segments in a dish and squeeze over any remaining juice from the pulp.

Slice the red onion very thinly. Chop the cucumber into small cubes. Crush the juniper berries and peppercorns in a pestle and mortar – or use a rolling pin – and sprinkle over the salmon in the dish. Add the red onion, cucumber, gin, vinegar, salt and walnut oil.

Mix everything together and then spread the salmon out again in a single layer. Cover and leave at room temperature for about 30 minutes or until the salmon starts to go opaque.

Just before you are about to serve, turn the salmon over in the dish and place on the table. Accompany with plenty of crusty country bread to mop up the gorgeous juices.

600g really fresh salmon
3 pink grapefruits
1 small red onion
½ cucumber
1 tablespoon
 juniper berries
½ teaspoon white or
 black peppercorns
4 tablespoons
 good-quality gin
1 tablespoon balsamic
 vinegar
½ teaspoon sea
 salt flakes
2 tablespoons walnut oil
crusty country bread,
 to serve

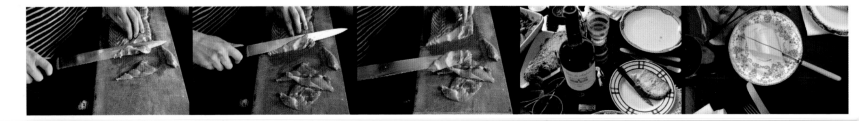

TURKEY SALTIMBOCCA WITH ANCHOVY BUTTER & CRUSHED RED WINE POTATOES

Tradtionally saltimbocca is veal topped with prosciutto and sage, but turkey works wonderfully well here.

Put the (unpeeled) potatoes in a clean cloth and, using a wooden mallet or rolling pin, gently thump them to crack them open but not in half. Crush the peppercorns in a pestle and mortar.

Heat the oil over a medium-to-high heat in a pan large enough to hold the potatoes in a single layer. Add the potatoes, crushed peppercorns and some salt and cook for 4–5 minutes until golden brown, turning occasionally. Then add the wine, bring to the boil and reduce the heat. Add the sprigs of thyme, cover with a lid and simmer gently for 25–30 minutes, shaking the pan and turning the potatoes occasionally, until tender.

To make the anchovy butter, place the butter in a bowl and beat until soft. Rinse the capers in warm water, drain and roughly chop. Crush the garlic. Squeeze the juice from the lemon. Drain the anchovies and finely crush them on a board with the back of a knife. Add the crushed anchovies, capers, garlic and lemon juice to the butter in the bowl, season with black pepper and mix well.

Cut the cabbage into large wedges. Bring a large pan of salted water to the boil, add the cabbage and boil for 3–4 minutes until just tender. Drain well and season with lots of black pepper.

Season the turkey breast steaks (or fillets) on both sides with salt and pepper. Place a few sage leaves on each turkey breast and lay a slice of Parma ham on top, pleating it in the middle to fit. Attach with a wooden cocktail stick or two.

Divide the oil and butter between 2 frying pans over a high heat, and add the saltimbocca, Parma-ham-side down. Fry for 1–2 minutes, adding a few more sage leaves to the pan as you cook. Turn over and cook for a further 1–2 minutes on the other side, or until the turkey is tender, spooning the butter over each saltimbocca as it cooks.

To serve, transfer to a plate, scoop a spoonful of the butter onto each saltimbocca and drizzle over some of the juices from the pan. Accompany with the cabbage and the potatoes on the side.

6 x 150g turkey breast
 steaks or fillets
15g sage leaves
6 slices of Parma ham
1 tablespoon olive oil
25g butter
1 savoy cabbage
sea salt and freshly
 ground black pepper

For the Anchovy Butter
100g unsalted butter
½ tablespoon capers
1 large garlic clove
juice of ½ lemon
8 anchovies in oil

For the Crushed
Red Wine Potatoes
1kg new potatoes
½ tablespoon whole
 black peppercorns
4 tablespoons olive oil
300ml red wine
15g fresh thyme
sea salt and freshly
 ground black pepper

CARAMELISED CLEMENTINES & POMEGRANATE WITH VANILLA ICE CREAM

The clementines and pomegranate give a bright, fresh zing in the cold, dark winter months.

Peel the clementines, making sure you remove all of the white pith. Slice 6 of the fruit into 3 slices across the middle and lay in a serving dish. Remove the seeds from the pomegranate (see page 27) and scatter over the clementines in the dish. Squeeze the juice from the 2 remaining clementines into a jug and set aside.

Place the sugar in a saucepan with 175ml water and bring to the boil, stirring to dissolve. Simmer over a moderate heat for about 10 minutes, or until the syrup starts to take on a caramel colour. Boil a kettle of water. Remove the hot caramel from the heat and, covering your hand with a tea towel first (because the caramel will spit and splutter), very carefully pour in 175ml boiling water from the kettle along with the reserved clementine juice. Stir to mix. If the sugar starts to set slightly, return the pan to the heat for a minute or two to melt it again.

Pour the caramel liquid over the sliced clementines, cover and leave to cool. To serve, place the dish on the table for everyone to help themselves. Accompany with the vanilla ice cream.

8 clementines
1 pomegranate
100g golden caster sugar
vanilla ice cream, to serve

ONION & CELERY HEART SOUP WITH STILTON CROÛTES.
ORANGE & HORSERADISH STEAK WITH CELERIAC & BEETROOT MASH.
POMEGRANATE TART.

60 min   Preheat your oven to 200°C/gas mark 6. Start with the soup. Slice the onions very thinly. Melt the butter and olive oil in a large saucepan, add the onions, a pinch of salt and the thyme and cook gently without colouring for 5 minutes.

Meanwhile, place the walnuts for the dessert on a baking sheet and toast in the oven for 5–10 minutes or until golden. Remove from the oven, cool and crush well.

50 min   Back to the soup. Finely chop the celery and its leaves and stir into the pot. Stir over a low heat for 5 minutes, and then cover and cook over a very low heat for a further 20 minutes, stirring occasionally, until very soft. Add the stock, season well and simmer for a further 25 minutes.

40 min   To prepare the marinade for the beef, combine the horseradish, olive oil and mustard in a shallow dish. Finely grate in the zest from the orange and season with salt, pepper and cayenne. Add the steaks, turn in the marinade to cover evenly and set aside.

Meanwhile, prepare the mash. Peel the beetroots and celeriac and cut into small chunks. Place in a pan, pour over enough water to cover, add a little salt and bring to the boil. Simmer for about 30 minutes or until tender.

30 min   Now for the tart. Remove the seeds from the pomegranate, making sure you discard all of the bitter white pith (see page 27). Dust a large baking tray with a little flour and lay the sheet of pastry on top. Scatter with the crushed walnuts and pomegranate seeds and spread out evenly. Using a rolling pin, roll the seeds and walnuts into the pastry so that it ends up about 2cm bigger on each side. Sift half of the icing sugar evenly over the surface and bake in the oven for 10 minutes.

20 min   Remove the tart from the oven, dust the edges with the remaining sugar and return to the oven for a further 10 minutes or until dark golden brown. Meanwhile, drain the celeriac and beetroot, return to the pan, then mash well. Season with salt and pepper and stir in the cream, if using. Keep warm.

10 min   To make the croûtes for the soup, lay the slices of bread in a single layer on a baking tray and crumble the Stilton over the top. Place in the oven and bake for 8–10 minutes, or until the Stilton is melted and golden.

Meanwhile, reheat the soup, stir in the cream and check the seasoning.

To serve the starter, ladle the soup into warmed soup bowls and top each one with a Stilton croûte.

To cook the steaks for the main course, heat a large frying pan until very hot. Add the steaks and cook for about 1–2 minutes on each side, or to your liking. Leave to rest for 5 minutes. To serve, spoon the mash onto warmed serving plates and top each one with a steak.

To serve the dessert, cut the pomegranate tart into 12 pieces and accompany with the Greek yogurt on the side.

Onion & Celery Heart Soup With Stilton Croûtes
4 small onions
big knob of butter
6 tablespoons olive oil
about 3 sprigs of thyme
200g celery heart with leaves
1.2 litres vegetable stock
100ml double cream
6 slices of crusty wholemeal bread
100g Stilton cheese
sea salt and freshly ground black pepper

Orange & Horseradish Steak with Celeriac & Beetroot Mash
1 teaspoon horseradish sauce
4 tablespoons olive oil
½ teaspoon Dijon mustard
1 large orange
pinch of cayenne
6 x 100g sirloin or fillet steaks
4 small, raw beetroots
1 celeriac
100ml double cream (optional)
sea salt and freshly ground black pepper

Pomegranate Tart
35g walnuts
½ fresh pomegranate (about 85g pomegranate seeds)
a little flour, for dusting
26 x 30cm sheet of puff pastry
25g golden icing sugar
Greek yogurt, to serve

ONION & CELERY HEART SOUP WITH STILTON CROÛTES

Celery heart leaves are the soft, sweet leaves you find nestled in the centre of a head of celery.

Peel and very thinly slice the onions. Melt the butter and olive oil in a large saucepan, add the onions, a pinch of salt and the thyme and cook gently without colouring for 5 minutes. Finely chop the celery and its leaves and stir into the pot. Stir for a further 5 minutes, and then cover and cook over a very low heat for a further 20 minutes, stirring occasionally, until very soft.

Add the stock, season well and simmer for a further 25 minutes. Preheat your oven to 200°C/gas mark 6.

To make the croûtes, lay the slices of bread in a single layer on a baking tray and crumble the Stilton over the top. Place in the oven and bake for 8–10 minutes, or until the Stilton is melted and golden.

To serve, stir the cream into the soup, ladle into warmed soup bowls and top each one with a Stilton croûte.

4 small onions
big knob of butter
6 tablespoons olive oil
about 3 sprigs of thyme
200g celery heart
 with leaves
1.2 litres vegetable stock
100ml double cream
sea salt and freshly
 ground black pepper

For the croûtes
6 slices crusty
 wholemeal bread
100g Stilton

ORANGE & HORSERADISH STEAK WITH CELERIAC & BEETROOT MASH

Coating the steaks in the tangy horseradish and zesty orange marinade gives the tender meat (and your tongue) a subtle kick.

First prepare the marinade. In a shallow dish, mix together the horseradish, olive oil and mustard. Finely grate in the zest from the orange and season with salt, pepper and cayenne. Turn the steaks in the marinade to cover evenly and set aside.

Peel the beetroots and celeriac and cut into small chunks. Place in a pan and pour over enough water to cover. Add a little salt, cover and bring to the boil. Simmer for about 30 minutes or until tender. Drain thoroughly and return to the pan, then mash well. Season with salt and pepper and stir in the cream, if using.

Heat a large frying pan until very hot. Add the steaks and cook for about 1–2 minutes on each side, or to your liking. Leave to rest for 5 minutes.

To serve, spoon the celeriac and beetroot mash onto warmed plates and top with a steak.

6 x 100g sirloin
 or fillet steaks
4 small, raw beetroots
1 celeriac
100ml double cream
 (optional)
sea salt and freshly
 ground black pepper

For the marinade
1 teaspoon horseradish
 sauce
4 tablespoons olive oil
½ teaspoon
 Dijon mustard
1 large orange
pinch of cayenne
sea salt and freshly
 ground black pepper

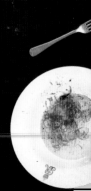

POMEGRANATE TART

Such a simple tart where you roll the pomegranate seeds into the pastry, which gives a crunchy texture once cooked.

Preheat your oven to 200°C/gas mark 6.

Place the walnuts on a baking sheet and toast in the oven for 5–10 minutes, or until golden brown. Remove from the oven, cool and crush well.

Remove the seeds from the pomegranate, making sure you discard all of the bitter white pith (see page 27).

Dust a large baking tray with a little flour and lay the sheet of pastry on top. Scatter with the crushed walnuts and pomegranate seeds and spread out evenly. Using a rolling pin, roll the seeds and walnuts into the pastry so it ends up about 2cm bigger on each side.

Sift half of the icing sugar evenly over the surface and bake in the oven for 10 minutes. Remove from the oven, dust the edges with the remaining sugar to make them golden and glossy and return to the oven for a further 10 minutes or until dark golden brown.

Remove from the oven and leave to cool slightly before cutting into 12 pieces. Serve with the Greek yogurt on the side.

35g shelled walnuts
½ fresh pomegranate
 (about 85g pomegranate
 seeds)
a little flour, for dusting
26 x 30cm sheet
 of puff pastry
25g golden icing sugar
Greek yogurt, to serve

GINGERY COCKLE & CARROT MISO SOUP.
OVEN-BAKED LEMON RISOTTO WITH PARMESAN CRISPS.
SAKE SOAKED FRUIT.

60 min   Preheat the oven to 180°C/gas mark 4. For the soup, scrub the cockles (or clams) and throw away any that are broken or those that stay open when tapped. Leave to soak in cold water for 30 minutes to clear some of their sand or grit.

To make the Parmesan crisps for the main course, line 2 baking trays with parchment paper. Sprinkle and shape half of the grated Parmesan into 12 little rounds, about 9cm in diameter. (Reserve the rest of the Parmesan for the risotto.) Place in the oven and bake for 5–10 minutes, or until the cheese has melted and is golden brown. Remove and set aside to cool and harden.

50 min   To make the dessert, peel the lychees or rambutans and place in a deep serving bowl. Peel the clementines, separate the segments, making sure none of the white pith is attached (see page 26) and add to the bowl. Place the sugar,* 200ml water and the sake in a pan. Heat gently until the sugar has dissolved, and then remove from the heat and pour over the fruit. Stir gently to combine and set aside.

* If you are using tinned lychees or rambutans, use the syrup they came in instead of the water and reduce the quantity of sugar to 30g.

40 min   Now for the risotto. Using a vegetable peeler, carefully remove the zest from the lemons in thin strips (taking care not to include any of the bitter white pith). Squeeze the juice into a jug. Finely chop the onion, celery and garlic. Pour the stock into a pan and bring to a simmer. Meanwhile, heat the olive oil in a large, flame-proof casserole, add the onion, celery, garlic and lemon zest and cook for 5–6 minutes, without colouring, or until soft.

30 min   Add the rice and stir for a minute or two to coat the grains in the oil. Stir in the hot stock and season with pepper. Cover and place in the oven for 25–30 minutes, or until the rice is just cooked and all the liquid has been absorbed. Drain the mozzarella and roughly grate.

20 min   Now for the soup. Peel the ginger, chop it roughly, and then squeeze it through a garlic press into a large pan (alternatively, bash it with a rolling pin to bruise it, chop roughly and add to the pan, and hook out the pieces at the end). Pour in 1.2 litres water and bring to the boil. Slice the carrot very thinly. Chop the spring onions. Drain and rinse the cockles and add to the pan with the sliced carrot.

10 min   Bring back to the boil, and then cover and cook for about 2 minutes or until all the cockles have opened. Drain the cockles through a colander into a clean pan, discarding any that have refused to open. Add the miso paste to the pan and stir to dissolve. Return the cockles to the pan, stir in the spring onions and remove from the heat.

Just before you sit down for the starter, quickly stir the butter, cream, mozzarella, reserved Parmesan and lemon juice into the cooked risotto. Taste to check the seasoning, adding more if needed, and keep warm while you eat the soup.

To serve the starter, ladle the miso soup into small bowls.

To serve the main course, stir the parsley into the risotto and accompany with the Parmesan crisps on the side to crack over it.

To serve the dessert, spoon the fruit into small bowls and accompany with a fortune cookie or a little biscuit.

Gingery Cockle & Carrot Miso Soup
500g cockles (or clams) in their shell
2 carrots
3 spring onions
8cm piece of fresh root ginger
4 tablespoons yellow, red or white miso paste

Oven-baked Lemon Risotto with Parmesan Crisps
200g Parmesan cheese, grated
2 unwaxed lemons
1 onion
2 celery sticks
2 garlic cloves
1.4 litres chicken or vegetable stock
1 tablespoon olive oil
400g risotto rice (such as Carnaroli or Arborio)
1 buffalo mozzarella cheese
25g butter
100ml double cream
25g flat-leaf parsley, chopped
sea salt and freshly ground black pepper

Sake Soaked Fruit
18 fresh lychees or rambutans, peeled (or 2 x 425g tins)
6 clementines, tangerines or satsumas
50g dark muscovado sugar
500ml sake
fortune cookies or other light biscuits, to serve

GINGERY COCKLE & CARROT MISO SOUP

Scrub the cockles (or clams) and throw away any that are broken or those that remain open when tapped. Leave to soak in cold water for 30 minutes to clear some of their sand or grit.

Slice the carrot very thinly. Chop the spring onions.

Peel the ginger, chop it roughly, and then squeeze it through a garlic press into a large pan. (Alternatively, bash the ginger with a rolling pin to bruise it, chop roughly and add to the pan, and hook out the pieces at the end.) Pour in 1.2 litres water and bring to the boil.

Drain and rinse the cockles and add them to the pan with the sliced carrot. Bring back to the boil, and then cover and cook for about 2 minutes, or until all the cockles have opened. Drain the cockles through a colander into another pan, discarding any that refused to open.

Add the miso paste to the cooking liquor in the pan and stir to dissolve. Return the cockles to the pan and stir in the spring onions. Serve immediately.

500g cockles (or
 clams) in their shell
2 carrots
3 spring onions
8cm piece of fresh
 root ginger
4 tablespoons yellow, red
 or white miso paste

OVEN-BAKED LEMON RISOTTO WITH PARMESAN CRISPS

Light and crunchy cheesy wafers crumbled over the creamy risotto makes a glorious combination of textures.

Preheat your oven to 180°C/gas mark 4.

To make the Parmesan crisps, line 2 baking trays with parchment paper. Sprinkle and shape half of the Parmesan into 12 little rounds, about 9cm in diameter. (Reserve the rest of the Parmesan for the risotto.) Place in the oven and bake for 5–10 minutes, or until the cheese has melted and is golden brown. Remove and set aside to cool and harden.

Using a vegetable peeler, carefully remove the zest from the lemons in thin strips (being careful not to include any of the bitter white pith). Squeeze the juice into a jug. Finely chop the onion, celery and garlic.

Pour the stock into a pan and bring to a simmer. Meanwhile, heat the olive oil in a large, flame-proof casserole, add the onion, celery, garlic and lemon zest and cook for 5–6 minutes without colouring, or until soft.

Add the rice and stir-fry for about a minute to coat the grains in the oil. Stir in the hot stock and season with pepper. Cover and place in the oven for 25–30 minutes, or until the rice is just cooked and all the liquid has been absorbed. Meanwhile, drain the mozzarella and roughly grate.

Stir the butter, cream, mozzarella, reserved Parmesan and lemon juice into the cooked risotto. Taste for seasoning, adding more if needed, and stir in the parsley. Serve at once with the Parmesan crisps on the side to crack over the risotto.

200g Parmesan cheese, grated
2 unwaxed lemons
1 onion
2 celery sticks
2 garlic cloves
1.4 litres chicken or vegetable stock
1 tablespoon olive oil
400g risotto rice (such as Carnaroli or Arborio)
1 buffalo mozzarella cheese
25g butter
100ml double cream
25g flat-leaf parsley, chopped
salt and freshly ground black pepper

SAKE SOAKED FRUIT

You can always use a combination of fruits, rather than just one type.

Peel the lychees or rambutans and place in a deep serving bowl. Peel the clementines, separate the segments, making sure none of the white pith is attached (see page 26), and add to the bowl.

Place the sugar,* 200ml water and the sake in a pan. Heat gently until the sugar has dissolved, and then remove from the heat and pour over the fruit. Stir gently to combine and set aside.

Serve in little bowls with a fortune cookie or biscuit on the side.

* If you are using tinned lychees or rambutans, use the syrup they came in instead of the water and reduce the quantity of sugar to 30g.

18 fresh lychees or rambutans, peeled (or 2 x 425g tins)
6 clementines, tangerines or satsumas
50g dark muscovado sugar
500ml sake
fortune cookies or other light biscuits, to serve

SEARED BROCCOLI WITH LEMON DIJON DRESSING.
CHICORY TARTE TATIN WITH BEETROOT & RED ONION SALAD.
CARDAMOM YOGURT BRÛLÉE.

60 min   Preheat your oven to 220°C/gas mark 7. To prepare the salad for the main course finely chop the beetroot and onion and place in a small bowl. Stir in the red wine vinegar and oil, season well and set aside. Trim the base of the chicory heads for the tarte tatin. Drain and finely chop the anchovies (if using) and remove the thyme leaves from the stalks.

50 min   To prepare the tarte tatin, melt the butter and sugar over a moderate heat in a 28cm oven-proof frying pan (or a cake tin with a fixed base). Simmer for about 5 minutes until the mixture starts to caramelise. Add the whole chicory, chopped anchovies and thyme leaves, season with salt and pepper and cook gently for 5–10 minutes, turning occasionally, or until the chicory just starts to soften and turn amber-coloured. Remove from the heat and poke the walnuts into the spaces in between.

40 min   Roll out the pastry so it is 2.5–5cm larger all round than the pan. Prick all over with a fork. Slide the pastry on top of the chicory, tucking the edges down inside the rim of the pan. Bake on the top shelf of an oven for 30–40 minutes, or until the pastry is crisp and golden.

30 min   Preheat the grill for the brûlées to high. Place the yogurt in a mixing bowl. Bash the cardamom pods in a pestle and mortar and crush really well, discarding the outer pods. Beat the crushed seeds into the yogurt with the honey. Divide the mixture between 6 125ml ramekins or heatproof dishes and level the tops.

20 min   Sprinkle evenly with the sugar and place on a baking tray. Set under the grill and cook for 5–7 minutes, or until the sugar has melted and is bubbling. Remove from the heat and leave to cool, and then place in the fridge until needed. Alternatively, you could use a blowtorch to melt the sugar.

10 min   Now for the starter. Trim the broccoli and cut in half lengthways. Cut the garlic into fine slivers. Squeeze the juice from the lemon. Heat the oil in a large, wide pan over a high heat. Add the broccoli pieces, chilli flakes (if using), garlic, olives and a pinch of salt and toss well. Pour in 200ml water – stand back as it will splutter – and bang a lid on straight away. Cook for 5–7 minutes, or until the broccoli is tender, shaking the pan occasionally.

Meanwhile, remove the tarte tatin from the oven and leave to cool in the pan for 5 minutes before inverting onto a plate.

To serve the starter, hook the broccoli stems out of the pan with a slotted spoon and arrange between 6 warmed plates. Add the lemon juice to the pan with the walnut oil and whisk in the mustard. Season with pepper. Boil the sauce for a moment or two, check the seasoning again, and then quickly spoon it over the broccoli. Serve immediately.

To serve the main course, crumble the goat's cheese over the tarte tatin, cut into wedges and place a slice on each dinner plate. Remove the core of the radicchio with a sharp knife and separate the leaves. Place a couple of whole radicchio leaves on each plate, to create a little bowl, and fill each one with a spoonful of the beetroot salad.

To serve the dessert, accompany the yogurt brûlées with a palmier or little biscuit on the side.

Seared Broccoli with Lemon Dijon Dressing
750g purple-sprouting or tenderstem broccoli
2 garlic cloves
1 lemon
4 tablespoons extra-virgin olive oil
small pinch of dried chilli flakes (optional)
18 dry black olives
2 tablespoons walnut oil
1 teaspoon Dijon mustard
sea salt flakes and freshly ground black pepper

Chicory Tarte Tatin
6 large whole heads of chicory
1 x 50g tin anchovies (optional)
few sprigs of thyme
100g butter
100g sugar
50g walnut halves
375g shortcrust pastry
100g goat's cheese
sea salt and freshly ground black pepper

Beetroot and Red Onion Salad
250g cooked beetroot (see page 24)
½ small red onion
½ tablespoon red wine vinegar
2 tablespoons extra-virgin olive oil
1 radicchio

Cardamom Yogurt Brûlée
750g Greek yogurt
3 green cardamom pods
2 tablespoons runny honey
6 tablespoons golden caster sugar
palmiers or other little pastries, to serve

SEARED BROCCOLI WITH LEMON DIJON DRESSING

Trim the broccoli and cut in half lengthways. Cut the garlic into fine slivers. Squeeze the juice from the lemon.

Heat the oil in a large, wide pan over a high heat. Add the broccoli pieces, chilli flakes (if using), garlic, olives and a pinch of salt and toss well. Pour in 200ml water – stand back, as it will splutter – and bang on a lid straight away.

Cook for 5–7 minutes, or until the broccoli is tender, shaking the pan occasionally. When it is cooked, hook out with a slotted spoon and divide between 6 warmed starter plates. Add the lemon juice to the pan with the walnut oil and whisk in the mustard. Season with pepper.

Boil the sauce for a moment or two, check the seasoning, and then quickly spoon it over the broccoli spears. Serve immediately.

750g purple-sprouting or tenderstem broccoli
2 garlic cloves
1 lemon
4 tablespoons extra-virgin olive oil
small pinch of dried chilli flakes (optional)
18 dry black olives
2 tablespoons walnut oil
1 teaspoon Dijon mustard
sea salt flakes and freshly ground black pepper

CHICORY TARTE TATIN WITH BEETROOT & RED ONION SALAD

If you are nervous about how to turn out your hot tarte tatin, read the helpful technique in Methods Most Useful on page 31.

Preheat your oven to 220°C/gas mark 7. Trim the base of the chicory heads. Drain and finely chop the anchovies (if using). Remove the thyme leaves from the stalks.

Melt the butter and sugar over a moderate heat in a 28cm oven-proof frying pan (or cake tin with a fixed base). Simmer for about 5 minutes until the mixture starts to caramelise. Add the whole chicory, chopped anchovies and thyme leaves, and season with salt and pepper. Cook gently for about 5–10 minutes, turning occasionally, or until the chicory just starts to soften and turn amber-coloured. Remove from the heat and poke the walnuts in the spaces in between.

Roll out the pastry so it is 2.5–5cm larger all round than the pan. Prick all over with a fork. Slide the pastry on top of the chicory, tucking the edges down inside the rim of the pan. Put the tart on the top shelf of the oven and bake for about 30–40 minutes, or until the pastry is crisp and golden.

Meanwhile, prepare the salad. Finely chop the beetroot and onion and place both in a small bowl. Stir in the red wine vinegar and olive oil and season well. Remove the core of the radicchio with a sharp knife, separate the leaves and set aside.

When the tart is cooked, remove it from the oven and leave to stand for 5 minutes before inverting it onto a plate. Crumble over the goat's cheese and cut into wedges.

To serve, place a couple of whole radicchio leaves on each dinner plate to create little bowls and fill each one with a spoonful of the beetroot salad. Place a wedge of tart on each plate.

6 large whole heads
  of chicory
1 x 50g tin anchovies
  (optional)
few sprigs of thyme
100g butter
100g sugar
50g walnut halves
375g shortcrust pastry
100g goat's cheese
sea salt and freshly
  ground black pepper

For the salad
250g cooked beetroot
  (see page 24)
½ small red onion
½ tablespoon red
  wine vinegar
2 tablespoons extra-virgin
  olive oil
1 radicchio
sea salt and freshly
  ground black pepper

CARDAMOM YOGURT BRÛLÉE

Preheat the grill to high. Place the yogurt in a mixing bowl. Bash the cardamom pods in a pestle and mortar and crush really well, discarding the outer pods. Beat the crushed seeds into the yogurt with the honey.

Divide the mixture between 6 125ml ramekins or heatproof dishes and level the tops.

Sprinkle evenly with the sugar and place on a baking tray. Set under the grill and cook for 5–7 minutes, or until the sugar has melted and is bubbling. Remove from the heat and leave to cool, and then place in the fridge until needed. Serve with the palmiers on the side.

Make sure your grill is really hot before setting the brûlées beneath it, otherwise you could curdle the yogurt. Alternatively, you could use a blowtorch to melt the sugar.

750g Greek yogurt
3 green cardamom pods
2 tablespoons runny
  honey
6 tablespoons golden
  caster sugar
palmiers or other little
  pastries, to serve

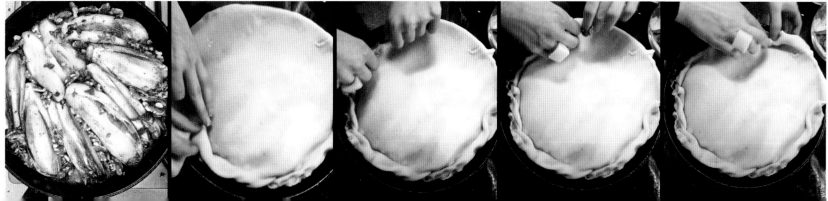

WATERCRESS & BLOODY MARY CHILLED SOUP.
BAKED CHORIZO EGGS WITH CURLY KALE.
EGG NOG TART.

60 min Chill 6 teacups or little bowls in the freezer for the starter. Preheat the oven to 180°C/gas mark 4. For the dessert, roll out the pastry thinly and use to line a 25cm tart tin. Cut a piece of parchment paper slightly bigger than the tin, place in the bottom of the tart and fill with baking beans (or dried pulses). Place on a baking sheet and bake in the oven for 15 minutes. Remove the paper and beans and return to the oven for a further 5 minutes. Finely grate the nutmeg.

50 min To make the custard, place the whole eggs, egg yolks and sugar in a bowl and whisk together until smooth. Gradually whisk in the cream, brandy and rum. Strain the mixture through a fine nylon sieve into a jug and stir in the grated nutmeg. Pour the custard mixture into the tart case and carefully place in the oven. Bake for about 25 minutes or until the custard is just set. Remove from the oven and allow to cool.

40 min Now for the main course. Remove any tough stalks from the kale or cabbge and wash really well. Drain and shred thinly. Slice the chorizo across into rounds 1cm thick. Heat a large pan over a moderate heat, add the chorizo slices and cook for 2–3 minutes, or until they start to yield their gorgeous, unctuous, red oil.

30 min Turn the heat up, stand back and pour in the sherry. Very carefully light the sherry with a match or, if you are cooking on gas, tilt the pan towards the flame so it ignites. Once the flames have died down, add the kale, season with a little salt and pepper and cover with a lid. Cook for 4–5 minutes, shaking the pan every now and then until tender. Meanwhile, finely grate the Manchego.

20 min Remove the pan from the heat and taste to check the seasoning. Spread out the kale and chorizo evenly in a large, oven-proof dish (or divide between 6 individual gratin-style dishes). Make 12 indentations in the cabbage mixture, like little nests, and break an egg into each one. Drizzle over the cream and sprinkle with the Manchego.

10 min Now for the starter. Shuck the oysters (if using) and place one in the bottom of each chilled teacup. Squeeze the juice from the lemon or lime, roughly chop the watercress and place in a blender with the rest of the ingredients and ice for the soup. Whizz until smooth. Pour into a jug and adjust the seasoning to taste.

To serve the starter, pour the soup into the teacups, sprinkle with a little more celery salt, garnish with celery leaves and accompany with the breadsticks and celery sticks on the side.

Just before you sit down for the starter, pop the chorizo eggs for the main course into the oven and bake for about 10 minutes, or until the whites are just set and the yolks are still runny. Serve immediately with crusty baguettes.

To serve the dessert, dust the tart lightly with icing sugar and cut into wedges.

Watercress & Bloody Mary Chilled Soup
½ lemon or lime
100g watercress
300ml vodka
4 tablespoons sherry
600ml tomato juice
squirt of Tabasco
½ teaspoon celery salt, plus extra to serve
½ teaspoon Worcestershire sauce
½ teaspoon grated horseradish or horseradish sauce
handful of ice
sea salt and freshly ground black pepper
6 native oysters, to serve (optional)
celery sticks and leaves, to serve
grissini breadsticks, to serve

Baked Chorizo Eggs with Curly Kale
400g curly kale or cabbage
3 whole cooking chorizo (total weight 250g)
100ml sherry
50g Manchego cheese
12 eggs
300ml single cream
sea salt and freshly ground black pepper
crusty baguettes, to serve

Egg Nog Tart
350g sweet shortcrust pastry
1 whole nutmeg
3 whole eggs, plus 6 egg yolks
125g caster sugar
500ml double cream
1½ tablespoons brandy
1½ tablespoons rum
icing sugar, to dust

WATERCRESS & BLOODY MARY CHILLED SOUP

Place 6 teacups or little bowls in the freezer.

Squeeze the juice from the lemon or lime, roughly chop the watercress and place in a blender with the rest of the ingredients and ice for the soup. Whizz until smooth. Check for seasoning, pour into a jug and chill in the fridge until ready to serve.

Shuck the oysters (if using) and place one in the bottom of each teacup. (Alternatively, you can serve the oysters separately.)

Pour the soup into the chilled teacups, sprinkle with a little more celery salt and garnish with a few celery leaves. Serve with the breadsticks and celery sticks on the side.

½ lemon or lime
100g watercress
300ml vodka
4 tablespoons sherry
600ml tomato juice
squirt of Tabasco
½ teaspoon celery salt,
 plus extra to serve
½ teaspoon
 Worcestershire sauce
½ teaspoon grated
 horseradish or
 horseradish sauce
handful of ice
sea salt and freshly
 ground black pepper

To serve
6 native oysters (optional)
celery sticks and leaves
grissini breadsticks

BAKED CHORIZO EGGS WITH CURLY KALE

Preheat your oven to 180°C/gas mark 4.

Remove any tough stalks from the kale or cabbage and wash really well. Drain and thinly shred. Slice the chorizo across into rounds 1cm thick. Heat a large pan over a moderate heat, add the chorizo slices and cook for 2–3 minutes, or until they start to yield their gorgeous, unctuous, red oil.

Turn the heat up, stand back and pour in the sherry. Very carefully use a match to light the sherry or, if you are cooking on gas, tilt the pan towards the flame so it ignites. Once the flames have died down, add the kale, season with a little salt and pepper and cover with a lid. Cook for 4–5 minutes, shaking the pan every now and again, or until the kale is tender.

Meanwhile, finely grate the Manchego.

Remove the pan from the heat and taste to check the seasoning. Spread the kale and chorizo out evenly in a large, oven-proof dish, or divide between 6 individual gratin-style dishes. Make 12 indentations in the cabbage mixture, like little nests, and break an egg into each one. Drizzle over the cream, sprinkle with the Manchego and bake for about 10 minutes – or until the whites have just set and the yolks are still runny. Serve immediately with crusty baguettes.

400g curly kale or
 cabbage
3 whole cooking chorizo
 (total weight 250g)
100ml sherry
50g Manchego cheese
12 eggs
300ml single cream
sea salt and freshly
 ground black pepper
crusty baguettes, to serve

EGG NOG TART

An egg nog nod to the past.

Preheat your oven to 180°C/gas mark 4.

Roll out the pastry thinly and use to line a 25cm tart tin. Cut a piece of parchment paper slightly bigger than the tin, place in the base of the tart and fill with baking beans (or dried pulses). Place on a baking sheet and bake in the oven for 15 minutes. Remove the paper and beans and return to the oven for a further 5 minutes (see page 35). Finely grate the nutmeg.

To make the custard, place the whole eggs, egg yolks and sugar in a bowl and whisk together until smooth. Gradually whisk in the cream, brandy and rum. Strain the mixture through a fine nylon sieve into a jug and stir in the grated nutmeg.

Pour the custard mixture into the tart case and carefully place in the oven. Bake for about 25 minutes or until the custard is just set. Remove from the oven and allow to cool slightly as it's delicious served warm. Dust lightly with icing sugar and cut into wedges.

350g sweet shortcrust
 pastry
1 whole nutmeg
3 whole eggs, plus 6
 egg yolks
125g caster sugar
500ml double cream
1½ tablespoons brandy
1½ tablespoons rum
icing sugar, to dust

BAY BAKED RICOTTA.

MUSSELS WITH SOMERSET CIDER & MUSTARD.

CHOCOLATE & HONEYCOMB FONDUE.

60 min   Begin with the starter. If the ricotta is very moist, tip it into a fine sieve to drain for 30 minutes.

Preheat your oven to 190°C/gas mark 5. Generously butter 6 200ml ramekins or other oven-proof moulds or cups. Place a bay leaf in the bottom of each one, and a couple around the sides. Slice the chorizo thinly (if using).

50 min   Now for the dessert. To make the honeycomb, grease a 25 x 18cm shallow tin. Place the syrup and sugar in a heavy-based pan. Set over a low heat and stir until dissolved. Increase the heat to medium and bring to the boil, stirring constantly. Once you see bubbles, reduce the heat slightly and simmer for about 5 minutes, stirring frequently, until the caramel is a deep golden-brown colour. (Be very careful that it doesn't burn.)

40 min   Remove from the heat and stir in the soda briefly, until it froths up into lava-like clouds. Pour immediately into the prepared tin and leave to cool completely. Break the chocolate into small pieces and place in a small pan with the honey and butter.

Check over the mussels for the main course and discard any that remain open when tapped, or any that are broken.

30 min   Back to the starter. Beat the eggs in a medium-sized bowl with a fork. Add the ricotta, season and mix well until smooth. Spoon the ricotta mixture into the buttered ramekins, pressing the bay leaves to the sides. Level the tops and, if using, place about 6 slices of chorizo on top of each one, overlapping them slightly. Bake in the oven for 15–20 minutes until just set. Remove from the oven and leave to cool slightly.

20 min   Meanwhile, prepare the pineapple for the dessert. Peel, core and cut into small chunks (see page 27).

For the main course, finely chop the shallots and celery leaves. Melt the butter in a pan large enough to hold all the mussels – or use 2 pans and divide the ingredients between them. Add the shallots and celery leaves and cook gently for 5 minutes until soft but not coloured.

10 min   Add the cider to the pan and bring to the boil. Add the mussels and cover the pan with a lid. Cook for 3–4 minutes, shaking the pan occasionally, until all the mussels have opened. Set a colander over a bowl to collect the cooking liquor, tip in the mussels and discard any that haven't opened. Strain the mussel liquor through muslin or a very fine sieve into a clean pan and place the mussels in a serving dish. Cover loosely with foil to keep warm. Toast the chunks of bread under the grill or place in the oven until golden on all sides.

To serve the starter, invert each ricotta mould onto a plate.

To finish the main course, put the mussel liquor back on the heat, add the mustard and crème fraîche and bring to the boil. Season with salt, pepper and nutmeg. Finely chop the dill and add to the pan with the mussels. Give everything a quick stir and then ladle into bowls. Serve with the toasted chunks of bread.

Just before you are ready to serve the dessert, set the pan with the fondue ingredients over a low heat and allow the chocolate to melt slowly. Meanwhile, break the hardened honeycomb into bite-sized pieces and put with the pineapple on a serving dish. Peel the bananas, cut into large chunks and place with the honeycomb and pineapple. Serve the warm fondue with skewers or forks to dip the fruit and honeycomb into the melted chocolate sauce.

Bay Baked Ricotta
750g ricotta
butter, for greasing
about 18 fresh bay leaves
150g cooking chorizo (optional)
3 eggs
sea salt and freshly ground black pepper

Mussels with Somerset Cider & Mustard
2kg mussels, scrubbed well and beards removed
3 shallots
handful of celery leaves
50g butter
500ml good-quality dry Somerset cider
2 tablespoons wholegrain mustard
500ml crème fraîche
freshly grated nutmeg, to taste
1 small bunch of dill
sea salt and freshly ground black pepper
chunks of bread, to serve

Chocolate & Honeycomb Fondue
oil, for greasing
4 tablespoons golden syrup
125g caster sugar
1½ teaspoons bicarbonate of soda
300g good-quality dark chocolate
1 tablespoon runny honey
50g butter
¼ fresh pineapple
3 bananas

BAY BAKED RICOTTA

An incredibly easy starter.

If the ricotta is moist, tip it into a fine sieve to drain for 30 minutes.

Preheat your oven to 190°C/gas mark 5.

Generously butter 6 200ml ramekins or other oven-proof moulds or cups. Place a bay leaf in the bottom of each one, and a couple around the sides. Slice the chorizo thinly (if using).

Beat the eggs in a medium-sized bowl with a fork. Add the ricotta, season and mix well. Spoon the ricotta mixture into the buttered ramekins, pressing the bay leaves to the sides. Level the tops and, if using, place about 6 slices of chorizo on top of each one, overlapping them slightly.

Bake for 15–20 minutes until just set. Leave to cool slightly before inverting each ricotta mould onto a starter plate.

750g ricotta
butter, for greasing
about 18 fresh bay leaves
150g cooking chorizo
 (optional)
3 eggs
sea salt and freshly
 ground black pepper

MUSSELS WITH SOMERSET CIDER & MUSTARD

Going back to my roots with Somerset cider!

Discard any mussels that remain open when tapped, or any that are broken. Finely chop the shallots and celery leaves. Melt the butter in a pan large enough to hold all the mussels. Add the shallots and celery leaves and cook gently for 5 minutes, or until softened but not coloured.

Add the cider to the pan and bring to the boil. Add the mussels and cover the pan with a lid. Cook for 3–4 minutes, shaking the pan occasionally, until all the mussels have opened.

Set a colander over a bowl, to collect the cooking liquor, and strain the mussels. Discard any mussels that haven't opened. Strain the mussel liquor through muslin or a very fine sieve into a clean pan and place the mussels in a serving dish. Cover loosely with foil to keep warm.

Toast the bread under the grill (or place in a preheated oven) until golden on all sides. Put the cooking liquor back on the heat, add the mustard and crème fraîche and bring to the boil. Season with salt, pepper and nutmeg. Finely chop the dill and add to the pan before pouring the sauce over the mussels. Serve with the toasted chunks of bread.

2kg mussels, scrubbed well and beards removed
3 shallots
handful of celery leaves
50g butter
500ml good-quality dry Somerset cider
2 tablespoons wholegrain mustard
500ml crème fraîche
freshly grated nutmeg, to taste
1 small bunch of dill
sea salt and freshly ground black pepper
chunks of bread, to serve

CHOCOLATE & HONEYCOMB FONDUE

Feel like a big kid by creating a bubbling golden lava in your own kitchen – how exciting!

Grease a 25 x 18cm shallow tin. Place the syrup and sugar in a heavy-based pan. Set over a low heat and stir until dissolved. Increase the heat to medium and bring to the boil, stirring constantly.

Once you see bubbles, reduce the heat slightly and simmer for about 5 minutes, stirring frequently, until the caramel is a deep golden-brown colour. (Be very careful that it doesn't burn.)

Remove from the heat and stir in the soda briefly, until it froths up into lava-like clouds. Pour immediately into the prepared tin and leave to cool completely. Once the honeycomb is set, break into bite-sized pieces.

Break the chocolate into small pieces and place in a small pan with the honey and butter. Set over a low heat and melt gently, stirring. Peel, core and cut the pineapple into small chunks (see page 27). Peel the bananas and cut into large chunks. Arrange the fruit and honeycomb on a serving dish.

Serve the warm fondue at the table, using skewers or forks to dip the fruit and honeycomb into the chocolate sauce.

oil, for greasing
4 tablespoons golden syrup
125g caster sugar
1½ teaspoons bicarbonate of soda
300g good-quality dark chocolate
1 tablespoon runny honey
50g butter
¼ fresh pineapple
3 bananas

WALNUT PESTO WALDORF SALAD.
PANCETTA-WRAPPED TURKEY & LEEK PATTIES WITH GOOSE FAT POTATOES.
CURRANT PIE & CHEESE.

60 min   Preheat your oven to 170°C/gas mark 3. Place the walnuts for the starter on a baking sheet and roast for 5–10 minutes until golden brown. Leave to cool. Meanwhile, for the main course finely slice the leeks for the patties. Crush the garlic. Melt the butter in a large frying pan, add the leeks and garlic and cook without colouring for about 10 minutes, or until soft. Leave to cool.

50 min   Back to the starter. To make the pesto, place the parsley in the bowl of a food processor with the toasted walnuts and a good slug of oil. Blitz until roughly chopped. Scrape into a bowl and stir in the remaining oil, the cheese (if using) and season lightly as the cheese is quite salty already. Spoon the crème fraîche into a small bowl and stir in about half of the pesto. (You can save the rest to use as a pasta sauce.) Squeeze the juice from the lemon, add half to the crème fraîche mixture, beat well together and set aside.

40 min   Increase the oven temperature to 200°C/gas mark 6. Cut the potatoes into 2cm cubes. Melt the goose fat in a large, heavy-based roasting tin over a high heat. Carefully tip in the potatoes, season and stir to coat. Transfer the tin to the top shelf of the oven and roast for 30–35 minutes, turning once or twice, until the potatoes are crisp and golden.

Meanwhile, roll out the pastry for the dessert to just over 30 x 20cm. Cut in half across the middle widthways, and then give one of the pieces another quick roll so it ends up 1cm larger all round than the other. Place on a baking sheet and chill in the fridge.

30 min   Melt the butter and sugar together in a small pan and stir until dissolved (this takes only a couple of minutes). Remove from the heat and stir in the currants and spices. Leave to cool.

To make the patties, finely chop the parsley leaves. Remove the leaves from the thyme. Finely grate the zest from the lemons into a large bowl and add the herbs with the turkey mince. Add the cooled leeks, season and mix together until well combined. Divide the mixture into 12 equal-sized patties and wrap each one in 2 slices of pancetta (or bacon rashers), criss-crossing them over the top.

20 min   Remove the pastry from the fridge and spread the currant mixture evenly over the smaller piece, leaving a 2cm gap all round. Top with the larger sheet of pastry and press the edges with a fork to seal. Beat the egg white lightly with a little salt in a bowl. Brush evenly over the top and pierce in a couple places with a skewer to allow the steam to escape. Sprinkle with the caster sugar and bake for about 20 minutes until golden and crisp.

10 min   Meanwhile, prepare the Waldorf salad. Pour the remaining lemon juice into a large bowl. Cut the apple into quarters (leave the skin on), core and cut across into thin slices. Toss the apple slices in the lemon juice in the bowl to prevent them discolouring. Slice the celery hearts (including any leaves) very thinly and add to the bowl with the sultanas. Spoon the pesto dressing over the salad ingredients and toss well to combine. Just before you eat your starter, finish the main course. Heat a little of the oil in a large frying pan and fry the patties for about 5 minutes on each side – you might need 2 frying pans for this. Transfer to a baking sheet and finish off in the oven for about 15 minutes, or until tender and cooked through.

To serve the starter, divide the little gem leaves between 6 plates and place a spoonful of the Waldorf salad on each.

To serve the main, divide the potatoes between 6 warm dinner plates and top each portion with 2 turkey patties. To serve the dessert, cut the currant pie into slices and accompany with the cheese (or single cream).

Walnut Pesto Waldorf Salad
50g walnut halves
50g flat-leaf parsley leaves
150ml extra-virgin olive oil
25g Parmesan or Pecorino cheese, finely grated (optional)
100g crème fraîche
½–1 lemon
1 large apple
300g celery hearts
50g sultanas
2 little gem lettuces
sea salt and freshly ground black pepper

Pancetta-wrapped Turkey & Leek Patties with Goose Fat Potatoes
2 leeks
2 garlic cloves
50g butter
1kg potatoes
8 tablespoons goose fat
a handful of flat-leaf parsley leaves
a few sprigs of fresh thyme
2 lemons
1kg turkey mince
24 thin slices pancetta (or streaky bacon rashers)
2 tablespoons groundnut oil
sea salt and freshly ground black pepper

Currant Pie & Cheese
500g shortcrust or puff pastry
50g butter
60g molasses or dark brown sugar
150g currants
½ teaspoon ground allspice
½ teaspoon grated nutmeg
1 egg white
sea salt
2 tablespoons golden caster sugar
Lancashire and/or Lincolnshire Poacher cheese
(or single cream), to serve

WALNUT PESTO WALDORF SALAD

Using walnuts to make a pesto brings the classic Waldorf salad bang up to date.

Preheat your oven to 170°C/gas mark 3.

To make the pesto, place the walnuts on a baking sheet and roast for 5–10 minutes until golden brown. Leave to cool.

Remove the leaves from the parsley, discarding the stalks, and place in the bowl of a food processor with the toasted walnuts and a good slug of oil. Blitz until roughly chopped. You want the mixture to be quite rough in texture. Scrape into a bowl and stir in the remaining oil, the cheese (if using) and some salt and black pepper – go easy on the salt if using cheese as it will be quite salty already.

Wash and dry the little gem leaves. Squeeze the juice from the lemon and pour half into a large bowl. Cut the apple into quarters (leave the skin on), remove the core and cut across into thin slices. Toss the apple slices in the lemon juice in the bowl to prevent them discolouring. Slice the celery hearts (including any leaves) very thinly and add to the bowl with the sultanas.

Spoon the crème fraîche into a small bowl and stir in about half of the pesto. (You can save the rest to use as a pasta sauce.) Add the reserved lemon juice and beat well together. Spoon over the salad and mix thoroughly.

To serve, divide the little gem leaves between 6 starter plates and place a good spoonful of the Waldorf salad on each.

2 little gem lettuces
½–1 lemon
1 large apple
300g celery hearts
50g sultanas

For the walnut
pesto dressing
50g walnut halves
50g flat-leaf parsley
150ml extra-virgin
 olive oil
25g Parmesan or Pecorino
 cheese, finely grated
 (optional)
100g crème fraîche
sea salt and freshly
 ground black pepper

PANCETTA-WRAPPED TURKEY & LEEK PATTIES WITH GOOSE FAT POTATOES

Preheat your oven to 200ºC/gas mark 6.

Finely slice the leeks, wash and drain well. Crush the garlic. Melt the butter in a large frying pan, add the leeks and garlic and cook over a low heat without colouring for about 10 minutes, or until soft. Tip onto a plate and leave to cool.

Cut the potatoes into 2cm cubes. Melt the goose fat in a large, heavy-based roasting tin over a high heat. Carefully tip in the potatoes, season and stir to coat. Transfer the tin to the top shelf of the oven and roast for 30–35 minutes, turning once or twice, until the potatoes are crisp and golden.

Finely grate the zest from the lemons. Remove the leaves from the parsley, discarding the stems, and chop finely. Also remove the leaves from the thyme. Place the herbs and lemon zest in a large bowl with the turkey mince. Add the cooled leeks, season and mix together until well combined.

Divide the mixture into 12 equal-sized patties and wrap each one in 2 slices of pancetta (or bacon rashers), criss-crossing them over the top. Secure with wooden cocktail sticks.

You will probably need to cook the patties in batches. Heat a little of the oil in a large frying pan and fry the patties for about 5 minutes on each side. Transfer to a baking sheet and finish off in the oven for about 15 minutes, or until tender and cooked through.

To serve, divide the roast potatoes between 6 warmed dinner plates and top each portion with 2 turkey patties.

2 leeks
2 garlic cloves
50g butter
1kg potatoes
8 tablespoons goose fat
2 lemons
a handful of flat-leaf parsley
a few sprigs of fresh thyme
1kg turkey mince
24 thin slices pancetta or streaky bacon
2 tablespoons groundnut oil
sea salt and freshly ground black pepper

CURRANT PIE & CHEESE

I made this with shortcrust pastry, but using puff makes it more like an Eccles cake. Traditionally, Lancashire cheese is served with Eccles cakes and that would be just right here – alternatively, try a few slivers of another great British cheese, Lincolnshire Poacher.

Roll out the pastry to just over 30 x 20cm. Cut in half across the middle widthways, and then give one of the pieces another quick roll so it ends up 1cm larger all round than the other. Place on a baking sheet and chill in the fridge.

Melt the butter and sugar together in a small pan and stir until dissolved (this takes only a couple of minutes). Remove from the heat and stir in the currants and spices. Leave to cool.

Preheat your oven to 190ºC/gas mark 5.

Remove the pastry from the fridge and spread the currant mixture evenly over the smaller piece, leaving a 2cm gap all round. Top with the larger sheet of pastry and press the edges with a fork to seal.

Beat the egg white lightly with a little salt in a bowl. Brush evenly over the top of the pie and pierce in a couple places with a skewer to allow the steam to escape. Sprinkle with the caster sugar and bake for about 20 minutes until golden and crisp.

Leave to cool slightly before cutting. Accompany with the cheese (or single cream).

500g shortcrust or puff pastry
50g butter
60g molasses or dark brown sugar
150g currants
½ teaspoon ground allspice
½ teaspoon grated nutmeg
1 egg white
sea salt
2 tablespoons golden caster sugar
Lancashire cheese and/or Lincolnshire Poacher (or single cream), to serve

SPINACH & WHITE BEAN SOUP WITH ANCHOVY FROTH.
SALMON EN CROÛTE WITH GINGER & CURRANTS.
WALNUT WHIP.

60 min To make the soup, chop the onion and garlic. Melt 25g of the butter in a large pan, add the onion and garlic and cook without colouring for 5–6 minutes until soft. Rinse the beans and add them to the pot with the milk and stock. Season. Bring to the boil, stir in the spinach and remove from the heat. Leave to cool slightly, and then purée in a liquidiser or food processor until smooth. Strain through a sieve into a clean pan. Check the seasoning and grate in nutmeg to taste.

50 min Preheat your oven to 170ºC/gas mark 3. To make the main course, soften the butter in a bowl, and finely grate the zest of the lemon into it. Finely chop the stem ginger and beat into the butter with the currants, mace and seasoning. Season both sides of the salmon. Roll out the pastry thinly to a rectangle 54 x 36cm. Cut into 6 18cm squares and set on a baking sheet. Place a piece of salmon on each pastry square and top with a spoonful of the prepared butter. Brush the edges of the pastry with water and bring up the edges like an envelope, pinching the 4 corners together in the middle. Brush with beaten egg yolk and chill in the fridge for about 15 minutes.

40 min Meanwhile, prepare the dessert. Place the walnuts on a baking tray and toast in the oven for 5–6 minutes until golden. Tip onto a plate and leave to cool. Reserve 6 walnut halves for the garnish and roughly crush the rest. Bring a small pan of water to the boil, reduce the heat to barely simmering and put a heatproof bowl on top. Break the chocolate into the bowl, remove the pan immediately from the heat and stir occasionally until the chocolate has melted. This will only take a few minutes. Increase the oven temperature to 200ºC/gas mark 6.

30 min Line a baking tray that will fit inside your fridge with parchment paper. Reserve one-third of the melted chocolate for the cream and use the rest to make the chocolate discs. To make the discs, pour 6 spoonfuls of melted chocolate onto the parchment paper and spread out with the back of a spoon to make 10cm rounds. Scatter with one-third of the crushed walnuts and place in the fridge to harden.

To cook the salmon parcels, remove them from the fridge, brush with beaten egg yolk again and bake in the oven for 20–25 minutes or until the pastry is golden.

20 min To prepare the filling for the dessert, put the bowl with the rest of the melted chocolate back over the hot water, tear the marshmallows into little pieces and add them to the chocolate in the bowl. Stir until melted. Whip the cream and honey in a large bowl with an electric whisk until thick. Whisk in the chocolate and marshmallow mixture, and then fold in half of the remaining walnuts. Cover with clingfilm and set in the fridge until needed.

10 min To make the anchovy froth, melt the remaining butter in a small saucepan until it starts to bubble. Roughly chop the anchovies and put in a food processor with the egg yolks and half of the lemon juice. Blitz until pale and creamy and then slowly pour in the hot butter with the motor still running until the sauce thickens. Add 50ml boiling water and blitz to a froth, then pour into a bowl, season with salt, pepper and cayenne and squeeze in a little more lemon juice if needed. Keep warm.

To serve the starter, reheat the soup, ladle into bowls and top with a swirl of anchovy froth. Serve the rest on the side for people to help themselves.

To serve the main course, divide the salmon parcels between 6 warmed dinner plates and accompany with a crisp green salad on the side.

To serve the dessert, carefully peel the hardened chocolate discs from the paper and place one on each of your dessert plates. Place a spoonful of the chocolate cream on each, top with a walnut half and scatter over the remaining crushed walnuts.

Spinach & White Bean Soup with Anchovy Froth
1 large onion
2 garlic cloves
175g butter
1 x 400g tin cooked haricot or cannellini beans (see page 8)
400ml milk
600ml chicken or vegetable stock
300g young leaf spinach
grated nutmeg, to taste
3 tinned anchovy fillets
3 egg yolks
2 tablespoons lemon juice
cayenne pepper
sea salt and freshly ground black pepper

Salmon en Croûte with Ginger & Currants
85g butter
1 lemon
2 knobs of stem ginger in syrup
2 tablespoons currants
pinch of ground mace
6 x 125g skinless salmon fillets
600g shortcrust pastry
1 egg yolk
sea salt and freshly ground black pepper
crisp green salad, to serve

Walnut Whip
85g walnut halves
150g good-quality dark chocolate
100g marshmallows
300ml whipping cream
4 tablespoons runny honey

SPINACH & WHITE BEAN SOUP WITH ANCHOVY FROTH

The intensity of the anchovy goes brilliantly with the creaminess of the white beans.

To make the soup, chop the onion and garlic. Melt 25g of the butter in a large pan, add the onion and garlic and cook without colouring for 5–6 minutes until soft. Rinse the beans and add them to the pot with the milk and stock. Season.

Bring to the boil, stir in the spinach and remove from the heat. Leave to cool slightly, and then purée in a liquidiser or food processor until smooth. Strain through a sieve into a clean pan. Check the seasoning, and grate in nutmeg to taste.

To make the anchovy froth, melt the remaining butter in a small saucepan until it starts to bubble. Roughly chop the anchovies and put in a food processor with the egg yolks and half of the lemon juice. Blitz until pale and creamy, and then slowly pour in the hot butter with the motor still running until the sauce thickens. Add 50ml boiling water and blitz to a froth, then pour into a bowl, season to taste with salt, pepper and cayenne and squeeze in a little more lemon juice if needed.

Reheat the soup, ladle into bowls and serve with a swirl of anchovy froth on top and the rest in a little bowl on the side so people can help themselves.

1 large onion
2 garlic cloves
175g butter
1 x 400g tin haricot or
  cannellini beans (see
  page 8)
400ml milk
600ml chicken or
  vegetable stock
300g young leaf spinach
whole nutmeg, to grate
  or ground
3 tinned anchovy fillets
3 egg yolks
2 tablespoons lemon juice
cayenne pepper
sea salt and freshly
  ground black pepper

SALMON EN CROÛTE WITH GINGER & CURRANTS

A nod of respect to George Perry-Smith, the inventor of this unusual but delicious dish and one-time owner of The Hole in the Wall restaurant in Bath.

Preheat your oven to 200ºC/gas mark 6.

Soften the butter in a bowl, and finely grate the zest of the lemon into it. Finely chop the stem ginger and beat into the butter with the currants, mace and seasoning. Season both sides of the salmon.

Roll out the pastry thinly to form a rectangle 54 x 36cm. Cut into 6 18cm squares and set on a baking sheet. Place a piece of salmon on each pastry square and top with a spoonful of the prepared butter. Brush the edges of the pastry with water and bring up the edges like an envelope, pinching the 4 corners together in the middle. Brush with beaten egg yolk and chill in the fridge for about 15 minutes.

Brush the salmon parcels with egg yolk again and bake for 20–25 minutes, or until the pastry is golden.

Serve with a crisp green salad on the side.

85g butter
1 lemon
2 knobs of stem
  ginger in syrup
2 tablespoons currants
pinch of ground mace
6 x 125g skinless
  salmon fillets
600g shortcrust pastry
1 egg yolk
sea salt and freshly
  ground black pepper
crisp green salad, to serve

WALNUT WHIP

A homemade version of an old sweetshop favourite.

Preheat your oven to 170°C/gas mark 3.

Place the walnuts on a baking tray and toast in the oven for 5–6 minutes until golden. Tip onto a plate and leave to cool. Reserve 6 walnut halves for the garnish and roughly crush the rest.

Bring a small pan of water to the boil, reduce the heat to barely simmering and put a heatproof bowl on top. Break the chocolate into the bowl, remove the pan immediately from the heat and stir occasionally until the chocolate has melted. This will only take a few minutes. Line a baking tray that will fit inside your fridge with parchment paper.

Reserve one-third of the melted chocolate for the cream and use the rest to make the chocolate discs. To make the discs, pour 6 spoonfuls of chocolate onto the parchment paper and spread out with the back of a spoon to make 10cm rounds. Scatter with one-third of the crushed walnuts and place in the fridge to harden.

Put the bowl with the rest of the melted chocolate back over the hot water, tear the marshmallows into little pieces and add them to the chocolate in the bowl. Stir until melted.

Whip the cream and honey in a large bowl with an electric whisk until thick. Whisk in the chocolate and marshmallow mixture, and then fold in half of the remaining walnuts. Cover with clingfilm and set in the fridge until needed.

To serve, carefully peel the hardened chocolate discs from the paper and place one on each of your dessert plates. Place a spoonful of the chocolate cream on each, top with a walnut half and scatter over the remaining crushed walnuts.

85g walnut halves
150g good-quality
 dark chocolate
100g marshmallows
300ml whipping cream
4 tablespoons
 runny honey

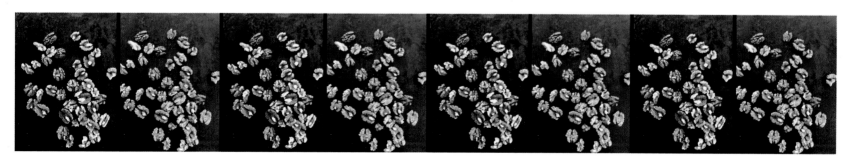

SPRING

SPRING ONION MISO SOUP.
CELERIAC & SAFFRON SARDINE GRATIN.
ROAST PINEAPPLE ON TOASTED GINGER CAKE.

60 min　Start with the main course. Preheat your oven to 220°C/gas mark 7. Crush the garlic cloves. Pour the cream into a small pan, add the saffron and crushed garlic, bring almost to the boil, and then remove from the heat and set aside to infuse. Thinly slice the onions. Use a little of the butter to grease a 38 x 28 x 8cm roasting tin. Melt the remaining butter in a large frying pan, add the onions with a sprinkle of salt, and then cover and cook for 5–10 minutes until soft. Peel the celeriac and slice very thinly and also slice the potatoes as thinly as possible (no need to peel). A mandolin is great for this job, otherwise use a large, sharp knife (see page 28).

50 min　Roughly chop the parsley and drain the sardines. Place the sliced potatoes, celeriac, cooked onions and parsley in the roasting tin, and then break the sardines over the top into large pieces. Season with salt and pepper and mix well together. Level the top and pour in the saffron cream. Place the tin directly on the heat, bring to the boil, and then cover with foil and place on the top shelf of the oven for 15 minutes.

40 min　Meanwhile, get on with the dessert. Using a serrated bread knife, peel the pineapple (see page 27). Cut it lengthways into very thin slices and place in a roasting tin. Finely grate half of the nutmeg into a bowl, add the sugar and mix well. Sprinkle the nutmeg sugar over the pineapple slices and turn to coat. Drizzle the rum over the top and place on the bottom shelf of the oven for 15–20 minutes, or until the pineapple is tender.

30 min　Slice the ginger cake into 12 slices and toast on each side – it won't brown very much. Leave to cool.

Remove the foil from the gratin and return it to the oven for a further 25 minutes, or until the potatoes and celeriac are tender and the top is golden brown.

20 min　Now for the starter. Slice the spring onions very thinly across into little rings. Trim the pak choi and separate the leaves, then chop across into about 4 pieces.

10 min　Bring 1.2 litres water to the boil in a large pan. Add the spring onions and pak choi and cook for 30 seconds. Add the miso paste, stir to dissolve and remove from the heat.

To serve the starter, ladle the soup into bowls, add a splash of soy sauce and a few mint and coriander leaves to each, and then drizzle with a few drops of sesame oil. Serve at once.

To serve the main course, spoon the gratin onto dinner plates and accompany with a few salad leaves on the side.

To serve the dessert, place a few slices of pineapple on each plate, top with a couple of slices of toasted ginger cake and finish with a ball of ice cream. Drizzle over the sugary juices and serve immediately.

Spring Onion Miso Soup
12 spring onions
250g pak choi
4 tablespoons yellow, red or white miso paste
a few coriander leaves
a few mint leaves
soy sauce, to taste
sesame oil, to taste

Celeriac & Saffron Sardine Gratin
4 garlic cloves
600ml single cream
pinch of saffron strands
2 large onions
50g butter
750g celeriac
750g potatoes
1 bunch of flat-leaf parsley
2 x 115g tins sardines in
  oil with chilli (piccante)
  or plain
sea salt and freshly
  ground black pepper
salad leaves, to serve

Roast Pineapple on Toasted Ginger Cake
1 large pineapple
1 whole nutmeg
100g dark soft brown sugar
3 tablespoons dark rum
300g Jamaican ginger cake
vanilla ice cream, to serve

SPRING ONION MISO SOUP.

It is really important not to cook the miso for too long, as it is a live food and enzymes are destroyed by boiling. I have also noticed it loses flavour the longer it is cooked.

Slice the spring onions very thinly across into little rings. Trim the pak choi, separate the leaves, and then chop each one across into about 4 pieces.

Bring 1.2 litres water to the boil in a large pan. Add the spring onions and pak choi and cook for 30 seconds.

Add the miso paste, stir to dissolve and remove from the heat. Rip the coriander and mint leaves roughly into the soup.

Ladle into 6 soup bowls, add a splash of soy sauce to each and drizzle with a few drops of sesame oil. Serve at once.

12 spring onions
250g pak choi
4 tablespoons yellow,
 red or white miso paste
a few coriander leaves
a few mint leaves
soy sauce, to taste
sesame oil, to taste

CELERIAC & SAFFRON
SARDINE GRATIN

Not only does the saffron give an amazing colour to this dish, it also gives a distinct musty spice flavour.

Preheat your oven to 220°C/gas mark 7.

Crush the garlic cloves. Pour the cream into a small pan, add the saffron and crushed garlic, bring almost to the boil, and then remove from the heat and set aside. Thinly slice the onions.

Use a little of the butter to grease a 38 x 28 x 8cm roasting tin. Melt the remaining butter in a large frying pan, add the onions with a sprinkle of salt, and then cover and cook for 5–10 minutes until soft. Peel the celeriac and slice very thinly and also slice the potatoes as thinly as possible (no need to peel). A mandolin is great for this job, otherwise use a large, sharp knife (see page 28).

Roughly chop the parsley and drain the sardines. Place the sliced potatoes, celeriac, cooked onions and parsley in the roasting tin and break the sardines over the top into large pieces. Season with salt and pepper and mix well together. Level the top and pour in the saffron cream. Place the tin directly on the heat and bring to the boil, and then cover with foil and place on the top shelf of the oven for 15 minutes. Remove the foil and return to the oven for a further 25 minutes, or until the potatoes and celeriac are tender and the top is golden brown. Serve with a few salad leaves on the side.

4 garlic cloves
600ml single cream
pinch of saffron strands
2 large onions
50g butter
750g celeriac
750g potatoes
1 bunch of flat-leaf
 parsley
2 x 115g tins sardines in
 oil with chilli (piccante)
 or plain
sea salt and freshly
 ground black pepper
salad leaves, to serve

ROAST PINEAPPLE ON TOASTED
GINGER CAKE

This is best eaten whilst listening to reggae!

Preheat your oven to 200°C/gas mark 6.

With a serrated bread knife, peel the pineapple (see page 27). Cut it lengthways into very thin slices and place in a roasting tin.

Finely grate half of the nutmeg into a bowl, add the sugar and mix well. Sprinkle the nutmeg sugar over the pineapple slices and turn to coat. Drizzle with the rum and place in the oven for 15–20 minutes, or until the pineapple is tender.

Meanwhile, slice the ginger cake into 12 slices and toast on each side – it won't brown very much. Leave to cool.

To serve, place a few slices of pineapple on each dessert plate, top with a couple of slices of toasted ginger cake and finish with a ball of ice cream. Drizzle over the sugary juices and serve immediately.

1 large pineapple
1 whole nutmeg
100g dark soft
 brown sugar
3 tablespoons dark rum
300g Jamaican
 ginger cake
vanilla ice cream, to serve

WHITE BEAN CROSTINI WITH ROSEMARY & POMEGRANATE.
PORK, PRUNE & PISTACHIO PATTIES WITH ANCHOVY DRESSING.
BANANA BRÛLÉE.

60 min   Preheat your oven to 180°C/gas mark 4. Begin with the main course. Chop the prunes into small pieces. Finely chop the pistachios. Finely chop the red onion. Place together in a bowl with the pork mince. Remove the leaves from the parsley and roughly chop. Set aside 6 tablespoons chopped parsley and place the rest in the bowl with the mince mixture. Add the cinnamon, allspice and chilli powder and season well. Mix well with your hands and shape into 12 equal-sized patties. Set aside.

50 min   Meanwhile, cut the baguette for the starter diagonally into thin slices. Lay out in a single layer on a large baking sheet and drizzle with 2 tablespoons of the extra-virgin olive oil. Place in the oven and bake for 5–7 minutes or until lightly golden.

40 min   Now for the dessert. Preheat the grill* to high. Place the yogurt in a bowl and stir in the vanilla extract. Peel the bananas and slice thinly. Place half of the sliced bananas in the bottom of 6 ramekins. Spoon the yogurt on top, level the surface with a knife and arrange the remaining banana slices over the yogurt. Sprinkle evenly with sugar, set on a baking tray and place under the grill for 5–7 minutes until the sugar has melted and is bubbling. Remove from the heat and leave to cool.

* Alternatively, you could use a blowtorch to melt the sugar.

30 min   Back to the starter. Wash and drain the haricot beans. Crush the garlic cloves. Remove the leaves from the rosemary and chop. Finely grate the zest from the lemon and squeeze half the juice. Using a vegetable peeler, pare the cheese into fine curls. Cut the pomegranate into quarters and pop the seeds off the skin onto a plate, making sure you discard all of the bitter pith (see page 27).

20 min   Heat 4 tablespoons of the remaining extra-virgin olive oil in a large frying pan over a low heat. Add the garlic and rosemary and cook gently without colouring for 2–3 minutes until soft. Add the drained beans, mash roughly with a fork and keep stirring until warmed through. Remove from the heat and stir in the lemon juice and zest, along with some salt and pepper to taste. Set aside.

10 min   To cook the patties for the main course, place the flour on a dinner plate and roll each one in the flour, shaking off any excess. Heat the olive oil over a moderate heat and cook the patties for 4–5 minutes on each side until golden brown and cooked through. Keep warm.

To prepare the dressing, rinse the capers, drain and chop. Drain the oil from the tins of anchovies into a frying pan and warm over a low heat. Finely chop the anchovies, add to the pan and cook gently until they start to dissolve and melt. Add the capers, raise the heat and add the vinegar. As the sauce starts to bubble, toss in the reserved parsley and remove from the heat.

To serve the starter, spread a little of the white bean mixture onto each toasted bread slice and arrange on a serving platter. Drizzle with the remaining extra-virgin olive oil and scatter with the cheese curls and pomegranate seeds.

To serve the main course, place 2 patties on each dinner plate, gently reheat the dressing and spoon a little over each patty. Accompany with the salad leaves on the side.

To serve the dessert, accompany the brûlées with a nut cookie on the side.

White Bean Crostini with Rosemary & Pomegranate
½ baguette
125ml extra-virgin olive oil
2 x 400g tins haricot beans
2 garlic cloves
1 branch of fresh rosemary
1 lemon
50g Pecorino or Parmesan cheese
1 pomegranate
sea salt and freshly ground black pepper

Pork, Prune & Pistachio Patties with Anchovy Dressing
200g ready-to-eat stoned prunes
50g shelled pistachios
1 red onion
900g pork mince
80g parsley
½ teaspoon ground cinnamon
1 teaspoon ground allspice
½ teaspoon chilli powder
4 tablespoons plain flour
3 tablespoons olive oil
2 tablespoons capers
2 x 50g tins anchovy fillets in olive oil
2 tablespoons red wine vinegar
sea salt and freshly ground black pepper
salad leaves, to serve

Banana Brûlée
500g Greek yogurt
1 teaspoon vanilla extract
4 small bananas
60g soft dark brown sugar
nut cookies, to serve

WHITE BEAN CROSTINI WITH ROSEMARY & POMEGRANATE

Scatter the vibrant and pretty pomegranate seeds all over your platter or tray for decoration.

Preheat your oven to 180°C/gas mark 4.

Cut the baguette diagonally into thin slices. Lay out in a single layer on a large baking sheet and drizzle with 2 tablespoons of the oil. Place in the oven and bake for 5–7 minutes until lightly golden.

Rinse and drain the haricot beans. Crush the garlic cloves. Remove the leaves from the rosemary and chop. Finely grate the zest from the lemon and squeeze half the juice. Using a vegetable peeler, pare the cheese into fine curls. Cut the pomegranate into quarters and pop the seeds off the skin onto a plate, making sure you discard all of the bitter pith (see page 27).

Heat 4 tablespoons of the remaining oil in a large frying pan over a low heat. Add the garlic and rosemary and cook gently without colouring for 2–3 minutes until soft. Add the drained beans, mash roughly with a fork and keep stirring until warmed through.

Remove from the heat and stir in the lemon juice and zest, along with some salt and pepper to taste. Spread a little of the white bean mixture onto each toasted bread slice and arrange on a serving platter. Drizzle with the remaining oil and scatter with the cheese curls and pomegranate seeds.

½ baguette
125ml extra-virgin olive oil
2 x 400g tins haricot beans
2 garlic cloves
1 branch of fresh rosemary
1 lemon
50g Pecorino or Parmesan cheese
1 pomegranate
sea salt flakes and freshly ground black pepper

PORK, PRUNE & PISTACHIO PATTIES WITH ANCHOVY DRESSING

Another of my favourite dishes – I love these patties!

Chop the prunes into small pieces. Finely chop the pistachios and the red onion. Place together in a bowl with the pork mince. Remove the leaves from the parsley and roughly chop. Set aside 6 tablespoons parsley and place the rest in the bowl with the mince mixture. Add the cinnamon, allspice and chilli powder and season well. Mix well with your hands and shape into 12 equal-sized patties.

Place the flour on a dinner plate and roll each of the patties in the flour, shaking off any excess. Heat the olive oil over a moderate heat and cook the patties for 4–5 minutes on each side, or until golden brown and cooked through. Keep warm while you prepare the dressing.

Rinse the capers, drain and chop. Drain the oil from the tins of anchovies into a frying pan and warm over a low heat. Finely chop the anchovies, add to the pan and cook gently until they start to dissolve and melt. Add the capers, raise the heat and add the vinegar. As the sauce starts to bubble, toss in the reserved parsley and remove from the heat.

To serve, place 2 patties on each dinner plate and spoon a little of the dressing on top. Accompany with the salad leaves on the side.

200g ready-to-eat stoned prunes
50g shelled pistachios
1 red onion
900g pork mince
80g parsley
½ teaspoon ground cinnamon
1 teaspoon ground allspice
½ teaspoon chilli powder
4 tablespoons plain flour
3 tablespoons olive oil
2 tablespoons capers
2 x 50g tins anchovy fillets in olive oil
2 tablespoons red wine vinegar
sea salt and freshly ground black pepper
salad leaves, to serve

BANANA BRULÉE

Try substituting the banana with other soft fruit for a super easy pud.

Preheat your grill* to high.

Place the yogurt in a bowl and stir in the vanilla extract. Peel the bananas and slice thinly. Place half of the sliced bananas in the bottom of 6 ramekins. Spoon the yogurt on top, level the surface and arrange the remaining banana slices over the yogurt.

Sprinkle evenly with sugar, set on a baking tray and place under the grill for 5–7 minutes until the sugar has melted and is bubbling. Remove from the heat and leave to cool.

Serve with some good nut cookies on the side.

* Alternatively, you could use a blowtorch to melt the sugar.

500g Greek yogurt
1 teaspoon vanilla extract
4 small bananas
60g soft dark brown sugar
nut cookies, to serve

EASTER EGGS WITH DUKKAH.

HARISSA-MARINATED LAMB WITH CRUSHED NEW POTATOES.

HOT CROSS BUN BREAD & BUTTER PUDDING.

60 min   Start with the dessert. Preheat your oven to 180°C/gas mark 4. Pour the milk and cream into a saucepan. Cut the vanilla pod in half, scrape the seeds into the pan and also add the pod. Place over a low heat and bring to just below boiling point. Remove from the heat, whisk to disperse the vanilla seeds, remove the pod and leave to cool for 5 minutes. Finely grate the zest from the orange. Whisk together the eggs, sugar and zest in a bowl and then gradually pour in the milk and cream mixture, whisking all the time. Cut each hot cross bun horizontally into 3 equal-sized slices and spread each piece with butter. Place the bottom third of each bun into the base of 6 200ml ramekins, or oven-proof cups or mugs.

50 min   Pour over a little of the custard, and then add the middle section of the buns. Pour in the rest of the custard and finish with the top section of each bun, cross uppermost – avoid submerging the tops. Place the ramekins in a roasting tin, pour boiling water into the tin, so it comes halfway up the sides of the ramekins, and carefully transfer to the oven. Cook for about 20 minutes, or until just cooked but still a bit wobbly in the centre.

40 min   Meanwhile, prepare the marinade for the main course. Drain the sundried tomatoes, reserving 3 tablespoons of the oil. Roughly chop the mint leaves. Crush the garlic cloves. Place the mint and garlic in a food processor, add the sundried tomatoes and harissa and blitz until roughly chopped. Add 2 tablespoons of the reserved tomato oil and blitz again until you have a thick paste. Scrape the paste into a large bowl, add the lamb fillets, turn to coat and set aside to marinate.

30 min   Increase the oven temperature to 200°C/gas mark 6. Spread the hazelnuts for the starter on a baking tray and toast for 5–10 minutes until golden. Remove from the oven and tip onto a plate to cool. Heat a heavy-based

frying pan over a moderate heat, add the coriander and cumin seeds and toast them in the dry pan, turning every now and again until they start to pop. Remove from the heat and tip onto the plate with the hazelnuts. Add the sesame seeds to the pan, return to a low heat and toast for 3–5 minutes until lightly golden. To make the dukkah, place the spices, seeds, nuts, sea salt and peppercorns in a spice grinder or food processor and grind until fine – don't overdo it or you will end up with a paste. Tip into a serving dish.

20 min   Back to the main course. Bring a large pan of salted water to the boil, add the new potatoes and return to the boil. Reduce the heat and simmer for 15–20 minutes until tender.

Meanwhile, cook the eggs for the starter. Fill a medium-sized pan with water and bring to the boil. Carefully lower in the duck's and hen's eggs and bring back to the boil. Boil the duck's eggs for 10 minutes and the hen's eggs for 8 minutes. Add the quail's eggs for the last 2½ minutes. Once the eggs are cooked, remove them from the pan and arrange in a large serving bowl. Remove the leaves from the lettuce and place in a serving bowl. Melt the butter in a small pan and pour into a small serving dish.

10 min   To cook the lamb, heat the remaining tablespoon of tomato oil over a high heat in an oven-proof frying pan. Season the marinated lamb all over with salt and black pepper and place in the hot pan. Brown all over for a total of 2–3 minutes, and then finish off in the oven for a further 8–10 minutes, or until tender but still pink.

Meanwhile, drain the potatoes and return them to the pan. Using a fork, crush gently to create a really rough mash and season with salt and pepper. Gently stir in the crème fraîche.

Once the lamb is cooked, remove it from the oven, wrap it in foil and leave to rest while you have your starter.

To serve the starter, place the dukkah, melted butter and sea salt on the table alongside the freshly boiled eggs and lettuce leaves. Allow everyone to peel the eggs themselves, and then dip them, and the leaves, into the melted butter, dukkah and sea salt.

To serve the main course, slice the lamb thinly and serve on top of the crushed new potatoes.

To serve the dessert, dust the bread and butter puddings with icing sugar and serve warm or at room temperature.

Easter Eggs with Dukkah
25g skinned hazelnuts
50g coriander seeds
1 tablespoon cumin seeds
100g sesame seeds
½ teaspoon ground cinnamon
2 teaspoons sea salt flakes, plus extra to serve
1 tablespoon black peppercorns
3 duck's eggs
6 free-range hen's eggs
12 quail's eggs
2 little gem lettuces
100g butter

Harissa-marinated Lamb with Crushed New Potatoes
50g sundried tomatoes in olive oil
25g fresh mint
2 garlic cloves
1 tablespoon rose harissa
1kg whole lamb neck fillets (2–3 fillets,
 depending on size)
750g new potatoes
150ml crème fraîche
sea salt and freshly ground black pepper

Hot Cross Bun Bread & Butter Pudding
300ml milk
300ml single cream
1 vanilla pod
1 orange
2 eggs
70g golden caster sugar
6 hot cross buns
50g butter, softened
icing sugar, to dust

EASTER EGGS WITH DUKKAH

An Egyptian fragrant spice mix to dip your (non-chocolate) Easter eggs into. A dish to share. I use any leftover dukkah sprinkled over salads, or mixed with crème fraîche to accompany cold lamb.

Preheat your oven to 200°C/gas mark 6. Spread the hazelnuts on a baking tray and toast for 5–10 minutes, or until golden. Remove from the oven and tip onto a plate to cool.

Heat a heavy-based frying pan over a moderate heat, add the coriander and cumin seeds and toast them in the dry pan, turning every now and then, until they start to pop. Remove from the heat and tip onto the plate with the hazelnuts. Add the sesame seeds to the pan and toast for 3–5 minutes, or until lightly golden.

To make the dukkah, place the spices, seeds, nuts, sea salt and peppercorns in a spice grinder or food processor and grind until fine – don't overdo it or you will end up with a paste. Transfer to a small serving bowl.

Fill a medium-sized pan with water and bring to the boil. Carefully lower in the duck's and hen's eggs and bring back to the boil. Boil the duck's eggs for 10 minutes and the hen's eggs for 8 minutes. Add the quail's eggs towards the end for the last 2½ minutes.

Drain the eggs once they are cooked and arrange in a large serving bowl. Remove the leaves from the lettuces. Melt the butter in a small pan, pour into a small dish and serve alongside the dukkah, freshly boiled eggs and lettuce leaves. Allow everyone to peel the eggs at the table, and then dip them and the leaves into the melted butter, dukkah and sea salt.

25g skinned hazelnuts
50g coriander seeds
1 tablespoon cumin seeds
100g sesame seeds
½ teaspoon ground cinnamon
2 teaspoons sea salt flakes, plus extra to serve
1 tablespoon black peppercorns
3 duck's eggs
6 free-range hen's eggs
12 quail's eggs
2 little gem lettuces
100g butter

HARISSA-MARINATED LAMB WITH CRUSHED NEW POTATOES

Lamb in spring is at its most tender and succulent.

First prepare the marinade. Drain the sundried tomatoes, reserving 3 tablespoons of the oil. Remove the leaves from the mint and roughly chop. Crush the garlic cloves. Place the mint and garlic in a food processor, add the sundried tomatoes and harissa and blitz until roughly chopped. Add 2 tablespoons of the reserved tomato oil and blitz again until you have a thick paste. Scrape the paste into a mixing bowl, add the lamb fillets, turn to coat and set aside to marinate for 20–30 minutes. Preheat your oven to 200°C/gas mark 6.

Heat the remaining tablespoon of tomato oil over a high heat in an oven-proof frying pan. Season the marinated lamb all over with salt and black pepper and place in the hot pan. Brown all over for a total of 2–3 minutes, and then finish off in the oven for a further 8–10 minutes, or until tender but still pink. Remove from the oven, cover with foil to keep warm and leave to rest.

Bring a large pan of salted water to the boil, add the new potatoes and return to the boil. Reduce the heat and simmer for 15–20 minutes until tender. Drain well, and then return to the pan. Using a fork, crush the potatoes gently to create a really rough mash. Season with salt and pepper and gently stir in the crème fraîche.

To serve, place a spoonful of the crushed potatoes on each plate, slice the meat thinly and arrange on top.

1kg whole lamb neck fillets (2–3 fillets depending on size)
750g new potatoes
150ml crème fraîche
sea salt and freshly ground black pepper

For the marinade
50g sundried tomatoes in olive oil
25g fresh mint
2 garlic cloves
1 tablespoon rose harissa

HOT CROSS BUN BREAD & BUTTER PUDDING

Preheat your oven to 180°C/gas mark 4.

Pour the milk and cream into a saucepan. Cut the vanilla pod in half, scrape the seeds into the pan and add the pod. Place over a low heat and bring to just below boiling point. Remove from the heat, whisk to disperse the vanilla seeds, remove the pod and leave to cool for 5 minutes.

Meanwhile, finely grate the zest from the orange. Whisk the eggs with the sugar and zest in a mixing bowl. Pour in the milk and cream mixture, whisking all the time until combined.

Cut each hot cross bun horizontally into 3 equal-sized slices and spread each piece with butter. Place the bottom third of each bun in the base of 6 200ml ramekins, or oven-proof cups or mugs. Pour a little of the custard over the top, and then add the middle section of the buns. Pour in the rest of the custard and finish with the top section of each bun, cross uppermost – don't submerge the top.

Place the ramekins in a roasting tin and pour boiling water into the tin, so it comes halfway up the sides of the ramekins. Carefully transfer the tin to the oven and cook for about 20 minutes, or until the puddings are just cooked but still a bit wobbly in the centre. Serve warm or at room temperature, dusted with icing sugar.

300ml milk
300ml single cream
1 vanilla pod
1 orange
2 eggs
70g golden caster sugar
6 hot cross buns
50g butter, softened
icing sugar, to dust

BROCCOLI & TOASTED ALMOND SOUP.
CHICKEN WITH RAISINS, PINE NUTS & SHERRY.
BANANA TARTE TATIN.

60 min   Begin with the starter. Preheat your oven to 180°C/gas mark 4. Spread the ground almonds evenly on a baking sheet and toast in the oven for about 8–10 minutes or until golden. Set aside. Increase the oven temperature to 220°C/gas mark 7. Trim the base of the broccoli and cut the stalks into thin slices and the broccoli heads into small florets. Slice the spring onions, crush the garlic cloves and deseed and finely chop the chilli (if using).

50 min   Melt the butter in a large pan and add the spring onions, broccoli stalks and chilli. Cook for 4–5 minutes or until soft. Add the stock or water and bring to the boil. Add the broccoli florets, bring back to the boil, and then reduce the heat and simmer for about 10 minutes or until tender. Leave to cool slightly, and then blend in a liquidiser until smooth with three-quarters of the toasted almonds. Reserve the rest.

40 min   For the dessert, melt the butter and sugar over a moderate heat in a 28cm oven-proof frying pan (or cake tin with a fixed base). Cook for about 5 minutes until the mixture is starting to go brown and caramelise. Peel the bananas and slice in half lengthways. Arrange in the pan, cut-side down. Remove from the heat.

30 min   Roll out the pastry so it is about 2.5–5cm larger than the pan and prick all over with a fork. Slide the pastry on top of the bananas, tucking the edges down inside the rim of the pan. Put the tarte tatin on the top shelf of the oven and bake for about 30–40 minutes or until the pastry is crisp and golden.

20 min   Meanwhile, get on with the main course. Cut the chicken breasts along the thickest edge, from the widest part to the tip, in half across the middle, nearly but not all the way through. Open out like a book and you will end up with a heart-shaped piece of chicken.

Crush the garlic cloves, squeeze the juice from the lemon and combine in a large bowl with the paprika and some salt and pepper. Add the chicken pieces, turn over in the marinade to coat and set aside. Trim, wash and dry the watercress. Bring a medium pan of salted water to the boil, add the new potatoes and simmer for 15–20 minutes or until tender.

10 min   Melt half of the butter over a moderate heat in a large frying pan and fry the raisins and pine nuts for 3–4 minutes, stirring constantly, or until the nuts turn golden. Using a slotted spoon, remove the nuts and raisins to a plate and add the remaining butter to the pan. Put in the opened-out chicken breasts (you may need to do this in batches) and cook for 5–10 minutes, or until tender and cooked through, turning once or twice. Remove the chicken pieces to a serving dish and keep warm. Place the pan on one side for later to make the sauce.

To serve the starter, pour the soup back into the pan, stir in the milk, bring back to the boil to reheat and season to taste with salt and pepper. Ladle into bowls, swirl a spoonful of cream on top and sprinkle with the reserved toasted almonds.

To serve the main course, return the pan (in which the chicken was cooked) to a moderate heat. Add the sherry, stand back and ignite with a match to flambé and cook out the alcohol. Once the flames have died down, return the nuts and raisins to the pan and allow the sauce to bubble away for a minute or two. Pour over the chicken pieces and serve with the watercress and new potatoes on the side.

To serve the dessert, remove the tarte tatin from the oven once it is cooked and leave to cool for 5 minutes before inverting it onto a plate. Cut it into wedges and accompany with a scoop of ice cream on the top.

Broccoli & Toasted Almond Soup
100g ground almonds
850g broccoli
2 bunches of spring onions
2 garlic cloves
1 red chilli (optional)
50g butter
850ml vegetable stock or water
300ml milk
150ml double cream
sea salt and freshly ground black pepper

Chicken with Raisins, Pine Nuts & Sherry
6 x 150g free-range chicken breasts
2 garlic cloves
1 lemon
½ teaspoon smoked paprika
25g butter
70g raisins
70g pine nuts
200ml medium-dry sherry
sea salt and freshly ground black pepper
watercress and new potatoes, to serve

Banana Tarte Tatin
70g butter
100g golden caster sugar
6 small bananas
375g ready-made sweetcrust pastry
chocolate ice cream, to serve

BROCCOLI & TOASTED ALMOND SOUP

The addition of toasted almonds gives a wonderful nutty undertone and creaminess.

Preheat your oven to 180°C/gas mark 4.

Spread the ground almonds evenly on a baking sheet and toast in the oven for about 8–10 minutes or until golden. Set aside.

Trim the base of the broccoli and cut the stalks into thin slices and the broccoli heads into small florets. Slice the spring onions, crush the garlic cloves and deseed and finely chop the chilli (if using).

Melt the butter in a large pan and add the spring onions, broccoli stalks and chilli. Cook for 4–5 minutes or until soft. Add the stock or water and bring to the boil. Add the broccoli florets, bring back to the boil, and then reduce the heat and simmer for about 10 minutes or until tender. Leave to cool slightly, then blend until smooth with three-quarters of the toasted almonds. Reserve the rest. Pour the soup back into the pan and stir in the milk. Bring back to the boil to reheat and season to taste with salt and pepper.

Ladle into bowls and serve with a swirl of cream and a sprinkling of the reserved almonds.

100g ground almonds
850g broccoli
2 bunches of
 spring onions
2 garlic cloves
1 red chilli (optional)
50g butter
850ml vegetable
 stock or water
300ml milk
150ml double cream
sea salt and freshly
 ground black pepper

CHICKEN WITH RAISINS, PINE NUTS & SHERRY

A Spanish-influenced recipe.

Cut the chicken breasts along the thickest edge, from the widest part to the tip, in half across the middle, nearly but not all the way through. Open out like a book and you will end up with a heart-shaped piece of chicken.

Peel and crush the garlic cloves, squeeze the juice from the lemon and combine in a large bowl with the paprika and some salt and pepper. Add the chicken pieces, turn over in the marinade to coat and set aside.

Melt half of the butter over a moderate heat in a large frying pan and fry the raisins and pine nuts for 3–4 minutes, stirring constantly, or until the nuts turn golden. Using a slotted spoon, remove the nuts and raisins to a plate and add the remaining butter to the pan. Put in the opened-out chicken breasts (you may need to do this in batches) and cook for 5–10 minutes, or until tender and cooked through, turning once or twice.

Remove the chicken pieces to a serving dish and keep warm. Add the sherry to the pan, stand back and ignite with a match to flambé and cook out the alcohol. Once the flames have died down, return the nuts and raisins to the pan and allow the sauce to bubble away for a minute or two. Pour over the chicken pieces and serve with the watercress and new potatoes on the side.

6 x 150g free-range
 chicken breasts
2 garlic cloves
1 lemon
½ teaspoon
 smoked paprika
25g butter
70g raisins
70g pine nuts
200ml medium-dry sherry
sea salt and freshly
 ground black pepper
watercress and new
 potatoes, to serve

BANANA TARTE TATIN

If you have time try making your own sweetcrust pastry, using the recipe on page 34.

Preheat your oven to 220°C/gas mark 7. Melt the butter and sugar over a moderate heat in a 28cm oven-proof frying pan (or cake tin with a fixed base). Cook for about 5 minutes until the mixture is starting to go brown and caramelise.

Peel the bananas and slice in half lengthways. Arrange in the pan, cut-side down. Remove from the heat.

Roll out the pastry so it is about 2.5–5cm larger than the pan and prick all over with a fork. Slide the pastry on top of the bananas, tucking the edges down inside the rim of the pan. Put the tarte tatin on the top shelf of the oven and bake for about 30–40 minutes or until the pastry is crisp and golden. Leave to cool for 5 minutes before inverting onto a plate.

Serve warm with a scoop of chocolate ice cream.

70g butter
100g golden caster sugar
6 small bananas
375g ready-made
 sweetcrust pastry
chocolate ice cream,
 to serve

BLOOD ORANGE, WATERCRESS & RADISH SALAD.
THAI-STYLE FISH FINGERS.
BABY BRIOCHE WITH CHOCOLATE & GINGER ICE CREAM.

MENU 31

60 min   Take the ice cream out of the freezer and leave to soften for 20–30 minutes.

Meanwhile, get on with the main course. Deseed and roughly chop the chillies; roughly chop the garlic; peel and roughly chop the ginger; roughly chop the coriander, including the stalks; roughly chop the spring onions; and finely grate the zest from the limes. Place all of these ingredients in the bowl of a food processor and blitz until finely chopped. Scrape out into a mixing bowl. Cut the fish into large chunks, place in the processor bowl and blitz until you have a rough paste. Spoon into the mixing bowl.

50 min   Squeeze the juice from one of the limes into the fish mixture, add the fish sauce and season with a little salt and pepper – go easy on the salt because the nam pla is quite salty already. Combine well with your hands, and then tip out into a 30 x 18 x 3cm tray. Flatten the top with the palm of your hand and set in the fridge to firm up slightly for about 30 minutes.

40 min   The ice cream should now be soft. Lift the stem ginger from the syrup and chop finely. Tip the ice cream into a large bowl and scatter in the chopped ginger, along with 2 tablespoons of the ginger syrup from the jar. Quickly beat together, and then place the bowl in the freezer until you are ready to serve.

30 min   Now for the starter. Wash and dry the watercress and place on a large serving platter. Remove the top and bottom from the oranges with a sharp knife and then, standing each orange upright on a board, cut off the peel from top to bottom, making sure you remove all of the white pith (see page 26). Cut the oranges into thin slices and arrange over the watercress. Thinly slice the carrots and radishes and scatter slices over the salad. Cover with clingfilm and place in the fridge until you are ready to serve.

20 min   Back to the main course. Place the egg whites in a bowl and whisk lightly with a fork. Tip the desiccated coconut onto a large tray. Cut the fish mixture in half lengthways, and then into 9 slices to create 18 fish fingers. Working with one piece at a time, carefully remove it from the tray and dip first into the egg white and then into the coconut. Shake off any excess and transfer to another tray.

10 min   Heat the oil in a large frying pan over a moderate heat and fry the fish fingers for about 6 minutes, turning once or twice (you may need to do this in batches). Drain on kitchen paper.

To serve the starter, crumble the goat's cheese (if using) over the salad and sprinkle with a little salt and pepper. To make the dressing, mix the 2 oils together in a small bowl and drizzle over the salad.

To serve the main course, accompany the fish fingers with little bowls of dipping sauce and mayonnaise.

To serve the dessert, cut the brioche in half horizontally, but not quite all the way through, and scoop a spoonful of the ice cream into the centre. Place on a dessert plate, dust with a little cocoa powder and serve immediately.

Blood Orange, Watercress & Radish Salad
100g watercress
4 blood oranges
6 baby carrots
12 radishes
100g fresh goat's cheese (optional)
salt and freshly ground black pepper
3 tablespoons extra-virgin olive oil
1 teaspoon sesame oil

Thai-style Fish Fingers
1–2 red chillies
3 garlic cloves
5cm piece of fresh root ginger
40g fresh coriander
8 spring onions
2 limes
1kg skinless pollock, haddock or other firm white fish
1 tablespoon Thai fish sauce (nam pla)
salt and freshly ground black pepper
2 egg whites
200g unsweetened desiccated coconut
5 tablespoons vegetable oil
sweet chilli dipping sauce and mayonnaise, to serve

Baby Brioche with Chocolate & Ginger Ice Cream
500g chocolate ice cream
3–4 knobs of stem ginger in syrup
6 baby brioche
cocoa powder, to dust

BLOOD ORANGE, WATERCRESS & RADISH SALAD

Wash and dry the watercress and place on a large serving platter. Remove the top and bottom from the oranges with a sharp knife and then, standing each orange upright on a board, cut off the peel from top to bottom, making sure you remove all of the white pith (see page 26). Cut the oranges into thin slices and arrange over the watercress.

Thinly slice the carrots and radishes and scatter over the salad. Crumble the goat's cheese (if using) over the top and sprinkle with a little salt and pepper.

To make the dressing, mix the 2 oils together in a small bowl and drizzle over the salad just before serving.

100g watercress
4 blood oranges
6 baby carrots
12 radishes
100g fresh goat's cheese
 (optional)
3 tablespoons extra-virgin
 olive oil
1 teaspoon sesame oil
sea salt and freshly
 ground black pepper

THAI-STYLE FISH FINGERS

The fish finger, an English children's staple, is turned on its head.

Deseed and roughly chop the chillies; roughly chop the garlic cloves; peel and roughly chop the ginger; roughly chop the coriander, including the stalks; roughly chop the spring onions; and finely grate the zest from the limes.

Place all of these ingredients in the bowl of a food processor and blitz until finely chopped. Scrape out into a mixing bowl. Cut the fish into large chunks, place in the processor bowl and blitz until you have a rough paste. Spoon into the mixing bowl.

Squeeze the juice from one of the limes into the fish mixture, add the fish sauce and season with a little salt and pepper – go easy on the salt because the nam pla is quite salty already. Combine well with your hands, and then tip out into a 30 x 18 x 3cm tray. Flatten the top with the palm of your hand and set in the fridge to firm up slightly for about 30 minutes.

Place the egg whites in a bowl and whisk lightly with a fork. Tip the desiccated coconut onto a large tray.

Cut the fish mixture in half lengthways, and then into 9 slices to create 18 fish fingers. Working with one piece at a time, carefully remove it from the tray and dip first into the beaten egg white and then coat in the coconut. Shake off any excess and transfer to another tray.

Heat the oil in a large frying pan over a moderate heat and fry the fish fingers for about 6 minutes, turning once or twice (you may need to do this in batches). Drain on kitchen paper and serve with the dipping sauce and mayonnaise on the side.

1–2 red chillies
3 garlic cloves
5cm piece of fresh
 root ginger
40g fresh coriander
8 spring onions
2 limes
1kg skinless pollock,
 haddock or other firm
 white fish
1 tablespoon Thai fish
 sauce (nam pla)
2 egg whites
200g unsweetened
 desiccated coconut
5 tablespoons
 vegetable oil
sea salt and freshly
 ground black pepper
sweet chilli dipping sauce
 and mayonnaise, to serve

BABY BRIOCHE WITH CHOCOLATE & GINGER ICE CREAM

Remove the ice cream from the freezer and leave to soften for about 20 minutes. Meanwhile, finely chop the stem ginger. Tip the ice cream into a large bowl and add the chopped ginger, along with 2 tablespoons of the ginger syrup from the jar. Quickly beat together, and then place the bowl in the freezer to allow the ice cream to harden up slightly until you are ready to serve.

When you are ready, cut the brioche in half horizontally, but not quite all the way through, and scoop a spoonful of the ice cream into the centre. Place on a dessert plate, dust with a little cocoa powder and serve immediately.

500g chocolate ice cream
3–4 knobs of stem ginger in syrup
6 baby brioche
cocoa powder, to dust

CAULIFLOWER, PARSNIP & PARSLEY TEMPURA.
PORK STEAKS WITH RED ONION RELISH & BAY-ROASTED HASSELBACK POTATOES.
PASSION FRUIT MESS.

60 min   Start with the marinade for the pork. Finely grate the zest and squeeze the juice from the orange. Crush the garlic. Combine the zest, juice, garlic and 2 tablespoons of the olive oil in a large, flat dish. Lay the pork steaks in the dish in a single layer and turn to coat. Set aside to marinate.

50 min   Meanwhile, prepare the red onion relish. Pull the leaves from the thyme and thinly slice the onions. Melt 50g of the butter in a large frying pan over a moderate heat. Add the mustard seeds, wait for them to pop, and then stir in the onions and thyme. Cover, reduce the heat and cook gently for 40 minutes until the onions are very soft but not coloured, stirring occasionally.

40 min   Preheat your oven to 190°C/gas mark 5. To prepare the Hasselback potatoes, place 2 chopsticks on a board and lay a potato lengthways in between them. Holding the sticks and potato in place with one hand, cut the potato across into 3mm thin slices, cutting down just to the sticks – not all the way through. Repeat with the rest of the potatoes. Insert a bay leaf into each sliced potato.

30 min   Heat the remaining butter with 3 tablespoons of the olive oil in a heavy-based roasting tin. Place over a moderate heat and carefully add the potatoes in a single layer – be careful because they may spit. Move the potatoes around for a couple of minutes to colour them slightly and season with freshly ground black pepper and sea salt flakes. Place the tin in the oven and roast for 25–30 minutes until golden brown and tender.

For the starter, cut the cauliflower into florets about the size of a walnut or smaller. Cut the parsnip into long, thin strips with a potato peeler. Divide the curly parsley into large sprigs, keeping the stalks intact.

20 min   Now for the dessert. Cut 4 of the passion fruits in half and scoop out the flesh and seeds into a large bowl. Add the sugar, pour in the cream and whisk until soft peaks have formed – use a hand whisk for this because an electric whisk will break up the seeds too much. Crumble the meringues into small pieces over the top of the cream and fold in gently. Spoon into dessert dishes or large wine glasses and place in the fridge.

Remove the pork from the marinade, season each side and set on a plate. Tip the marinade into the pan with the onions and add the vinegar and sugar. Increase the heat and boil rapidly to reduce the sauce. Keep warm until ready to serve.

Back to the starter. Heat the oil for the tempura in a large, deep pan or wok. To check it is hot enough, drop in a cube of bread – it should turn golden brown in 40 seconds.

10 min   While the oil is heating, make the batter. Lightly beat the egg yolk in a large bowl with a pinch of salt. Measure the fizzy water into a jug and add a few ice cubes, as it needs to be really cold. Whisk the water into the egg, tip in the flour all at once and whisk quickly together. Don't overmix and don't worry about the lumps – it is meant to be lumpy! Use immediately.

To make the tempura, dip a large handful of the cauliflower florets, parsnip strips or parsley sprigs in the batter, shake off any excess and deep-fry for about 3–4 minutes or until tender and crisp. Drain on kitchen paper, sprinkle lightly with salt and keep warm while you cook the rest. To serve, pile up the tempura on a platter and accompany with small bowls of soy sauce and chilli sauce for dipping.

To finish the main course, heat the remaining oil in a large frying pan, add the steaks – you may need to do this in batches – and cook over a medium-high heat for 3–4 minutes on each side, or until tender and cooked through.

To serve the main course, place a pork steak on each warmed dinner plate, top with the red onion relish and accompany with the Hasselback potatoes on the side.

To serve the dessert, cut the remaining 2 passion fruits in half, scoop out the seeds and spoon over each dessert.

Cauliflower, Parsnip & Parsley Tempura
½ small cauliflower
1 large parsnip
25g curly parsley
groundnut oil for deep-frying
1 egg yolk
sea salt
250ml sparkling water
a few ice cubes
200g plain flour
soy sauce and sweet chilli sauce, for dipping

Pork Steaks with Red Onion Relish & Bay-Roasted Hasselback Potatoes
1 orange
2 small garlic cloves
100ml olive oil
6 x 150g pork loin steaks
10g fresh thyme
4 large red onions
70g butter
2 teaspoons mustard seeds
24 small potatoes
about 24 fresh bay leaves
1 tablespoon balsamic vinegar
1 tablespoon caster sugar
sea salt flakes and freshly ground black pepper

Passion Fruit Mess
6 passion fruits
3 tablespoons golden caster sugar
450ml double cream
4 ready-made meringue nests

CAULIFLOWER, PARSNIP & PARSLEY TEMPURA

Cut the cauliflower into florets about the size of a walnut or smaller. Cut the parsnip into long, thin strips with a potato peeler. Divide the curly parsley into large sprigs, keeping the stalks intact.

Heat the oil in a large, deep pan or wok. To check it is hot enough, drop in a cube of bread – it should turn golden brown in 40 seconds.

While the oil is heating, make the batter. Lightly beat the egg yolk in a large bowl with a pinch of salt. Measure the fizzy water into a jug and add a few ice cubes, as it needs to be really cold. Whisk the water into the egg, tip in the flour all at once and whisk quickly together. Don't overmix and don't worry about the lumps – it is meant to be lumpy! Use immediately.

To make the tempura, dip a large handful of the cauliflower florets, parsnip strips or parsley sprigs in the batter, shake off any excess and deep-fry for about 3–4 minutes or until tender and crisp. Drain on kitchen paper, lightly sprinkle with salt and keep warm while you cook the rest.

To serve, pile the tempura up on a platter and accompany with small bowls of soy sauce and chilli sauce for dipping.

½ small cauliflower
1 large parsnip
25g curly parsley
groundnut oil,
 for deep-frying
1 egg yolk
sea salt
250ml sparkling water
a few ice cubes
200g plain flour
soy and sweet chilli
 sauce, for dipping

PORK STEAKS WITH RED ONION RELISH & BAY-ROASTED HASSELBACK POTATOES

Finely cutting slits in the potatoes allows the bay to infuse.

First make the marinade. Finely grate the zest and squeeze the juice from the orange. Crush the garlic cloves. Mix the zest, juice, garlic and 2 tablespoons of the olive oil in a large, flat dish. Lay the pork steaks in the dish in a single layer and turn to coat. Leave to marinate for about 50 minutes–1 hour.

Meanwhile, prepare the red onion salad. Pull the leaves from the thyme and thinly slice the onions. Melt 50g of the butter in a large frying pan over a moderate heat. Add the mustard seeds, wait for them to pop, and then stir in the onions and thyme. Cover, reduce the heat and cook gently for 40 minutes until very soft but not coloured, stirring occasionally.

Preheat your oven to 190°C/gas mark 5. To prepare the Hasselback potatoes, place 2 chopsticks on a board and lay a potato lengthways in between them. Holding the sticks and potato in place with one hand, cut the potato across into 3mm thin slices, cutting down just to the sticks – not all the way through. Repeat with the rest of the potatoes. Insert a bay leaf into each sliced potato.

Heat the remaining butter with 3 tablespoons of the olive oil in a heavy-based roasting tin. Place over a moderate heat and carefully add the potatoes in a single layer – be careful because they may spit. Move them around for a couple of minutes to colour them slightly and season with freshly ground black pepper and sea salt flakes. Place the tin in the oven and roast for 25–30 minutes until golden brown and tender.

Remove the pork from the marinade and season each side, reserving the marinade.

Heat the remaining oil in a large frying pan, add the pork steaks – you may need to do this in batches – and cook over a medium-high heat for 3–4 minutes on each side, or until tender and cooked through. Keep warm while you finish off the sauce.

The onions should now be soft. Remove the lid from the pan, stir in the pork marinade, vinegar and sugar and boil rapidly to reduce the sauce.

Serve a pork steak on each warmed dinner plate, top with the red onion relish and accompany with the Hasselback potatoes.

1 orange
2 small garlic cloves
100ml olive oil
6 x 150g pork loin steaks
10g fresh thyme
4 large red onions
70g butter
2 teaspoons mustard
  seeds
24 small potatoes
about 24 fresh bay leaves
1 tablespoon balsamic
  vinegar
1 tablespoon caster sugar
sea salt flakes and freshly
  ground black pepper

PASSION FRUIT MESS

The passion fruit seeds look like little jewels amongst the cream.

Cut 4 of the passion fruits in half and scoop out the flesh and seeds into a large bowl. Add the sugar, pour in the cream and whisk until soft peaks have formed – use a hand whisk for this because an electric whisk will break up the seeds too much. Crumble the meringues into small pieces over the top of the cream and fold in gently.

Spoon into dessert dishes or large wine glasses and place in the fridge. To serve, cut the remaining 2 passion fruits in half, scoop out the seeds and spoon over each dessert.

6 passion fruits
3 tablespoons
  golden caster sugar
450ml double cream
4 ready-made
  meringue nests

ASPARAGUS & PROSCIUTTO SOLDIERS WITH DUCK'S EGGS.
CRUSHED JERSEY ROYAL CRAB CAKES WITH LEMONY BROCCOLI.
BROWN SUGAR FLOATING ISLANDS.

60 min   Start with the main course. Bring a large pan of salted water to the boil, add the potatoes and boil for 15–20 minutes or until tender. Meanwhile, finely chop the spring onions and remove the leaves from the parsley and roughly chop. Set aside. Beat the whole egg and egg yolk in a large bowl, add the crab, season and mix thoroughly.

50 min   Once they are tender, drain the potatoes well and return to the dry pan. Add half the butter and crush the potatoes roughly with a fork. Fold in the crab mixture, spring onions and two-thirds of the parsley. Set aside.

40 min   Now for the dessert. Pour the custard and milk into a wide, shallow saucepan or frying pan and bring to just below simmering point. Meanwhile, whisk the egg whites with the salt in a large mixing bowl until they are thick and foamy. Add the sugar a spoonful at a time and continue beating until the mixture is very thick and glossy.

30 min   Using a large spoon, gently lower 6 scoops of the meringue into the custard mixture. Poach for 3 minutes, and then turn over carefully and poach for a further 3 minutes on the other side. Lift the meringues out with a slotted spoon and place on kitchen paper to drain. Pour the remaining custard mixture through a fine sieve into a bowl, cover the surface with clingfilm to stop a skin from forming and transfer to the fridge to cool.

20 min   Melt the butter for the starter in a small pan. Snap the coarse ends off the asparagus. Cut each slice of prosciutto in half lengthways and wrap a piece around the middle of each asparagus spear. Brush with melted butter and sprinkle lightly with sea salt.

10 min   Bring a pan of water to the boil, gently lower in the eggs, bring back to the boil and cook for 6–8 minutes. Heat a griddle or non-stick frying pan over a moderate heat and gently pan-fry the asparagus, turning occasionally, for a minute or two until just tender. Remove from the heat.

To serve the starter, drain the eggs and place each one in a pretty eggcup. Serve the asparagus soldiers on the side.

To finish the main course, steam the broccoli until tender, toss with the remaining butter and squeeze in the juice of the lemon. Season with black pepper and keep warm. Meanwhile, to cook the crab cakes, heat the oil in a large frying pan over a moderate heat. Divide the mixture roughly into 12 and spoon into the pan – you may need to use 2 frying pans or you can cook the crab cakes in batches. Fry the crab cakes for about 3–4 minutes on each side, or until golden and slightly crispy on the outside.

To serve the main course, top each crab cake with a spoonful of soured cream or crème fraîche, a teaspoon of fish roe and a sprinkling of chopped parsley. Serve with the broccoli on the side.

To serve the dessert, spoon the custard into your dessert dishes and top each one with a floating island.

Asparagus & Prosciutto Soldiers with Duck's Eggs
50g butter
12–18 asparagus spears
6–9 thin slices prosciutto
sea salt flakes
6 duck's or hen's eggs

Crushed Jersey Royal Crab Cakes with Lemony Broccoli
1kg Jersey Royals or other new potatoes
6 spring onions
15g parsley
1 egg and 1 egg yolk
100g white crabmeat
50g brown crabmeat
85g butter
400g purple-sprouting broccoli
½ lemon
2–3 tablespoons olive oil
soured cream or crème fraîche, to serve
55g Aruba, Arena or Onega herring roe
  or lumpfish roe (see page 10), to serve
sea salt and freshly ground black pepper

Brown Sugar Floating Islands
1 litre good-quality vanilla custard
700ml milk
3 egg whites
a pinch of salt
100g light muscovado sugar

ASPARAGUS & PROSCIUTTO SOLDIERS WITH DUCK'S EGGS

Very well dressed soldiers!

Melt the butter in a small pan. Snap the coarse ends off the asparagus. Cut each slice of prosciutto in half lengthways and wrap a piece around the middle of each asparagus spear. Brush with melted butter and sprinkle lightly with sea salt.

Heat a griddle or non-stick frying pan over a moderate heat and gently pan-fry the asparagus for a minute or two, turning occasionally, until just tender. Remove from the heat.

Bring a pan of water to the boil, gently lower in the eggs, bring back to the boil and cook for 6–8 minutes. Drain and place each egg into a pretty eggcup. Serve with the asparagus soldiers on the side.

50g butter
12–18 asparagus spears
6–9 thin slices prosciutto
sea salt flakes
6 duck's or hen's eggs

CRUSHED JERSEY ROYAL CRAB CAKES WITH LEMONY BROCCOLI

You could always serve a poached egg on top of the crab cakes instead.

Bring a large pan of salted water to the boil, add the potatoes and boil for 15–20 minutes or until tender. Meanwhile, finely chop the spring onions and remove the leaves from the parsley and roughly chop. Set aside.

Beat the whole egg and egg yolk in a large bowl, add the crab, season and mix thoroughly.

Once they are tender, drain the potatoes well and return to the dry pan. Add half the butter and crush the potatoes roughly with a fork. Fold in the crab mixture, spring onions and two-thirds of the parsley.

Steam the broccoli until tender, toss with the remaining butter and squeeze in the juice of the lemon. Season with black pepper and keep warm.

To cook the crab cakes, heat the oil in a large frying pan over a moderate heat. Divide the mixture roughly into 12 and spoon into the pan – you may need to use 2 frying pans or you can cook the crab cakes in batches. Fry the crab cakes for about 3–4 minutes on each side, or until golden and slightly crispy on the outside.

To serve, top each crab cake with a spoonful of soured cream or crème fraîche, a teaspoon of fish roe and a sprinkling of chopped parsley. Serve with the broccoli on the side.

1kg Jersey Royals or
 other new potatoes
6 spring onions
15g flat-leaf parsley
1 egg and 1 egg yolk
100g white crabmeat
50g brown crabmeat
85g butter
400g purple-sprouting or
 tenderstem broccoli
½ lemon
2–3 tablespoons olive oil
soured cream or
 crème fraîche, to serve
55g Aruba, Arena or
 Onega herring roe or
 lumpfish roe
 (see page 10), to serve
sea salt and freshly
 ground black pepper

BROWN SUGAR FLOATING ISLANDS

To give this a stronger vanilla flavour, you could scrape the seeds of a whole vanilla pod into the custard.

Pour the custard and milk into a wide, shallow saucepan or frying pan and bring to just below simmering point.

Meanwhile, whisk the egg whites with the salt in a large mixing bowl until they are thick and foamy. Add the sugar a spoonful at a time and continue beating until the mixture is very thick and glossy.

Using a large spoon, gently lower 6 scoops of the meringue into the custard mixture. Poach for 3 minutes, and then turn over carefully and poach for a further 3 minutes on the other side.

Lift the meringues out with a slotted spoon and place on kitchen paper to drain. Pour the remaining custard mixture through a fine sieve into a bowl, cover the surface with clingfilm to stop a skin from forming and transfer to the fridge to cool.

To serve, divide the custard between 6 dessert dishes and top each one with a floating island.

1 litre good-quality
 vanilla custard
700ml milk
3 egg whites
a pinch of salt
100g light
 muscovado sugar

JERSEY ROYAL & WATERCRESS SOUP.
SEA BASS WITH SPRING ONION & OLIVE RELISH.
MARSALA MASCARPONE CREAMS.

60 min First make the soup. Chop the garlic, onion and leek. Melt the butter in a large, heavy-based pan, add the onion, leek and garlic and cook for about 8–10 minutes or until lightly golden.

50 min Scrub the potatoes, slice into 5mm slices and add to the pan with the mint and stock. Season with salt and pepper and bring to the boil, then reduce the heat and simmer for about 15 minutes until the potatoes are tender.

40 min Meanwhile, get on with the dessert. To make the mascarpone cream, separate the eggs and whisk the egg yolks, sugar and Marsala in a large bowl until creamy, then beat in the mascarpone until well combined. Whisk the egg whites until stiff but not dry and carefully fold into the mascarpone mixture. Roughly crumble two of the chocolate flakes and gently fold in. Divide the mixture between 6 pretty glasses and place the glasses in the fridge.

30 min Now for the main course. To make the onion and olive relish, chop the spring onions and garlic, deseed and chop the chilli and roughly chop the olives. Place the onion, garlic, vinegar and 2 tablespoons of the oil in the bowl of a food processor and blitz until finely chopped. Scrape into a bowl and stir in the olives. Remove the leaves from the herbs and chop finely. Stir the herbs into the onion and olive mixture, season with salt and pepper and set aside.

20 min Back to the soup. Chop the watercress and stir into the soup until wilted. Remove from the heat, leave to cool for about 10 minutes, and then purée in a blender until smooth. Pass through a fine sieve into a clean pan.

10 min Wash and dry the baby spinach for the main course and divide between 6 dinner plates.

To serve the starter, pour the milk into the soup and reheat gently. Check the seasoning and ladle into warmed soup bowls. Finish with a swirl of cream in the centre of each.

To finish the main course, season the bass fillets with salt and pepper. Heat the remaining oil in a large frying pan over a high heat and add the bass fillets, skin-side down – you may need to do this in batches. Cook for a minute or two, and then turn over and cook for less than a minute on the other side or until just tender. To serve, lay a bass fillet on top of each pile of spinach on the dinner plates and spoon over some of the onion and olive relish.

To serve the dessert, crumble the remaining flake over the top of each mascarpone cream, then dust with a little icing sugar, followed by a little cocoa powder.

Jersey Royal & Watercress Soup
1 garlic clove
1 onion
1 leek
50g butter
500g Jersey Royal potatoes
1 large sprig of mint
1.2 litres chicken or vegetable stock
200g watercress
300ml milk
200ml thick Jersey cream
sea salt and freshly ground black pepper

Sea Bass with Spring Onion & Olive Relish
12 spring onions
1 garlic clove
1 red chilli
16 pitted Kalamata olives
1 teaspoon balsamic vinegar
2 tablespoons extra-virgin olive oil
3 sprigs of mint
5g parsley
100g baby leaf spinach
6 x 150g fillets of sea bass, skin on
sea salt flakes and freshly ground black pepper

Marsala Mascarpone Creams
2 eggs
2 tablespoons caster sugar
2 tablespoons Marsala
500g mascarpone
3 chocolate flakes
icing sugar and cocoa powder, to dust

JERSEY ROYAL & WATERCRESS SOUP

Chop the garlic, onion and leek. Melt the butter in a large, heavy-based pan, add the onion, leek and garlic and cook for 8–10 minutes or until lightly golden.

Scrub the potatoes, slice into 5mm slices and add to the pan with the mint and stock. Season with salt and pepper and bring to the boil, then reduce the heat and simmer for about 15 minutes until the potatoes are tender.

Chop the watercress and stir into the soup until wilted. Remove from the heat, leave to cool for about 10 minutes, and then purée in a blender until smooth. Pass through a fine sieve into a clean pan.

Add the milk and reheat gently, check the seasoning and ladle into warmed soup bowls. Swirl with a spoonful of cream.

1 garlic clove
1 onion
1 leek
50g butter
500g Jersey Royal potatoes
1 large sprig of mint
1.2 litres chicken or vegetable stock
200g watercress
300ml milk
200ml thick Jersey cream
sea salt and freshly ground black pepper

SEA BASS WITH SPRING ONION & OLIVE RELISH

Chop the spring onions and garlic, deseed and chop the chilli and roughly chop the olives. Place the onions, garlic, vinegar and 2 tablespoons of the oil in the bowl of a food processor and blitz until finely chopped.

Scrape into a bowl and stir in the olives. Remove the leaves from the herbs and chop finely. Stir the herbs into the onion and olive mixture and season with salt and pepper.

Wash and dry the baby spinach.

Season the bass fillets with salt and pepper. Heat the remaining oil in a large frying pan over a high heat and add the bass fillets, skin-side down – you may need to do this in batches. Cook for a minute or two, and then turn over and cook for less than a minute on the other side or until just tender.

To serve, divide the leaf spinach between the dinner plates, lay a bass fillet on top and spoon over some of the onion and olive relish.

12 spring onions
1 garlic clove
1 red chilli
16 pitted Kalamata olives
1 teaspoon balsamic vinegar
4 tablespoons extra-virgin olive oil
3 sprigs of mint
5g parsley
100g baby leaf spinach
6 x 150g fillets of sea bass, skin on
sea salt flakes and freshly ground black pepper

MARSALA MASCARPONE CREAMS

Separate the eggs and whisk the egg yolks, sugar and Marsala in a large bowl until creamy, then beat in the mascarpone until well combined.

Whisk the egg whites until stiff but not dry and carefully fold into the mascarpone mixture. Roughly crumble two of the chocolate flakes and gently fold in.

Divide the mixture between 6 pretty glasses and place the glasses in the fridge.

To serve, crumble the remaining flake over the top of each mascarpone cream, then dust with a little icing sugar, followed by a little cocoa powder.

2 eggs
2 tablespoons caster sugar
2 tablespoons Marsala
500g mascarpone
3 chocolate flakes
icing sugar and cocoa powder, to dust

PICKLED CUCUMBER SOUP.
SESAME PLAICE WITH COCONUT BROCCOLI.
LEMON & FIG MILLE FEUILLE

60 min Preheat your oven to 200°C/gas mark 6. Begin with the starter. Place 6 teacups into the fridge to chill. Peel the cucumber, cut one-eighth into tiny dice and the rest into thin slices. Place the diced cucumber in a bowl, cover and place in the fridge. Place the sliced cucumber in a colander, sprinkle with the salt and mix together. Place the colander over a bowl and set aside in the fridge for 30 minutes. Chop the figs, tip into a heatproof bowl and pour over boiling water to cover and leave to soak for about 45 minutes–1 hour.

50 min Divide the pastry in half and roll out each piece on a floured work surface to a 28 x 30cm rectangle. Cut in half lengthways and prick all over with a fork. Place 2 rectangles onto each of 2 baking sheets, dust evenly with the icing sugar and bake for 20 minutes (swap the trays around halfway through) or until crisp and golden and the pastry has a dark glaze on top. Remove from the oven and place the pastries onto cooling racks until cold. Now for the main course. Place the coconut in a heatproof bowl and pour over enough boiling water to cover. Leave to soak for 20 minutes.

40 min Remove the crusts from the bread and cut the bread into large cubes. Place the nuts in the bowl of a food processor and blitz until finely chopped. Add the bread cubes and sesame seeds and blitz again so that you end up with fine breadcrumbs (see page 27).

Melt the butter in a large frying pan and season with salt and pepper. Dip each plaice fillet into the seasoned butter, turning to coat, then lift out onto the tray of breadcrumbs. Carefully turn each fillet over to evenly coat both sides with the breadcrumb mixture and transfer to 2 baking trays in a single layer, flesh-side up. Keep to one side while you finish off the starter.

30 min Rinse the sliced cucumber with cold water and tip into the bowl of a blender. Finely chop the dill and add to the blender with the garlic, yogurt, 2 tablespoons of

the vinegar and the chilli (if using). Blitz until smooth, and then pour into a bowl. Stir in the sugar and add a little more vinegar to taste. Season well with black pepper and return to the fridge to keep cold until you are ready to serve.

20 min Back to the main course. Prepare the dressing for the broccoli. Crush the garlic, squeeze the juice from the limes, and remove the leaves from the mint and chop. Place together in a small bowl, add the honey and soy sauce and mix well. Trim the broccoli and cut into small florets. Spoon the lemon curd into a bowl. Drain and chop the dried figs into little pieces and stir into the lemon curd. Whip the cream to soft peaks. Lay 3 of the pastry slices onto a work surface and spread a third of the lemon curd and fig mixture evenly onto each piece. Spread each with a third of the whipped cream. Place 1 of the covered pastry pieces onto a serving dish and stack the other 2 on top. Finally top with the remaining pastry piece. Set aside.

10 min To cook the plaice fillets, place the baking trays in the oven and cook for 10–15 minutes or until golden brown and cooked through.

To cook the broccoli, heat the oil in a large frying pan over a high heat. Add the broccoli florets, sprinkle with a little salt and stir-fry for a minute or two. Add a small cup of cold water and put on the lid. Cook for 3–4 minutes, shaking the pan occasionally, until the broccoli is tender and the water has just evaporated. Remove from the heat, stir in the reserved coconut, pour over the dressing, season with black pepper and sprinkle with the sesame oil.

To serve the starter, thinly slice the baguette and toast until golden. Ladle the soup into the chilled teacups and sprinkle with the diced cucumber. Serve the toasts on the side.

To serve the main course, place 2 plaice fillets on each dinner plate and accompany with the broccoli.

To serve dessert, dust the mille feuille liberally with icing sugar and use a serrated bread knife to cut into thick slices.

Pickled Cucumber Soup
1 large cucumber
1 tablespoon sea salt
10g fresh dill
1 garlic clove
300g natural yogurt
2–3 tablespoons sherry or cider vinegar
½ green chilli (optional)
freshly ground black pepper
1 tablespoon caster sugar
1 baguette, to serve

Sesame Plaice with Coconut Broccoli
40g unsweetened desiccated coconut
1 x 400g loaf of bread
100g cashew nuts (or a mixture of cashews, peanuts, almonds and Brazil nuts)
100g sesame seeds
100g butter
12 plaice fillets, skin on, about 1kg total weight
1 large garlic clove
2 limes
10g fresh mint
1 tablespoon runny honey
2 tablespoons soy sauce
700g broccoli
3 tablespoons vegetable oil
2 tablespoons sesame oil
sea salt and freshly ground black pepper

Lemon & Fig Mille Feuille
500g puff pastry
325g jar lemon curd
100g dried figs
600ml whipping cream
3 tablespoons icing sugar, plus extra for dusting

PICKLED CUCUMBER SOUP

Place 6 teacups into the fridge to chill. Peel the cucumber, cut one-eighth into tiny dice and the rest into thin slices. Place the diced cucumber in a bowl, cover and place in the fridge. Place the sliced cucumber in a colander, sprinkle with the salt and mix together. Place the colander over a bowl and set aside in the fridge for 30 minutes. Meanwhile, finely chop the dill.

Rinse the sliced cucumber with cold water and tip into the bowl of a blender. Add the dill, garlic, yogurt, 2 tablespoons of the vinegar and the chilli (if using), and then blitz until smooth. Pour into a bowl, stir in the sugar and add a little more vinegar to taste. Season well with black pepper and return to the fridge to keep cold until you are ready to serve.

Slice the baguette thinly and toast until golden.

Ladle the soup into the chilled teacups, scatter with the diced cucumber and serve with the toasts.

1 large cucumber
1 tablespoon sea salt
10g dill
1 garlic clove
300g natural yogurt
2–3 tablespoons sherry
 or cider vinegar
½ green chilli (optional)
1 tablespoon caster sugar
freshly ground black
 pepper
1 baguette, to serve

SESAME PLAICE WITH COCONUT BROCCOLI

Adding cashews to the coating gives it a gentle nuttiness.

Place the coconut in a heatproof bowl and pour over enough boiling water to cover. Leave to soak for 20 minutes, then strain through a sieve, gently pressing the coconut against the sides with the back of a spoon to squeeze out any excess moisture. Set aside.

Preheat your oven to 200°C/gas mark 6.

Remove the crusts from the bread and cut the bread into large cubes. Place the nuts in the bowl of a food processor and blitz until finely chopped. Add the bread cubes and sesame seeds and blitz again so that you end up with fine breadcrumbs (see page 27). Tip out onto a tray.

Melt the butter in a large frying pan and season with salt and pepper. Dip each plaice fillet one at a time into the seasoned butter, turning to coat, and then lift out onto the tray of breadcrumbs. Carefully turn each fillet over to ensure both sides are evenly covered with the breadcrumb mixture and transfer to 2 baking trays in a single layer, flesh-side up. Bake in the oven for 10–15 minutes or until golden brown and cooked through.

Meanwhile, make the dressing for the broccoli. Crush the garlic, squeeze the juice from the limes, and remove the leaves from the mint and finely chop. Place together in a small bowl, add the honey and soy sauce and mix well. Trim the broccoli and cut into small florets.

To cook the broccoli, heat the oil in a large frying pan over a high heat. Add the broccoli florets, sprinkle with a little salt and stir-fry for a minute or two. Add a small cup of cold water and immediately bang on the lid. Cook for 3–4 minutes, shaking the pan occasionally, until the broccoli is tender and the water has just evaporated.

Remove from the heat, stir in the reserved coconut, pour in the dressing, season with black pepper and sprinkle with the sesame oil.

To serve, place 2 fillets on each plate and accompany with the broccoli on the side.

40g unsweetened desiccated coconut
1 x 400g loaf of bread
100g cashew nuts (or a mixture of cashews, peanuts, almonds and Brazil nuts)
100g sesame seeds
100g butter
12 plaice fillets, skin on (about 1kg total weight)
1 large garlic clove
2 limes
10g mint
1 tablespoon runny honey
2 tablespoons soy sauce
700g broccoli
3 tablespoons vegetable oil
2 tablespoons sesame oil
sea salt and freshly ground black pepper

LEMON & FIG MILLE FEUILLE

A decadent, leaning tower of joy.

Preheat your oven to 200°C/gas mark 6.

Chop the figs, tip into a heatproof bowl and pour over boiling water to cover and leave to soak for about 45 minutes–1 hour.

Divide the pastry in half and roll out each piece on a floured work surface to a 28 x 30cm rectangle. Cut in half again lengthways and prick all over with a fork.

Place 2 rectangles onto each of 2 baking sheets, dust evenly with the icing sugar and bake for about 20 minutes (swap trays around halfway through) until crisp and golden and the pastry has a dark glaze on top. Remove from the oven and place the pastries onto cooling racks until completely cold.

Spoon the lemon curd into a bowl. Drain and chop the dried figs into little pieces and stir into the lemon curd. Whip the cream to soft peaks.

Lay 3 of the pastry slices onto a work surface and spread a third of the lemon curd and fig mixture evenly onto each piece. Spread each with a third of the whipped cream. Place 1 of the covered pastry pieces onto a serving dish and then top with the further 2. Finally top with the remaining pastry piece and dust liberally with icing sugar.

Use a serrated bread knife to cut into thick slices.

500g puff pastry
325g jar lemon curd
100g dried figs
600ml whipping cream
3 tablespoons icing sugar,
 plus extra for dusting

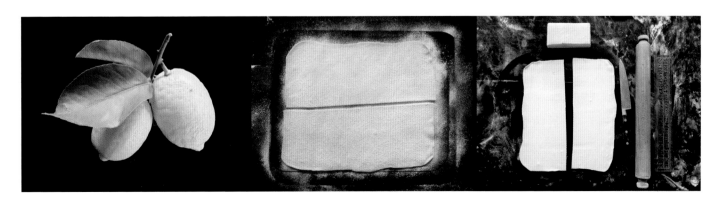

SMOKED SALMON POPPY SEED PIZZAS WITH PRESERVED LEMON & CAPER DRESSING.
FRESH PEA & MINT CLAFOUTIS.
CAMPARI SORBET SLUSH.

60 min   Begin with the pizza dough for the starter. Place the pizza or bread mix in a large bowl and mix in a pinch of salt flakes and the poppy seeds. Make a well in the centre and add 2 tablespoons of the oil and 150ml warm water. Mix together with a fork until a dough starts to form, and then tip out onto a work surface and knead well for 5 minutes. Place the dough back into the bowl, cover and set aside for 30 minutes.

50 min   Meanwhile, get on with the dessert. Place 6 pretty glasses in the freezer to chill. Cut a thin slice from each end of the oranges and place upright on a board. Using a sharp knife, peel the oranges from top to bottom, removing all the bitter white pith as you go (see page 26). Holding the oranges over a bowl to catch the juice, cut into segments by cutting down on either side of each piece of membrane. Place the segments in a bowl, squeeze over any remaining juice from the pulp and stir in the Campari and Grand Marnier.

40 min   Preheat your oven to 170°C/gas mark 3. To make the dressing for the pizzas, cut the preserved lemon into quarters, remove the flesh and discard, then finely chop the skin. Place the skin in a small bowl and squeeze in the juice from the fresh lemon. Finely chop the dill and parsley and add to the bowl with the capers. Mix everything together with the remaining olive oil, season and mix again.

30 min   To make the main course, crack the eggs into a large bowl and beat with a fork. Remove the leaves from the mint and chop finely. Grate the cheese and chop the spring onions. Add the mint, cheese and spring onions to the eggs and stir in the cream and peas. Season well and beat again to combine.

Grease 6 250ml ramekins or oven-proof dishes and use a ladle to divide the mixture between them. Place on a baking tray and bake in the oven for 15–20 minutes or until slightly risen and lightly golden but still a little wobbly in the centre.

20 min   The pizza dough for the starter should now be ready. Lightly dust your work surface with flour, divide the dough into 6 balls and roll out each ball as thinly as possible to form a rough circle. Transfer to greased baking sheets.

Once the clafoutis are cooked, remove them from the oven and increase the oven temperature to 220°C/gas mark 7.

10 min   To finish the pizzas, drizzle them with a little olive oil and sprinkle them with sea salt flakes. Bake in the oven for about 10 minutes or until lightly crisp and golden.

To serve the starter, divide the smoked salmon between the pizzas and drizzle with the dressing. Place a spoonful of crème fraîche in the middle of each one, grind over some black pepper and serve immediately.

To serve the main course, put the clafoutis back in the oven for 5 minutes to warm up and accompany with a rocket salad on the side.

When you are ready for your dessert, drain the orange segments over a jug to catch the juice mixture. Scoop the sorbet into the bowl of a food processor, switch on the motor and pour in the juice through the feeder tube. Process briefly and pour into the chilled glasses. Divide the fruit between the glasses and serve immediately.

Smoked Salmon Poppy Seed Pizzas with
Preserved Lemon & Caper Dressing
250g pizza or bread mix, suitable for hand baking
2 tablespoons poppy seeds
125ml extra-virgin olive oil, plus extra for drizzling
50g preserved lemons
1 lemon
15g dill
15g parsley
2 tablespoons capers, rinsed in warm water
a little flour, for dusting
200g smoked salmon
200ml crème fraîche
sea salt flakes and freshly ground black pepper

Fresh Pea & Mint Clafoutis
6 medium eggs
25g mint
200g Comté or Gruyère cheese
6 spring onions
300ml double cream
400g fresh peas
a little butter, for greasing
sea salt and freshly ground black pepper
rocket salad, to serve

Campari Sorbet Slush
3 oranges
3 tablespoons Campari
1 tablespoon Grand Marnier
500g strawberry or orange sorbet

SMOKED SALMON POPPY SEED PIZZAS WITH PRESERVED LEMON & CAPER DRESSING

You can use the pulp of preserved lemons, but it is the intensely flavoured zest and pith which is used most often.

Preheat your oven to 220°C/gas mark 7.

Place the pizza or bread mix in a large bowl and mix in a pinch of salt flakes and the poppy seeds. Make a well in the centre and add 2 tablespoons of the oil and 150ml warm water. Mix together with a fork until a dough starts to form, and then tip out onto a work surface and knead well for 5 minutes.

Place the dough back into the bowl, cover and set aside to rise for 30 minutes.

To make the dressing, cut the preserved lemon into quarters, remove the flesh and discard, then finely chop the skin. Place the skin in a small bowl and squeeze in the juice from the fresh lemon. Finely chop the dill and parsley and add to the bowl with the capers. Mix everything together with the remaining olive oil, season and mix again.

Divide the dough into 6 balls. Lightly dust your work surface with flour and roll out each ball as thinly as possible to form a rough circle. Transfer to greased baking sheets, drizzle with olive oil and sprinkle with sea salt flakes. Bake for about 10 minutes or until lightly crisp and golden.

Divide the smoked salmon between the pizzas and drizzle with the dressing. Scoop a spoonful of crème fraîche into the middle of each, grind over some black pepper and serve immediately.

250g pizza or bread mix, suitable for hand baking
2 tablespoons poppy seeds
125ml extra-virgin olive oil, plus extra for drizzling
50g preserved lemons
1 lemon
15g dill
15g parsley
2 tablespoons capers, rinsed in warm water
a little flour, for dusting
200g smoked salmon
200ml crème fraîche
sea salt flakes and freshly ground black pepper

FRESH PEA & MINT CLAFOUTIS

For a simple salad dressing to serve with your rocket salad see page 32.

Preheat your oven to 170°C/gas mark 3.

Crack the eggs into a large bowl and beat with a fork. Remove the leaves from the mint and chop finely. Grate the cheese and chop the spring onions. Add the mint, cheese and spring onions to the eggs and stir in the cream and peas. Season well and beat again to combine.

Grease 6 250ml ramekins or oven-proof dishes with butter and use a ladle to divide the mixture between them. Place on a baking tray and bake in the oven for 15–20 minutes or until slightly risen, and lightly golden but still a little wobbly in the centre.

Serve immediately with a rocket salad on the side.

6 medium eggs
25g fresh mint
200g Comté or
  Gruyère cheese
6 spring onions
300ml double cream
400g fresh peas
a little butter, for greasing
sea salt and freshly
  ground black pepper
rocket salad, to serve

CAMPARI SORBET SLUSH

A mix of an after-dinner cocktail and fruity dessert.

Place 6 pretty glasses in the freezer to chill.

Cut a thin slice from each end of the oranges and place upright on a board. Using a sharp knife, peel the oranges from top to bottom, removing all the bitter white pith as you go (see page 26). Holding the oranges over a bowl to catch the juice, cut into segments by cutting down on either side of each piece of membrane. Place the segments in a bowl, squeeze over any remaining juice from the pulp and stir in the Campari and Grand Marnier.

When you are ready to serve, drain the orange segments over a jug to catch the juice mixture. Scoop the sorbet into the bowl of a food processor, switch on the motor and pour in the juice mixture through the feeder tube. Process briefly and pour into the chilled glasses. Divide the fruit between the glasses and serve immediately.

3 oranges
3 tablespoons Campari
1 tablespoon Grand
  Marnier
500g strawberry or
  orange sorbet

GOAT'S CHEESE CUSTARDS.
ONION & ANCHOVY PUFF PASTRY TARTS.
RHUBARB, BLOOD ORANGE & ELDERFLOWER COMPOTE.

60 min   Start with the main course. Pull the leaves from the rosemary; finely chop the garlic and finely slice the onions. Heat the oil in a large pan, add the onions, garlic, rosemary and a pinch of salt and stir over a low heat. Cover with a lid and cook gently for 30 minutes, stirring occasionally, until the onions are very soft and starting to collapse.

50 min   Now for the starter. Preheat your oven to 180°C/gas mark 4. Beat the eggs in a large bowl. Remove the leaves from the parsley and thyme and chop finely. Add the herbs and cream to the eggs, season with nutmeg, cayenne, salt and pepper and beat to combine. Crumble in the goat's cheese and stir again.

40 min   Divide the mixture between 6 150ml ramekins and stand them in a roasting tin. Boil a kettle of water and pour into the tin so it comes halfway up the sides of the ramekins. Carefully transfer the custards to the oven and cook for about 15–20 minutes, or until they are just cooked but still a bit wobbly in the centre.

30 min   Back to the main course. Cut each rectangle of pastry across widthways into 3 so that you end up with 6 small rectangles. Transfer to 2 baking sheets. Using a small knife, score a 2cm border around the inside edge of each pastry rectangle and prick the centres all over with a fork. Chill in the fridge while you finish off the topping. The onions should now be completely soft. Increase the heat, add the vinegar and cook until it has almost evaporated, stirring constantly. Season with pepper and set aside to cool slightly while you prepare the dessert.

20 min   Trim the rhubarb, cut into 5cm lengths and place in a large pan. Finely grate the orange zest into the pan, squeeze in the juice and add the elderflower cordial. Sprinkle with sugar and toss well together. Place over a

low heat, bring to a simmer, and then cover and cook very gently for 10–12 minutes until tender. Set aside and leave to cool – it's best served at room temperature.

10 min   Increase the oven temperature to 220°C/gas mark 7. To assemble the tarts for the main course, spoon the onions onto the pastry rectangles, spreading them out evenly and leaving a 2cm border all around the outside. Scatter with olives, cut the anchovies in half lengthways and crisscross over the top. Sprinkle the pastry borders with Parmesan and bake in the oven for 10–15 minutes or until the pastry is golden.

To serve the starter, take the warm goat's cheese custards to the table and accompany with the grissini breadsticks on the side.

To serve the main course, place an onion tart on each of the 6 dinner plates. Serve with the baby salad leaves.

To serve the dessert, spoon the rhubarb compote into 6 pretty glasses and stand a shortbread biscuit upright in each one. Serve a few more biscuits on the side.

Goat's Cheese Custards
6 eggs
handful of flat-leaf parsley
3 sprigs of thyme
200ml double cream
pinch of grated nutmeg
pinch of cayenne pepper
100g goat's cheese
sea salt and freshly ground black pepper
grissini breadsticks, to serve

Onion & Anchovy Puff Pastry Tarts
2 sheets of ready-rolled puff pastry, about 28 x 21cm each
2 sprigs of rosemary
2 garlic cloves
1kg red onions
75ml olive oil
2 tablespoons red wine vinegar
18 black olives
50g tinned anchovies
25g Parmesan cheese, grated
sea salt and freshly ground black pepper
baby salad leaves, to serve

Rhubarb, Blood Orange & Elderflower Compote
800g rhubarb
1 orange, preferably a blood orange
75ml elderflower cordial
50g soft brown sugar
shortbread fingers, to serve

GOAT'S CHEESE CUSTARDS

Preheat your oven to 180°C/gas mark 4.

Beat the eggs in a large bowl. Remove the leaves from the parsley and thyme and chop finely. Add the herbs and cream to the eggs, season with nutmeg, cayenne, salt and pepper and beat well to combine. Crumble in the goat's cheese and stir again.

Divide the mixture between 6 150ml ramekins and stand them in a roasting tin. Boil a kettle of water and pour into the tin so it comes halfway up the sides of the ramekins. Carefully transfer the custards to the oven and cook for about 15–20 minutes, or until they are just cooked but still a bit wobbly in the centre.

Serve with the breadsticks on the side.

6 eggs
handful of flat-leaf
 parsley
3 sprigs of thyme
200ml double cream
pinch of grated nutmeg
pinch of cayenne pepper
100g goat's cheese
sea salt and freshly
 ground black pepper
grissini breadsticks,
 to serve

ONION & ANCHOVY PUFF PASTRY TARTS

It may seem like a lot of onions, but they will cook down.

Cut each rectangle of pastry across widthways into 3 so that you end up with 6 small rectangles. Transfer to 2 baking sheets. Using a small knife, score a 2cm border around the inside edge of each pastry rectangle and prick the centres all over with a fork. Chill in the fridge while you prepare the topping.

Pull the leaves from the rosemary, finely chop the garlic and finely slice the onions. Heat the oil in a large pan, add the onions, garlic, rosemary and a pinch of salt and stir over a low heat. Cover with a lid and cook gently for 30 minutes, stirring occasionally, until the onions are very soft and starting to collapse. Raise the heat, add the vinegar and cook until it has almost evaporated, stirring constantly. Season with pepper and set aside to cool slightly.

Preheat your oven to 220°C/gas mark 7.

Spoon the onions onto the pastry rectangles, spreading them out evenly and leaving a 2cm border all around the outside. Scatter with olives, cut the anchovies in half lengthways and crisscross over the top. Sprinkle the pastry borders with Parmesan and bake in the oven for 10–15 minutes or until the pastry is golden. Serve with the baby salad leaves on the side.

2 sheets of ready-rolled
 puff pastry, about
 28 x 21cm each
2 sprigs of rosemary
2 garlic cloves
1kg red onions
75ml olive oil
2 tablespoons red wine
 vinegar
18 black olives
50g tinned anchovies
25g Parmesan cheese,
 grated
sea salt and freshly
 ground black pepper
baby salad leaves,
 to serve

RHUBARB, BLOOD ORANGE & ELDERFLOWER COMPOTE

You could always use this compote in a spring crumble or brûlée.

Trim the rhubarb, cut into 5cm lengths and place in a large pan. Finely grate the orange zest into the pan, squeeze in the juice and add the elderflower cordial. Sprinkle with sugar and toss well together.

Place the pan over a low heat, bring to a simmer, and then cover and cook very gently for 10–12 minutes or until tender. Set aside and leave to cool.

To serve, spoon the rhubarb compote into 6 pretty glasses and stand a shortbread finger upright in each one. Serve a few extra biscuits on the side.

800g rhubarb
1 orange, preferably
 a blood orange
75ml elderflower cordial
50g soft brown sugar
shortbread fingers,
 to serve

WARM CRAB, CUCUMBER & CHICORY SALAD.
CHEAT'S SOLE VÉRONIQUE.
APRICOT & ROSEMARY PIES.

60 min   Preheat your oven to 200°C/gas mark 6. Cut the grapes for the main course in half and place in a bowl in the fridge.

Cut the apricots for the dessert in half, remove the stones, and place the fruit in a bowl. Reserve 2 tablespoons of the sugar for sprinkling and add the rest to the apricots with the vanilla extract.

50 min   Roll out the pastry thinly and cut out 6 18cm circles, using a small plate as a guide. Transfer to a baking sheet and place 4 or 5 apricot halves in the centre of each. Add a sprig of rosemary (if using) and bring up the edges of the pastry to enclose the fruit partially. Dot the apricots with butter, brush the pastry with a little water and sprinkle with the remaining sugar. Bake for 15–20 minutes or until the pastry is golden and crisp.

40 min   To make the salad for the starter, trim the chicory and separate the leaves into a large bowl. Finely chop the parsley and chives. Slice the cucumber as thinly as possible – a mandolin makes this a lot easier (see page 18). Combine the chicory, cucumber and herbs together in the bowl, separating out the slices of cucumber as much as possible. Cover and place in the fridge until needed.

30 min   To prepare the sauce for the main course, very finely chop the shallots (or onion). Melt the butter in a small pan, add the shallots and cook gently for 5–6 minutes until softened but not coloured.

Meanwhile, lightly season the sole fillets. Roll each one loosely from head to tail and secure with a wooden cocktail stick. Place in a baking dish.

Remove the apricot pies from the oven and turn down the temperature to 150°C/gas mark 2.

20 min   Bring a pan of lightly salted water to a boil, add the new potatoes and cook for 15-20 minutes or until tender. Drain and keep warm. Once the shallots are soft, increase the heat, add the wine and let it bubble away to reduce by half. Add the crème fraîche and season. Simmer for 5 minutes until the sauce has thickened slightly, and then remove from the heat.

Place the egg yolks in a small bowl. Beat together with a fork, and then add a couple of spoonfuls of the sauce and beat again. Stir this mixture back into the pan, check the seasoning and pour over the sole fillets.

10 min   Just before you are ready to serve the starter (this needs to be done at the last minute), melt the butter in a frying pan over a gentle heat and add the oil, vinegar, mustard, honey and lemon juice. Raise the heat, add the crab and stir-fry briefly until hot. Tip the hot crab mixture into the bowl with the chicory salad, season well with salt and pepper and toss everything together to combine. Divide the crab salad between 6 starter plates and serve immediately with some crusty bread on the side.

To finish the main course, place the dish of sole in the oven and bake for about 10 minutes or until the fish is tender. Meanwhile, separate the lettuce leaves and wash and drain well. Place in a large bowl. Make a dressing with the olive oil, lemon juice and seasoning. Pour over the leaves and toss well.

To serve the main course, divide the lettuce leaves between your dinner plates, top with 2 fillets of sole, spoon over some of the sauce and scatter with the chilled grape halves. Serve immediately with the new potatoes on the side.

To serve the dessert, accompany the apricot pies warm with a dollop of Greek yogurt on the side.

Warm Crab, Cucumber & Chicory Salad
4 heads of chicory
10g flat-leaf parsley
10g chives
½ cucumber
50g butter
1½ tablespoons extra-virgin olive oil
½ tablespoon sherry vinegar
1 tablespoon wholegrain mustard
1 tablespoon runny honey
juice of 1 small lemon
100g fresh white crabmeat
sea salt and freshly ground black pepper
crusty bread, to serve

Cheat's Sole Véronique
300g seedless green grapes
2 shallots (or ½ small onion)
25g butter
12 x 125g skinless sole fillets (there are 4 fillets per whole fish)
100ml dry white wine
200ml crème fraîche
2 egg yolks
2 tablespoons extra-virgin olive oil
juice of ½ lemon
sea salt and freshly ground black pepper
new potatoes, to serve
3 little gem lettuces, to serve

Apricot & Rosemary Pies
600g apricots
125g light soft brown sugar
1 teaspoon vanilla extract
500g shortcrust pastry
6 small sprigs of rosemary (optional)
25g butter
thick Greek yogurt, to serve

WARM CRAB, CUCUMBER AND CHICORY SALAD

MENU 38

A little bit of a good thing goes a long way here.

Trim the chicory and separate the leaves into a large bowl. Finely chop the parsley and chives. Slice the cucumber as thinly as possible – a mandolin makes this a lot easier (see page 18). Combine the chicory, cucumber and herbs together, separating out the slices of cucumber as much as possible.

Melt the butter in a frying pan over a gentle heat. Add the oil, vinegar, mustard, honey and lemon juice. Raise the heat, add the crab to the pan and stir-fry briefly until hot. Tip the hot crab mixture into the bowl with the salad, season with salt and pepper and toss everything together to combine.

Divide the crab salad between 6 starter plates and serve immediately with some crusty bread on the side.

4 heads of chicory
10g flat-leaf parsley
10g chives
½ cucumber
50g butter
1½ tablespoons
 extra-virgin olive oil
½ tablespoon
 sherry vinegar
1 tablespoon wholegrain
 mustard
1 tablespoon runny honey
juice of 1 small lemon
100g fresh white
 crabmeat
sea salt and freshly
 ground black pepper
crusty bread, to serve

CHEAT'S SOLE VÉRONIQUE

This is preschool, old school – a speedy version of a French classic. Cool fresh grapes with a warm rich creamy sauce, served over delicate sole.

Preheat your oven to 150°C/gas mark 2.

Cut the grapes in half and place in a bowl in the fridge. Very finely chop the shallots (or onions). Melt the butter in a small pan, add the shallots and cook gently for 5–6 minutes until softened but not coloured.

Meanwhile, lightly season the sole fillets. Roll each one loosely from head to tail and secure with a wooden cocktail stick. Place in a baking dish.

Once the shallots are soft, increase the heat, add the wine and let it bubble away to reduce by half. Add the crème fraîche and season. Simmer for 5 minutes until the sauce has thickened slightly, and then remove from the heat.

Bring a pan of lightly salted water to the boil, add the new potatoes and cook for 15–20 minutes or until tender. Drain and keep warm. Separate the lettuce leaves and wash and drain them well. Place in a large bowl.

Place the egg yolks in a small bowl. Beat together with a fork, and then add a couple of spoonfuls of the hot sauce and beat again. Stir this mixture back into the pan, check the seasoning and pour over the sole fillets. Place the dish in the oven and bake for about 10 minutes or until the fish is tender.

Meanwhile, make a dressing with the olive oil, lemon juice and seasoning. Pour over the lettuce leaves and toss together.

To serve, divide the salad between your dinner plates, top with 2 sole fillets, spoon over some of the sauce and scatter with the grape halves. Serve with some new potatoes on the side.

300g green seedless grapes
2 shallots (or ½ small onion)
25g butter
12 x 125g skinless sole fillets (there are 4 fillets per whole fish)
100ml dry white wine
200ml crème fraîche
3 little gem lettuces
2 egg yolks
2 tablespoons extra-virgin olive oil
½ lemon
sea salt and freshly ground black pepper
new potatoes, to serve

APRICOT & ROSEMARY PIES

As you may have noticed, I like combining fruit and herbs. In autumn, try using plums and thyme instead.

Preheat your oven to 200°C/gas mark 6.

Cut the apricots in half, remove the stones and place the fruit in a bowl. Reserve 2 tablespoons of the sugar for sprinkling and add the rest to the apricots with the vanilla extract.

Roll out the pastry thinly and cut out 6 18cm circles, using a small plate as a guide. Transfer to a baking sheet and place 4 or 5 apricot halves in the centre of each. Add a sprig of rosemary (if using) and bring up the edges of the pastry to enclose the fruit partially.

Dot the apricots with butter, brush the pastry with a little water and sprinkle with the remaining sugar. Bake for 15–20 minutes or until the pastry is golden and crisp.

Serve the pies with Greek yogurt on the side.

600g apricots
125g light soft brown sugar
1 teaspoon vanilla extract
500g shortcrust pastry
6 small sprigs of rosemary (optional)
25g butter
thick Greek yogurt, to serve

PEA CROSTINI.

LAMB WITH ALMOND & DIJON CRUST.

WINE-STEEPED APRICOTS & RASPBERRIES.

60 min Begin with the starter. Finely slice the spring onions, crush the garlic and deseed and finely chop the chilli (if using). Remove the leaves from the herbs and chop finely and set aside. Heat 1 tablespoon of the olive oil in a large frying pan, add the spring onions, garlic and chilli and stir-fry over a high heat for about a minute. Add the peas, lemon juice and 1 tablespoon of water, bang on the lid and cook for about 3 minutes, or until the peas are nearly tender. Remove the lid and boil to reduce the liquid and finish cooking the peas.

50 min Stir in the chopped herbs and season well. Leave to cool slightly, then place the mixture in a food processor. Add 2 tablespoons of the remaining olive oil and blitz to form a rough paste. Scrape the paste into a bowl, crumble in the feta, fold in gently and check for seasoning. Set aside. Preheat your oven to 200°C/gas mark 6.

40 min Slice the ciabatta into thin slices about 5mm thick (from one regular-sized ciabatta you will get about 24 slices). Lay in a single layer on a baking tray, drizzle with the remaining oil and bake in the oven for 4–5 minutes or until crisp and golden. Remove the ciabatta from the oven and increase the temperature to 220°C/gas mark 7.

30 min To make the dessert, cut the apricots in half and remove the stones. Pour the wine into a large saucepan, add the sugar and bring to the boil. Slide in the apricots, reduce the heat and simmer for 8–10 minutes or until tender. Stir in the raspberries, remove from the heat and set aside to cool.

20 min For the main course, tip the potatoes into a large roasting tin, drizzle over the oil, season, add the bay leaves and toss well together. Place in the oven and roast for 15–20 minutes or until tender, turning once or twice.

To make the coating for the lamb, remove the leaves from the parsley and chop fairly finely. Tip onto a tray, add the almonds, season well and toss together. Spread a little mustard onto each side of the lamb steaks and dip them into the herby almond mixture. Transfer in a single layer to 2 baking sheets and keep to one side.

10 min Cut the broccoli into small florets and steam until tender. Beat the crème fraîche in a bowl with some salt and pepper. Place the lamb in the oven and cook for 5–7 minutes or until the lamb is tender and golden.

To serve the starter, scatter the pea shoots (if using) over a large serving platter. Spread the ciabatta slices with the pea purée, lay on top of the pea shoots and allow everyone to help themselves.

To serve the main course, divide the potatoes and broccoli between 6 dinner plates. Add 2 lamb steaks to each one and finish with a spoonful of crème fraîche. Serve immediately.

To serve the dessert, serve the fruit warm or cold in small dishes, with some macaroons on the side.

Pea Crostini
6 spring onions
2 garlic cloves
1 green chilli (optional)
5g dill
5g mint
5g basil
120ml olive oil
200g fresh shelled (or frozen) peas
juice of ½ lemon
100g feta cheese
sea salt and freshly ground black pepper
1 regular-sized ciabatta, to serve
50g pea shoots (optional), to serve

Lamb with Almond and Dijon Crust
500g Jersey Royals
 or other new potatoes
4 tablespoons olive oil
a few bay leaves
25g flat-leaf parsley
50g ground almonds
12 x 100g lamb steaks
4 tablespoons Dijon mustard
400g broccoli
200ml crème fraîche
sea salt flakes and freshly
 ground black pepperr

Wine-Steeped Apricots and Raspberries
12 apricots
200ml Muscat or other dessert wine
50g golden caster sugar
150g raspberries
macaroons, to serve

PEA CROSTINI

Finely slice the spring onions, crush the garlic and deseed and finely chop the chilli (if using). Remove the leaves from the herbs, chop finely and set aside

Heat 1 tablespoon of the olive oil in a large frying pan, add the spring onions, garlic and chilli and stir-fry over a high heat for about a minute. Add the peas, lemon juice and 1 tablespoon of water, bang on the lid and cook for about 3 minutes, or until the peas are nearly tender. Remove the lid and boil rapidly to reduce the liquid and to finish cooking the peas.

Stir in the chopped herbs and season well with salt and pepper. Leave to cool slightly, then place the mixture in a food processor. Add 2 tablespoons of the remaining olive oil and blitz to form a rough paste. Scrape the paste into a bowl, crumble in the feta, fold in gently and check for seasoning. Set aside. Preheat your oven to 200°C/gas mark 6.

Slice the ciabatta into thin slices about 5mm thick (from one regular-sized ciabatta you will get about 24 slices). Lay the slices in a single layer on a baking tray, drizzle with the remaining oil and bake in the oven for 4–5 minutes or until crisp and golden.

To serve, scatter the pea shoots (if using) over a large serving platter. Spread the ciabatta slices with the pea purée, lay on top of the pea shoots and allow everyone to help themselves.

6 sping onions
2 garlic cloves
1 green chilli (optional)
5g dill
5g mint
5g basil
120ml olive oil
200g fresh shelled (or frozen) peas
juice of ½ lemon
100g feta cheese
salt and freshly ground black pepper
1 regular-sized ciabatta, to serve
50g pea shoots, to serve (optional)

LAMB WITH ALMOND AND DIJON CRUST

Preheat your oven 220°C/gas mark 7.

Tip the potatoes into a large roasting tin. Drizzle over the oil, season, add the bay leaves to the tin and toss well together. Place in the oven and roast for 15–20 minutes or until tender, turning once or twice.

To make the coating for the lamb, remove the leaves from the parsley and chop fairly finely. Tip onto a tray, add the almonds, season well and toss together.

Spread a little mustard onto each side of the lamb steaks and dip them into the herby almond mixture. Transfer in a single layer to 2 baking sheets and bake in the oven for 5–7 minutes or until the lamb is tender and golden. Meanwhile, cut the broccoli into small florets and steam until tender. Beat the crème fraîche in a bowl with some salt and freshly ground black pepper.

To serve, divide the potatoes and broccoli between 6 dinner plates. Add 2 lamb steaks and finish with a spoonful of crème fraîche. Serve immediately.

500g Jersey Royals or other new potatoes
4 tablespoons olive oil
a few bay leaves
25g flat-leaf parsley
50g ground almonds
12 x 100g lamb steaks
4 tablespoons Dijon mustard
400g broccoli
200ml crème fraîche
sea salt flakes and freshly ground black pepper

WINE-STEEPED APRICOTS AND RASPBERRIES

Cut the apricots in half and remove the stones. Pour the wine into a large saucepan, add the sugar and bring to the boil. Slide in the apricots, reduce the heat and simmer for 8–10 minutes or until tender. Stir in the raspberries, remove from the heat and set aside to cool.

Serve the fruit warm or cold in small dishes, with some macaroons on the side.

12 apricots
200 ml Muscat or other dessert wine
50g golden caster sugar
150g raspberries
macaroons, to serve

SUMMER

FENNEL FRITTERS WITH ORANGE & LEMON MAYONNAISE.
ROAST PLAICE WITH PROSCIUTTO & PEA PURÉE.
POACHED APRICOTS STUFFED WITH MARZIPAN.

60 min   Begin with the starter. Bring a large pan of salted water to the boil. Add the fennel bulbs and cook for about 10–15 minutes or until tender, then drain and leave to cool.

Meanwhile, get on with the dessert. Make a slit in one side of the apricots and squeeze gently to remove the stones. Place the apricots in a large pan and finely grate over the orange zest. Squeeze in the orange juice and add the sugar. Cover with a lid and simmer over a low heat for about 8–10 minutes or until tender, turning them from time to time. Remove from the heat and leave to cool.

50 min   Spoon the mayonnaise for the starter into a small bowl. Finely grate in the orange and lemon zest and squeeze in the juice. Stir well to combine and season with black pepper. Mix together the breadcrumbs, five-spice, ground pepper and salt flakes in a shallow tray.

40 min   To prepare the fish for the main course, lay a slice of prosciutto on a board or work surface and lay a fillet of plaice (or sole) on top. Season with salt and freshly ground black pepper and roll up, not too tightly, so that the prosciutto is on the outside. Secure with a wooden cocktail stick or skewer and place the rolled fillets on a baking tray.

30 min   Back to the dessert. The apricots should now be cool enough to handle. Knead the marzipan with the orange flower water (if using) – go easy on the orange flower water as it is quite potent and you do really need only a couple of drops. Lift out each apricot with a spoon and poke a small ball of marzipan into the cavity. Place the apricots back in the cooking liquid and set aside.

Once the fennel bulbs for the starter are cool enough to handle, slice each one lengthways into 4 pieces so each piece is still attached to the root.

20 min   Back to the main course. Bring a pan of lightly salted water to the boil and cook the potatoes and boil for 10–20 minutes or until just tender. Drain and keep warm.

To make the pea purée, chop the spring onions. Remove the leaves from the mint and chop finely. Melt the butter in a pan, add the onions and mint and cook over a moderate heat for about 2 minutes. Add the peas, cover with a lid and cook for about 5–7 minutes, stirring occasionally, until tender. Tip the peas into the bowl of a food processor and blitz until smooth. Return to the pan and season to taste. Keep warm.

10 min   Preheat your oven to 200°C/gas mark 6. Back to the starter. Beat the eggs in a shallow dish. Dip the fennel slices first into the beaten egg and then into the breadcrumb mixture, patting and turning to coat. Heat the oil in a large frying pan over a moderate heat and fry the fennel slices for 3–4 minutes on each side or until golden – you will probably need to do this in batches or use 2 pans.

Meanwhile, place the tray of fish for the main course in the oven and cook for 6–8 minutes or until the plaice is just tender and the prosciutto is starting to crisp.

To serve the starter, place 2 fennel fritters on each plate and accompany with the mayonnaise on the side.

To serve the main course, divide the pea purée between 6 warmed dinner plates. Top with a piece of fish, scatter with a few mint leaves and accompany with the boiled new potatoes on the side.

To serve the dessert, place 3 apricots in each dessert bowl, spoon over some of the cooking juices and accompany with the clotted cream or yogurt on the side.

Fennel Fritters with Orange & Lemon Mayonnaise
3 fennel bulbs
200g mayonnaise
½ orange
½ lemon
100g fresh breadcrumbs (see page 27)
½ teaspoon Chinese five-spice powder
½ teaspoon ground black pepper, plus extra for seasoning
1 teaspoon sea salt flakes, plus extra for seasoning
2 eggs
6 tablespoons olive or vegetable oil

Roast Plaice with Prosciutto & Pea Purée
1 bunch of spring onions
2 sprigs of mint, plus a few extra little leaves to garnish
50g butter
450g fresh or frozen peas
6 slices of prosciutto
6 skinless double fillets of plaice (or sole)
sea salt and freshly ground black pepper
new potatoes, to serve

Poached Apricots Stuffed with Marzipan
18 fresh apricots
1 orange
225g caster sugar
85g natural undyed marzipan
a few drops of orange flower water (optional)
clotted cream or Greek yogurt, to serve

FENNEL FRITTERS WITH ORANGE & LEMON MAYONNAISE

Crunchy fritters with a creamy and citrussy mayonnaise.

Bring a large pan of salted water to the boil. Add the whole fennel bulbs and cook for about 10–15 minutes or until tender. Drain and set aside to cool. Cut each bulb lengthways into 4 pieces so each piece is still attached to the root.

Spoon the mayonnaise into a small bowl. Finely grate in the orange and lemon zest and squeeze in the juice. Stir the mayonnaise and season with black pepper.

Mix together the breadcrumbs, five-spice, ground pepper and salt flakes in a shallow tray. Beat the eggs in a shallow dish.

Dip the fennel slices into the egg and then into the breadcrumb mixture, patting and turning to coat.

Heat the oil in a large frying pan over a moderate heat and fry the fennel slices for 3–4 minutes on each side or until golden – you will probably need to do this in batches or use 2 pans. Serve with the orange and lemon mayonnaise.

3 fennel bulbs
200g mayonnaise
½ orange
½ lemon
100g fresh breadcrumbs
 (see page 27)
½ teaspoon Chinese
 five-spice powder
½ teaspoon ground
 black pepper, plus
 extra for seasoning
1 teaspoon sea salt
 flakes, plus extra
 for seasoning
2 eggs
6 tablespoons olive
 or vegetable oil

ROAST PLAICE WITH PROSCIUTTO & PEA PURÉE

Rolling the fish with prosciutto not only keeps the fish moist, but also adds another level of flavour and texture.

Chop the spring onions. Remove the leaves from the mint and chop finely. Melt the butter in a pan, add the onions and mint and cook over a moderate heat for about 2 minutes. Add the peas, cover with a lid and cook for about 5–7 minutes, stirring occasionally, until tender. Tip the peas into the bowl of a food processor and blitz until smooth. Return to the pan and season to taste.

Preheat your oven to 200°C/gas mark 6. Bring a pan of lightly salted water to the boil and cook the potatoes for 15–20 minutes or until just tender.

Lay a slice of prosciutto on a board or work surface and lay a fillet of plaice (or sole) on top. Season with salt and freshly ground black pepper and roll up, not too tightly, so that the prosciutto is on the outside. Secure with a wooden cocktail stick or skewer. Repeat with the remaining prosciutto/fish.

Place the rolled fillets on a baking tray and bake in the oven for 6–8 minutes or until the fish is just tender and the prosciutto is starting to crisp.

To serve, divide the pea purée between 6 warmed dinner plates. Top with a piece of fish and scatter with a few mint leaves. Accompany with the boiled new potatoes.

1 bunch of spring onions
2 sprigs of mint, plus a few extra little leaves to garnish
50g butter
450g fresh or frozen peas
6 slices of prosciutto
6 skinless double fillets of plaice (or sole)
sea sea salt and freshly ground black pepper
new potatoes, to serve

POACHED APRICOTS STUFFED WITH MARZIPAN

The apricots become soft and the marzipan gooey.

Make a slit in one side of the apricots and squeeze gently to remove the stones.

Place the apricots in a large pan and finely grate over the orange zest. Squeeze in the orange juice and add the sugar. Cover and simmer over a low heat for about 8–10 minutes or until tender, turning them from time to time. Remove from the heat and leave to cool.

Knead the marzipan with the orange flower water (if using) – go easy on the orange flower water as it is quite potent and you do really need only a couple of drops.

When the apricots are cool enough to handle, lift out each one with a spoon and poke a small ball of marzipan into the cavity.

Serve warm or cold, accompanied by the cooking juices from the pan and a dollop of clotted cream or Greek yogurt.

18 fresh apricots
1 orange
225g caster sugar
85g marzipan
a few drops of orange flower water (optional)
clotted cream or Greek yogurt, to serve

WARM FRESH PEA SALAD WITH LEMON, MINT & CRISPY PROSCIUTTO.
MACKEREL ESCABECHE.
CHERRIES ON TOAST.

60 min   Start with the main course. Thinly slice the red onion, carrots and garlic clove. Season the mackerel fillets on both sides. Heat 2 tablespoons of the olive oil in a non-stick frying pan, add the mackerel fillets in a single layer and cook for about 2 minutes on each side or until just tender – you will need to do this in batches. Lay the fillets in a non-metallic dish in a single layer and set aside.

50 min   Wipe out the pan and add half of the remaining oil. Add the sliced onion, carrots and garlic, along with the coriander seeds, saffron and allspice, and cook gently for about 5 minutes or until the onion is soft. Add the remaining oil and the vinegar, bring to the boil and check the seasoning. Spoon over the fish, making sure each fillet is well covered, and set aside to cool completely.

40 min   Now for the dessert. Remove the stalks and stones from the cherries and place the fruit in a pan. Using a vegetable peeler, cut a thin strip of peel from the orange and add to the pan. Squeeze in the orange juice and add half of the sugar. Place the pan over a low heat and stir gently to dissolve the sugar. Bring to the boil, and then cover and simmer for 5–8 minutes or until the cherries are tender. Remove from the heat and set aside.

30 min   Cut the brioche into slices. Combine the cinnamon with the remaining sugar on a plate.

Melt the butter in a large frying pan, add the brioche slices in a single layer – you may have to do this in batches – and cook for 3–5 minutes, turning once, until golden and lightly crisp. Remove to a baking tray, sprinkle lightly with the cinnamon sugar and set aside while you cook the rest.

20 min   To prepare the starter, chop the spring onions, very finely chop the garlic and chop the parsley and mint. Finely grate the zest from the lemon and squeeze the juice. Slice the mangetouts in half diagonally. Place the pea shoots (or baby spinach) in a large serving bowl.

Heat the oil over a low heat, add the spring onions, garlic and lemon zest and cook gently for a minute or two, without colouring. Add the peas, mangetouts and sugar snaps and season with salt and pepper. Increase the heat and cook for a further minute, stirring all the time. Remove from the heat and stir in the mint and parsley. Add some lemon juice to taste, check the seasoning and then quickly tip the mixture over the pea shoots in the bowl. Keep the pan to one side to fry the prosciutto.

10 min   Preheat the oven to 190°C/gas mark 5. Cook the Jersey Royals in boiling salted water for 15–20 minutes or until just tender. To finish the starter, reheat the frying pan over a high heat, rip the prosciutto into strips and add to the pan in a single layer. Cook for about 30 seconds– 1 minute until crispy. Drain on kitchen paper.

To serve the starter, toss the salad ingredients together, lay the crispy prosciutto over the top and allow everyone to help themselves.

To serve the main course, chop the parsley and sprinkle over the escabeche. Serve the fish at room temperature with the hot Jersey Royals on the side.

To serve the dessert, warm the brioche in the oven for a minute or two and then place a few slices on each dessert plate. Spoon over the warm poached cherries, sprinkle with a little more cinnamon sugar and serve immediately with the soured cream or crème fraîche on the side.

Warm Fresh Pea Salad with Lemon,
Mint & Crispy Prosciutto
3 spring onions
2 garlic cloves
25g flat-leaf parsley
15g mint
1 unwaxed lemon
200g mangetouts
50g pea shoots (or baby spinach)
3 tablespoons olive oil
200g fresh shelled peas
200g sugar snaps
6 slices of prosciutto
sea salt and freshly ground black pepper

Mackerel Escabeche
1 red onion
2 carrots
1 garlic clove
12 x 100g mackerel fillets
150ml olive oil
½ teaspoon coriander seeds
good pinch of saffron strands
pinch of ground allspice
75ml white wine vinegar
25g flat-leaf parsley
sea salt and freshly ground black pepper
Jersey Royals or other new potatoes, to serve

Cherries on Toast
500g fresh cherries
1 orange
50g caster sugar
6 mini brioche (chocolate or plain)
¼ teaspoon ground cinnamon
50g butter
200g soured cream or crème fraîche, to serve

WARM FRESH PEA SALAD WITH LEMON, MINT & CRISPY PROSCIUTTO

Fresh peas remind me of being a kid, sitting on the back step, podding peas.

Chop the spring onions, very finely chop the garlic and chop the parsley and mint. Finely grate the zest from the lemon and squeeze the juice. Slice the mangetouts in half diagonally. Place the pea shoots (or baby spinach) in a large serving bowl.

Heat the oil over a low heat, add the spring onions, garlic and lemon zest and cook gently for a minute or two, without colouring. Add the peas, mangetouts and sugar snaps, season with salt and freshly ground black pepper and raise the heat. Cook over a moderate heat for a further minute, stirring all the time. Remove from the heat and stir in the mint and parsley. Add some lemon juice to taste, check the seasoning and then tip the mixture onto the pea shoots in the bowl.

Return the pan to a high heat, rip the prosciutto into strips and add them to the pan in a single layer. Cook for about 30 seconds–1minute until crispy. Drain on kitchen paper.

To serve, toss the salad ingredients together, lay the crispy prosciutto over the top and allow everyone to help themselves.

3 spring onions
2 garlic cloves
25g flat-leaf parsley
15g mint
1 unwaxed lemon
200g mangetouts
50g pea shoots
 (or baby spinach)
3 tablespoons olive oil
200g fresh shelled peas
200g sugar snaps
6 slices of prosciutto
sea salt and freshly
 ground black pepper

MACKEREL ESCABECHE

Escabeche is a way of cooking and marinading fish in an acidic liquid. It lightly pickles the fish and gives it a delicious sweet and sour flavour, which is perfect with the rich and oily mackerel.

Thinly slice the red onion, carrots and garlic clove. Season the mackerel fillets on both sides. Heat 2 tablespoons of the olive oil in a non-stick frying pan, add the mackerel fillets in a single layer and cook for about 2 minutes on each side or until just tender – you will need to do this in batches. Lay the fillets in a non-metallic dish in a single layer and set aside.

Wipe out the pan and add half of the remaining oil. Add the sliced onion, carrots and garlic, along with the coriander seeds, saffron and allspice, and cook gently for about 5 minutes or until the onion is soft. Add the remaining oil and the vinegar, bring to the boil and check the seasoning. Spoon over the fish, making sure each fillet is well covered, and set aside to cool completely. It should be served at room temperature.

Bring a pan of lightly salted water to the boil and cook the Jersey Royals for 15–20 minutes or until just tender.

To serve, finely chop the parsley and sprinkle over the fish. Accompany with the Jersey Royals.

1 red onion
2 carrots
1 garlic clove
12 x 100g mackerel fillets
150ml olive oil
½ teaspoon coriander
 seeds
good pinch of saffron
 strands
pinch of ground allspice
75ml white wine vinegar
25g flat-leaf parsley
sea salt and freshly
 ground black pepper
Jersey Royals or other
 new potatoes, to serve

CHERRIES ON TOAST

If you can, buy brioche buns and cut them into slices across the middle; as you can see from the pictures below, they make pretty shapes.

Remove the stalks and stones from the cherries and place the fruit in a pan. Using a vegetable peeler, cut a thin strip of peel from the orange and add to the pan. Squeeze in the orange juice and add half of the sugar.

Place the pan over a low heat and stir gently to dissolve the sugar. Bring to the boil, and then cover and simmer for 5–8 minutes or until the cherries are tender. Remove from the heat and set aside.

Cut the brioche into slices. Combine the cinnamon with the remaining sugar on a plate.

Melt the butter in a large frying pan, add the brioche slices in a single layer – you may have to do this in batches – and cook for 3–5 minutes, turning once, until golden and lightly crisp. Remove to a baking tray, sprinkle lightly with the cinnamon sugar and set aside while you cook the rest.

To serve, place a few slices of the brioche on each plate, divide the warm poached cherries between them, sprinkle with a little more cinnamon sugar and serve immediately with the soured cream or crème fraîche on the side.

500g fresh cherries
1 orange
50g caster sugar
6 mini brioche
 (chocolate or plain)
¼ teaspoon
 ground cinnamon
50g butter
200g soured cream or
 crème fraîche, to serve

PEA & LETTUCE SOUP WITH BACON CRUMBS.
TROUT WITH LIME BUTTER SAUCE.
GOLDEN GOOSEBERRY MESS.

60 min   Start with the dessert. Place the gooseberries in a pan with the sugar, cover and gradually bring to the boil. Reduce the heat and simmer for 5–10 minutes or until tender. Remove from the heat and leave to cool completely.

Now for the soup. Chop the spring onions, crush the garlic and shred the lettuces. Melt half of the butter in a large pan, add the spring onions and garlic and cook without colouring for 3–5 minutes until soft.

50 min   Add the shredded lettuces and peas, 1 litre water and some salt and freshly ground black pepper. Bring to the boil and then simmer for about 5 minutes or until the peas are just cooked. Remove from the heat and leave to cool slightly.

40 min   Tear the bread into little pieces (or alternatively blitz in a food processor until large crumbs are formed). Very finely chop the bacon or pancetta.

Melt the remaining butter in a large frying pan, add the bacon and fry for 3–4 minutes over a moderate heat until lightly golden. Using a slotted spoon, lift the bacon pieces into a bowl.

Add the ripped breadcrumbs to the pan and cook until crispy and golden brown, stirring frequently. Remove from the heat and combine with the bacon pieces.

30 min   Purée the soup in a blender until smooth, and then pass through a fine sieve back into the pan. Preheat your oven to 200°C/gas mark 6.

20 min   To finish the dessert, crush the meringue nests into a small bowl with your fingers. Whip the cream in a large bowl until soft peaks are formed, and then carefully fold in the cooled gooseberries, crushed meringues and rose water (if using). Spoon the mixture into 6 dessert glasses or bowls and chill in the fridge until ready to serve.

Bring a pan of lightly salted water to a boil and cook the potatoes for 15-20 minutes or until just tender.

10 min   To cook the fish, rub a little oil into both sides of the trout and season inside and out. Place on 2 baking sheets and bake in the oven for 15–20 minutes or until just tender. To prepare the sauce for the fish, squeeze the juice from the limes into a small saucepan, add 3 tablespoons water and heat gently until reduced by half. Cut the butter into small cubes. Gradually whisk the cubes of butter into the pan, piece by piece, until you have a creamy sauce. Season well and keep warm.

To serve the starter, add the cream to the soup and reheat. Adjust the seasoning, ladle into soup bowls and sprinkle with the crumbs and a tiny pinch of cinnamon,(if using).

To serve the main course, place a whole trout on each dinner plate, spoon over some of the sauce and accompany with the boiled new potatoes on the side.

To serve the dessert, bring the glasses or bowls of gooseberry mess to the table straight from the fridge.

Pea & Lettuce Soup with Bacon Crumbs
8 spring onions
1 garlic clove
2 little gem lettuces
50g butter
600g fresh shelled peas
3 thick slices of crusty bread
100g bacon rashers or sliced pancetta
200ml double cream
pinch of ground cinnamon (optional)
sea salt and freshly ground black pepper

Trout with Lime Butter Sauce
6 x 300g whole trout, gutted and cleaned
2 tablespoons olive oil
2 limes
250g butter
sea salt and freshly ground black pepper
small new potatoes, to serve

Golden Gooseberry Mess
500g gooseberries
100g light brown sugar
4 meringue nests
500ml whipping cream
1 teaspoon rose water (optional)

PEA & LETTUCE SOUP WITH BACON CRUMBS

The bacon crumbs are a great way of adding crunch and texture.

Chop the spring onions, crush the garlic and shred the lettuce.

Melt half of the butter in a large pan, add the spring onions and garlic and cook without colouring for 3–5 minutes until soft. Add the shredded lettuces and peas, 1 litre water and some sea salt and freshly ground black pepper. Bring to the boil and then simmer for about 5 minutes or until the peas are just cooked. Remove from the heat, leave to cool slightly and then purée in a blender until smooth. Pass through a fine sieve.

Tear the bread into little pieces (or alternatively blitz in a food processor until large crumbs are formed). Very finely chop the bacon (or pancetta).

Melt the remaining butter in a large frying pan, add the bacon and fry for 3–4 minutes over a moderate heat until lightly golden. Using a slotted spoon, lift the bacon pieces into a bowl.

Add the ripped breadcrumbs to the pan and cook until crispy and golden brown, stirring frequently. Remove from the heat and combine with the bacon pieces.

To serve, add the cream to the soup and reheat. Adjust the seasoning, ladle into bowls and sprinkle with the crunchy crumbs and a tiny pinch of cinnamon, (if using).

8 spring onions
1 garlic clove
2 little gem lettuces
50g butter
600g fresh shelled peas
3 thick slices of
 crusty bread
100g bacon rashers
 (or sliced pancetta)
200ml double cream
pinch of ground cinnamon
 (optional)
sea salt and freshly
 ground black pepper

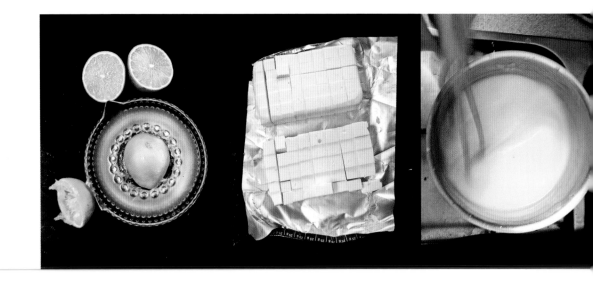

TROUT WITH LIME BUTTER SAUCE

Preheat your oven to 200°C/gas mark 6.

Rub a little oil into both sides of the trout and season inside and out. Place the fish onto 2 baking sheets and bake for 15–20 minutes or until just tender.

Squeeze the juice from the limes into a small saucepan, add 3 tablespoons water and heat gently until reduced by half. Cut the butter into small cubes and gradually whisk them into the pan, one by one, until you have a creamy sauce. Season well.

Meanwhile, cook the potatoes in boiling salted water for 15–20 minutes until just tender.

To serve, place a whole trout on each dinner plate, spoon over some of the sauce and accompany with the new potatoes on the side.

6 x 300g whole trout,
  gutted and cleaned
2 tablespoons olive oil
2 limes
250g butter
sea salt and freshly
  ground black pepper
small new potatoes,
  to serve

GOLDEN GOOSEBERRY MESS

Another fruit that reminds me of Dad's garden – hairy, ripe gooseberries warm from the sun.

Place the gooseberries in a pan with the sugar, cover and gradually bring to the boil. Reduce the heat and simmer for 5–10 minutes or until tender. Remove from the heat and leave to cool completely.

Crush the meringue nests into a small bowl with your fingers. Whip the cream in a large bowl until soft peaks are formed, and then carefully fold in the cooled gooseberries, crushed meringues and rose water (if using).

Spoon the mixture into 6 dessert glasses or bowls and chill in the fridge until ready to serve.

500g gooseberries
100g light brown sugar
4 meringue nests
500ml whipping cream
1 teaspoon rose
  water (optional)

COURGETTE & FENNEL SOUP WITH PECORINO CROÛTONS.
LAMB WITH SKORTHALIA.
STRAWBERRIES WITH BALSAMIC SYRUP & VANILLA ICE CREAM.

60 min   Begin with the starter. Finely chop the onion and garlic. Cut the fennel and courgettes into quarters lengthways and then slice across into 1cm pieces. Melt the butter in a large saucepan, add the onion, garlic and fennel and cook over a low heat, without colouring, for about 10 minutes or until soft.

50 min   Stir in the courgettes and cook for a further 2 minutes. Add the stock, bring to the boil, then reduce the heat and simmer for 5 minutes or until the courgettes are just tender. Remove from the heat and leave to cool slightly before blending until smooth – you might need to do this in batches.

40 min   Prepare the marinade for the main course. Peel the ginger and finely grate into a mixing bowl. Add 3 tablespoons of the olive oil, with the ground spices, and finely grate in the lemon zest. Remove the leaves from the fresh coriander, chop finely and add to the bowl. Mix well together. Coat the cutlets in the marinade and set aside.

30 min   To make the skorthalia, first remove the crusts from the bread and discard. Place the bread in a clean bowl, cover with cold water and leave to soak for 5 minutes. Squeeze out any excess liquid from the bread and transfer the bread to the bowl of a food processor. Squeeze the lemon juice into a small bowl, and crush the garlic. Add the garlic and half of the lemon juice to the food processor, along with the ground almonds. Process briefly until mixed and then, with the motor running, gradually pour in the remaining olive oil through the feeder tube in a thin stream until the mixture resembles mayonnaise. Add more lemon juice and salt and freshly ground black pepper to taste.

20 min   To make the balsamic syrup for the dessert, place the sugar in a small pan with 50ml cold water and stir over a low heat until the sugar has dissolved. Bring to the boil and simmer, without stirring, until the syrup turns a light caramel colour. Remove from the heat and very carefully pour in a further 50ml water and the balsamic vinegar – be very careful because it will spit. Stir well.

Bring a large pan of water to the boil. Place the sweetcorn in a steamer, place over the water and steam for 15–20 minutes or until tender. Alternatively brush the sweetcorn with a little olive oil and griddle or barbecue, turning occasionally, for 20–30 minutes.

10 min   Preheat your oven to 200°C/gas mark 6. To make the croûtons, cut the bread (crusts and all) into 2cm cubes and place on a non-stick baking sheet (or a tray lined with parchment paper). Drizzle with the olive oil, toss well together, and then spread out in a single layer. Finely grate the cheese over the top and place in the oven for 5–6 minutes or until golden and crispy, turning once.

Meanwhile, for the dessert, destalk and dehull the strawberries, slice them if they are large and divide between 6 little bowls.

To serve the starter, reheat the soup and season well. Ladle into soup bowls, add a swirl of cream to each and scatter the croûtons over the top.

To cook the lamb for the main course, preheat your grill to high or heat a griddle on the stove. Season the cutlets and grill for about 3 minutes on each side or until tender but still pink in the middle. To serve, place a spoonful of skorthalia on each plate, top with 2 lamb cutlets and accompany with the steamed or grilled sweetcorn

To serve the dessert, add a scoop of vanilla ice cream to each bowl (or spoon over single cream), drizzle with the balsamic syrup and serve with the shortbread fingers on the side.

Courgette & Fennel Soup
1 onion
1 garlic clove
1 fennel bulb (about 250g)
500g courgettes
25g butter
600ml chicken or vegetable stock
100ml double cream
sea salt and freshly ground black pepper

Pecorino Croûtons
100g country bread, sliced
3 tablespoons olive oil
50g Pecorino (or Parmesan) cheese

Lamb with Skorthalia
5cm piece of fresh root ginger
200ml extra-virgin olive oil
½ teaspoon ground turmeric
1 teaspoon ground coriander
½ teaspoon ground ginger
½ teaspoon ground cumin
1 lemon
25g fresh coriander
12 lamb cutlets
70g white country bread
4 garlic cloves
85g ground almonds
sea salt and freshly ground black pepper
6 whole sweetcorn cobs, trimmed, to serve

Strawberries with Balsamic Syrup & Vanilla Ice Cream
175g caster sugar
2 tablespoons balsamic vinegar
750g strawberries
vanilla ice cream (or single cream), to serve
shortbread fingers, to serve

COURGETTE & FENNEL SOUP WITH PECORINO CROÛTONS

A cheesy variation of the croûton!

Finely chop the onion and garlic. Cut the fennel and courgettes into quarters lengthways and then slice across into 1cm pieces. Melt the butter in a large saucepan, add the onion, garlic and fennel and cook over a low heat, without colouring, for about 10 minutes or until soft.

Stir in the courgettes and cook for a further 2 minutes. Add the stock, bring to the boil, and then reduce the heat and simmer for 5 minutes or until the courgettes are just tender. Remove from the heat and leave to cool slightly before blending until smooth – you might need to do this in batches.

Preheat your oven to 200°C/gas mark 6. To make the croûtons, cut the bread (crusts and all) into 2cm cubes and place on a non-stick baking sheet (or a tray lined with parchment paper). Drizzle with the olive oil, toss well together, and then spread out in a single layer. Finely grate the cheese over the top and place in the oven for 5–6 minutes or until golden and crispy, turning once.

Just before serving, reheat the soup and season well. Ladle into bowls and swirl in a little of the cream on top. Scatter with croûtons to serve.

1 onion
1 garlic clove
1 fennel bulb
 (about 250g)
500g courgettes
25g butter
600ml chicken or
 vegetable stock
100ml double cream
sea salt and freshly
 ground black pepper

For the croûtons
100g country bread, sliced
3 tablespoons olive oil
50g Pecorino (or Parmesan)
 cheese

LAMB WITH SKORTHALIA

Peel the ginger and finely grate into a mixing bowl. Add 3 tablespoons of the olive oil, along with the ground spices, and finely grate in the zest from the lemon. Remove the leaves from the fresh coriander, chop finely and add to the bowl. Mix well together. Coat the cutlets in the mixture and set aside to marinade for 30 minutes.

Steam the sweetcorn over a large pan of boiling water for 15–20 minutes or until tender. Alternatively brush the sweetcorn with a little olive oil and griddle or barbecue, turning occasionally, for 20–30 minutes.

Meanwhile make the skorthalia. Remove the crusts from the bread and discard. Place the bread in a clean bowl and cover with cold water. Leave to soak for 5 minutes.

Squeeze out any excess liquid from the bread and transfer the bread to the bowl of a food processor. Squeeze the juice of the lemon into a small bowl, and crush the garlic. Add the garlic and half of the lemon juice to the food processor, along with the ground almonds.

Process briefly until mixed and then, with the motor running, gradually pour in the remaining olive oil through the feeder tube in a thin stream until the mixture resembles mayonnaise. Add more lemon juice and salt and freshly ground black pepper to taste.

When you are ready to cook, preheat your grill to high or heat a griddle on the hob. Season the cutlets and place them under the grill or on the griddle. Cook for about 3 minutes on each side or until tender but still pink in the middle.

To serve, place a spoonful of skorthalia on each plate, top with 2 lamb cutlets and accompany with the steamed or grilled sweetcorn on the side.

5cm piece of fresh
 root ginger
200ml extra-virgin olive oil
½ teaspoon ground turmeric
1 teaspoon ground coriander
½ teaspoon ground ginger
½ teaspoon ground cumin
1 lemon
25g fresh coriander
12 lamb cutlets
70g white country bread
4 garlic cloves
85g ground almonds
sea salt and freshly
 ground black pepper
6 whole sweetcorn cobs,
 trimmed to serve

STRAWBERRIES WITH BALSAMIC SYRUP & VANILLA ICE CREAM

Sticky, sweet balsamic syrup really does marry beautifully with the strawberries.

Place the sugar in a small pan with 50ml cold water and stir over a low heat until the sugar has dissolved. Bring to the boil and simmer, without stirring, until the syrup turns a light golden caramel colour. Remove from the heat and very carefully pour in a further 50ml water and the balsamic vinegar – be very careful because it will spit. Stir well.

Destalk and dehull the strawberries, slice them if they are large and divide between 6 small bowls. Add a scoop of ice cream (or pour over a little single cream), drizzle with the balsamic syrup and serve with some shortbread fingers on the side.

175g caster sugar
2 tablespoons
 balsamic vinegar
750g strawberries
vanilla ice cream
 (or single cream),
 to serve
shortbread fingers,
 to serve

WATERMELON GAZPACHO.
GREEN BUTTER SOLE.
BAKED RICOTTA WITH RASPBERRY SAUCE.

60 min   Begin with the starter. Place 6 little cups or bowls in the fridge or freezer to chill. Peel the melon, cut into large chunks and place in a food processor. Blitz briefly until smooth but don't overdo it or you will break up the seeds too much. Pour into a sieve set over a bowl to catch the juice, and press through as much of the pulp as possible with the back of a wooden spoon. Pour the liquid back into the food processor.

Remove crusts from the bread (if using) and discard. Break the bread into small pieces and add to the food processor.

50 min   Finely chop one-third of the cucumber for the garnish, place in a bowl, cover with clingfilm and set aside in the fridge. Roughly chop the rest of the cucumber and add to the food processor. Chop the onion and crush the garlic and add these to the food processor as well.

40 min   Blend the gazpacho until very smooth, and then pour into a bowl. Season well with salt, pepper and the vinegar, and stir in the oil. Cover with clingfilm and place in the fridge until needed. Wash and dry the food processor bowl.

30 min   Now for the main course. Remove the leaves from the parsley and tarragon and place in the bowl of a food processor with the spring onions. Blitz together until very finely chopped, and then squeeze in the juice from the lemon. Soften the butter very slightly if necessary and scrape into the processor bowl. Add the five-spice powder, salt and pepper and blitz again until combined. Set aside.

20 min   Preheat your oven to 180°C/gas mark 4. To make the dessert, grease 6 175ml ramekins with a little butter. Cut the vanilla pod in half lengthways and scrape out the seeds into a large bowl. Add the eggs and the sugar and beat well. Add the ricotta and mix again. Divide

the mixture between the ramekins and smooth the tops. Place on a baking sheet and bake in the oven for 15–20 minutes until slightly puffed up and lightly golden.

Bring a pan of lightly salted water to the boil and cook the potatoes for 15–20 minutes or until just tender.

10 min   Meanwhile, make the raspberry sauce for the dessert. Place half of the raspberries in a saucepan with the honey. Cook over a moderate heat for about 2–3 minutes, stirring with a wooden spoon to break up the fruit. Reduce the heat and simmer for about 5 minutes to thicken the sauce. Remove from the heat, stir in the rest of the raspberries and set aside until needed.

Back to the main course. Bring a pan of lightly salted water to the boil and cook the beans for 5–8 minutes or until just tender.

Prepare the sole fillets by brushing them with oil, seasoning well and placing them in a single layer on a large baking tray. Preheat your grill to high.

When you are ready to serve the starter, check the seasoning – you may need a little more salt or pepper – and then pour the gazpacho into your chilled cups or bowls. Add an ice cube to each one, sprinkle with some of the reserved chopped cucumber and finish with a tiny pinch of sweet smoked paprika (if using).

To cook the sole, grill for 3–4 minutes, (no need to turn), or until just tender.

To serve the main course, place 2 fillets on each plate, scoop a spoonful of the green butter onto each and serve immediately with the boiled new potatoes and green beans on the side.

To serve the dessert, accompany each warm baked ricotta in its dish with the raspberry sauce and single cream in jugs on the side for everyone to share.

Watermelon Gazpacho
1½kg piece of watermelon
2 slices of slightly stale country bread (optional)
½ cucumber
½ small red onion
1 garlic clove
1 tablespoon balsamic vinegar
5 tablespoons extra-virgin olive oil
sea salt and freshly ground black pepper
a few ice cubes, to serve
sweet smoked paprika, to serve (optional)

Green Butter Sole
25g flat-leaf parsley
1 sprig of tarragon
3 spring onions
½ lemon
125g butter
pinch of Chinese five-spice powder
12 x 125g sole fillets, skin on
2 tablespoons olive oil
sea salt and freshly ground black pepper
new potatoes and green beans, to serve

Baked Ricotta with Raspberry Sauce
a little butter, for greasing
1 vanilla pod
2 eggs
40g soft dark brown sugar
600g ricotta
500g raspberries
3 tablespoons honey
single cream, to serve

WATERMELON GAZPACHO

Adding bread to the gazpacho gives the soup a thicker consistency. You could leave it out completely if preferred.

Place 6 little cups or bowls in the fridge or freezer to chill.

Peel the melon, cut into large chunks and place in the bowl of a food processor. Blitz briefly until smooth but don't overdo it or you will break up the seeds too much. Pour into a sieve placed over a bowl to catch the juice, and push through as much of the pulp as possible with the back of a wooden spoon. Pour the liquid back into the food processor.

Remove the crusts from the bread (if using) and discard. Break the bread into little pieces and add to the food processor.

Finely chop one-third of the cucumber for the garnish, place in a bowl, cover with clingfilm and set aside in the fridge until needed. Roughly chop the rest of the cucumber and add to the food processor. Chop the onion and crush the garlic and add these to the food processor as well.

Blend everything together until very smooth, and then pour into a bowl. Season well with salt, pepper and the vinegar, and stir in the oil. Cover with clingfilm and place in the fridge until needed.

When you are ready to serve, check the gazpacho for seasoning – it may need a little more salt and pepper – and pour into the chilled cups or bowls. To serve, add an ice cube to each one, sprinkle with some of the reserved chopped cucumber and finish with a tiny pinch of sweet smoked paprika (if using).

1½kg piece of watermelon
2 slices of slightly stale
 country bread (optional)
½ cucumber
½ small red onion
1 garlic clove
1 tablespoon balsamic
 vinegar
5 tablespoons extra-virgin
 olive oil
sea salt and freshly
 ground black pepper
a few ice cubes, to serve
sweet smoked paprika,
 to serve (optional)

GREEN BUTTER SOLE

Delicate sole with a fragrant, herby butter.

Bring a pan of lightly salted water to the boil and cook the potatoes for 15–20 minutes or until just tender. Remove the leaves from the parsley and tarragon and place in the bowl of a food processor with the spring onions. Blitz together until very finely chopped, and then squeeze in the juice from the lemon. Bring another pan of lightly salted water to the boil and cook the beans for 5–8 minutes or until just tender.

Soften the butter very slightly if necessary and scrape into the bowl of the food processor. Add the five-spice powder, salt and pepper and blitz again until combined. Set aside.

Preheat the grill to high. Brush the sole fillets with oil, season well and lay in a single layer on a large baking tray. Grill for about 3–4 minutes, (no need to turn), or until just tender.

To serve, place 2 fillets on each plate, top with a spoonful of the green butter and serve immediately with the boiled new potatoes and green beans on the side.

25g flat-leaf parsley
1 sprig of tarragon
3 spring onions
½ lemon
125g butter
pinch of Chinese
 five-spice powder
12 x 125g sole fillets,
 skin on
2 tablespoons olive oil
sea salt and freshly
 ground black pepper
new potatoes and
 green beans, to serve

BAKED RICOTTA WITH RASPBERRY SAUCE

Preheat your oven to 180°C/gas mark 4.

Grease 6 175ml ramekins with a little butter. Cut the vanilla pod in half lengthways and scrape out the seeds into a large bowl. Add the eggs and the sugar and beat well. Add the ricotta and mix again. Divide the mixture between the ramekins and smooth the tops. Place on a baking sheet and bake in the oven for 15–20 minutes until slightly puffed up and lightly golden.

To make the sauce, place half of the raspberries in a saucepan with the honey. Cook over a moderate heat for about 2–3 minutes, stirring with a wooden spoon to break up the fruit. Reduce the heat and simmer for about 5 minutes to thicken the sauce.

Remove from the heat and stir in the rest of the raspberries. Set aside.

Serve each warm baked ricotta in its dish with the raspberry sauce and single cream in jugs on the side for everyone to share.

a little butter, for
 greasing
1 vanilla pod
2 eggs
40g soft dark brown sugar
600g ricotta
500g raspberries
3 tablespoons honey
single cream, to serve

WARM COURGETTE DIP.
PAN-FRIED MACKEREL WITH FRIED POLENTA TOMATOES & ROASTED NEW POTATOES.
BAKED NECTARINES WITH MARSALA & CLOTTED CREAM.

60 min   Preheat your oven to 200°C/gas mark 6. Begin with the starter. Boil the whole courgettes (don't trim them yet) in salted water for about 30–40 minutes or until the courgettes are very soft – but still holding together.

50 min   Meanwhile, get on with the dessert. Cut the nectarines (or peaches) in half across the middle and remove the stones. Lay the halves, cut-side up, in a baking dish and drizzle with the Marsala and vanilla. Coat evenly with sugar. Cover with a lid or some tin foil and bake in the middle of the oven for 30–40 minutes or until the fruit is soft and tender.

40 min   Now for the main course. Tip the new potatoes into a roasting tin, sprinkle with salt and 3 tablespoons of the oil and mix well with your hands. Place in the top of the oven and roast for about 40–45 minutes or until tender.

Cut the preserved lemon into quarters, remove the flesh and discard, and finely chop the skin. Finely chop the parsley and coriander, squeeze the juice from the fresh lemon and roughly chop the green olives. Place everything together in a bowl, season and mix well.

30 min   To make the marinade for the tomatoes, crush the garlic and place in a large flat dish with the ginger, cumin, chilli and 2 tablespoons of the oil. Season with salt and black pepper and mix well. Slice the tomatoes thickly and lay in the spiced oil, turning to coat. Set aside.

20 min   The courgettes should now be cooked. Drain them into a colander, top and tail them and return to the pan. Mash well with a fork, squeeze in the juice from half the lemon and stir in the harissa and olive oil. Season to taste, adding more lemon juice if needed. Stir in the black olives, spoon into a serving dish and set aside.

10 min   Remove the nectarines from the oven and set aside. Turn the oven down to 170°C/gas mark 3.

Back to the main course. Tip the polenta onto a large plate. Heat 2 large frying pans and add 1–2 tablespoons of the oil to each. Dip each slice of tomato into the polenta, coating both sides, and transfer in a single layer to the pans. Fry over a moderate heat for 1–2 minutes on each side or until crispy and lightly golden. Cover to keep warm.

Place the flatbread on a baking tray in a single layer and place in the oven to warm for a few minutes To serve the starter, place the dish of courgette dip on the table with the warm flatbread on the side.

To finish the main course, season the mackerel fillets on both sides. Wipe out the frying pans, divide the remaining olive oil between them and set over a medium-to-high heat. Carefully put in the mackerel fillets, skin-side down, and cook for 1–2 minutes or until the skin is crisp – the secret to crisp skin is not to be tempted to touch the fish or the pan while they are cooking. Turn the fillets over and cook for a further minute on the other side, or until just tender. Remove the fillets, tip in the preserved lemon and olive mixture and bring to a simmer.

To serve the main course, transfer a few fried tomato slices to each dinner plate, top with 2 mackerel fillets and spoon over the olive and lemon dressing. Hand around the roasted new potatoes and the yogurt (if using) separately.

To serve the dessert, place 2 nectarine halves in each dessert dish and accompany with some clotted cream and amaretti biscuits on the side.

Warm Courgette Dip
750g courgettes
1 lemon
½ tablespoon rose harissa
2 tablespoons extra-virgin olive oil
18 pitted black olives
sea salt and freshly ground black pepper
flatbread, to serve

Pan-fried Mackerel with Fried Polenta Tomatoes & Roasted New Potatoes
1kg new potatoes
150ml extra-virgin olive oil
1 preserved lemon
10g flat-leaf parsley
10g coriander
1 lemon
50g large pitted green olives
2 garlic cloves
teaspoon ground ginger
½ teaspoon ground cumin
½ teaspoon chilli powder
6 large ripe tomatoes
100g coarse polenta
6 x 100g mackerel fillets, skin on
sea salt and freshly ground black pepper
natural yogurt, to serve (optional)

Baked Nectarines with Marsala & Clotted Cream
6 nectarines (or peaches)
200ml Marsala
1 teaspoon vanilla extract
50g brown sugar
clotted cream, to serve
amaretti biscuits, to serve

WARM COURGETTE DIP

This dip also makes a great snack for those nights sat in the garden, watching the stars with a gin and tonic.

Leave the courgettes whole and place them in a large pan with a pinch of salt and enough water to cover. Bring to the boil, reduce the heat and simmer for about 30–40 minutes or until the courgettes are very soft.

Drain the courgettes, top and tail them and return to the pan. Mash well with a fork, squeeze in the juice from half the lemon and stir in the harissa and olive oil. Season to taste, adding more lemon juice if needed. Stir in the black olives, spoon into a serving dish and set aside.

Preheat your oven to 190°C/gas 5. Place the flatbread on a baking tray in a single layer and place in the oven to warm for a few minutes before serving with the warm dip.

750g courgettes
1 lemon
½ tablespoon rose harissa
2 tablespoons extra-virgin
 olive oil
18 pitted black olives
sea salt and freshly
 ground black pepper
flatbread, to serve

PAN-FRIED MACKEREL WITH FRIED POLENTA TOMATOES & ROASTED NEW POTATOES

Spiced juicy tomatoes with a crunchy coating.

Preheat your oven to 200°C/gas mark 6. Crush the garlic and place in a large, flat dish with the ginger, cumin, chilli powder and 2 tablespoons of the oil. Season with salt and freshly ground black pepper and mix well. Slice the tomatoes thickly and lay in the spiced oil, turning to coat. Set aside.

Tip the potatoes into a roasting tin, sprinkle with salt and 3 tablespoons of the oil and mix well with your hands. Place in the oven and roast for about 40–45 minutes or until tender.

Cut the preserved lemon into quarters, remove the flesh and discard, and finely chop the skin. Finely chop the parsley and coriander, squeeze the juice from the fresh lemon and roughly chop the olives. Place everything together in a bowl, season and mix well.

Tip the polenta onto a large plate. Heat 2 large frying pans and add 1–2 tablespoons of the oil to each. Dip each slice of tomato into the polenta, coating both sides, and transfer in a single layer to the pans. Fry over a moderate heat for 1–2 minutes on each side or until crispy and lightly golden. Cover to keep warm.

Season the mackerel fillets on both sides. Wipe out the frying pans, divide the remaining olive oil between them and set over a medium-to-high heat. Carefully put in the mackerel fillets, skin-side down, and cook for 1–2 minutes or until the skin is crisp – the secret to crisp skin is not to be tempted to touch the fish or the pan while they are cooking. Turn the fillets over and cook for a further minute on the other side, or until just tender. Remove the fillets to a plate. To make the dressing, tip the preserved lemon and olive mixture into one of the pans and bring to a simmer.

To serve, transfer a few fried tomato slices to each dinner plate, top with 2 mackerel fillets and spoon over the olive and lemon dressing. Hand around the roasted new potatoes and yogurt (if using) separately.

2 garlic cloves
½ teaspoon ground ginger
½ teaspoon ground cumin
½ teaspoon chilli powder
150ml extra-virgin
 olive oil
6 large ripe tomatoes
1kg new potatoes
1 preserved lemon
10g flat-leaf parsley
10g coriander
1 lemon
50g large pitted
 green olives
100g coarse polenta
6 x 100g mackerel
 fillets, skin on
sea salt and freshly
 ground black pepper
natural yogurt, to serve
 (optional)

BAKED NECTARINES WITH MARSALA & CLOTTED CREAM

Marsala wine adds sweetness and depth to the baked nectarines.

Preheat your oven to 200°C/gas mark 6.

Cut the nectarines (or peaches) in half across the middle and remove the stones. Lay the halves, cut-side up, in a baking dish and drizzle with the Marsala and vanilla. Coat evenly with sugar.

Cover with a lid or some tin foil and bake in the oven for 30–40 minutes or until the fruit is soft and tender.

Serve with clotted cream and amaretti biscuits.

6 nectarines (or peaches)
200ml Marsala
1 teaspoon vanilla extract
50g brown sugar
clotted cream, to serve
amaretti biscuits, to serve

SUMMER HERB SOUP.
LAMB PARCELS WITH BLACK OLIVE STUFFING & SUMMER SLAW.
RHUBARB, RASPBERRY & AMARETTO SYLLABUB.

60 min   Begin with the dessert. Cut the rhubarb into 2cm pieces and place in a pan with the raspberries and 150g of the sugar. Cover and cook over a moderate heat, stirring occasionally, for 8–10 minutes or until tender. Meanwhile, get on with the starter . Chop the leek, wash and drain well. Separate the leaves from the parsley and coriander stalks and roughly chop the stalks; set aside a small handful of the herb leaves for the garnish.

50 min   Melt the butter in a large pan, stir in the chopped leeks and chopped herb stalks and cook over a low heat without colouring for about 15 minutes.

The rhubarb should now be cooked. Tip the rhubarb and raspberry mixture into a nylon sieve set over a bowl to catch the juices. Return the juices to the pan and simmer until reduced by half. Place the strained fruit in a bowl, stir in the thickened juices and leave to cool.

40 min   Chop the potato for the soup and add to the pan with the softened leek. Pour in the stock, bring to the boil and simmer for 10 minutes or until the potato is tender. Add the chives and the parsley and coriander leaves and cook for a further 5 minutes. Remove from the heat and leave to cool slightly.

Preheat your oven to 220°C/gas mark 7. Finely grate the zest from the lemon and bash in a pestle and mortar with the fennel seeds. Chop the anchovies and roughly chop the olives. Add to the lemon and fennel seed mixture and bash everything again to create a very rough paste. Season and mix again.

30 min   Place a lamb steak into a plastic bag or between 2 sheets of clingfilm and, using a rolling pin, gently bash out the meat, turning as you go, until it is about 8mm thick. Repeat with the remaining lamb steaks.

20 min   Season the steaks well on each side and lay out on a board. Place a spoonful of the olive mixture into the middle of each steak, fold over and use a wooden cocktail stick or skewer to close. Place the lamb parcels in a roasting tin, squeeze over the juice from the lemon and drizzle with the olive oil. Place in the oven and cook for about 10 minutes or until the lamb is tender but still slightly pink in the middle. Remove from the oven, cover with foil to keep warm and leave to rest.

10 min   To make the slaw, cut the beetroot, carrots and cucumber into very thin slices with a potato peeler or a mandolin (see page 28). Halve the fennel, remove the core and slice very thinly. Thinly slice the radishes and cut the celery into very thin sticks. Place all the vegetables together in a large bowl. To make the dressing, mix the cream with the mustard and vinegar in a small bowl. Season with salt, pepper and a pinch of sugar.

To serve the starter, blend the soup until smooth and return to the pan to reheat. Finely chop the reserved herb leaves for the garnish. Season the soup to taste and ladle into soup bowls. Add a swirl of cream and garnish with a sprinkling of the reserved chopped herbs.

To serve the main course, spoon the dressing over the slaw and mix well together. Divide the slaw between 6 dinner plates and top with a lamb parcel.

To finish the dessert, squeeze the juice from the lemon into a large bowl and add the double cream, the remaining sugar and the Amaretto. Whisk until soft peaks are formed. Gently marble the cooled fruit into the cream mixture and spoon into 6 dishes or glasses. Crumble the amaretti biscuits over the top and serve decorated with a few extra raspberries.

Summer Herb Soup
1 large leek
50g flat-leaf parsley
25g coriander
50g butter
1 large potato
1 litre chicken or vegetable stock
25g chives
100ml double cream
sea salt and freshly ground black pepper

Lamb Parcels with Black Olive Stuffing & Summer Slaw
1 lemon
1 teaspoon fennel seeds
3 tinned anchovy fillets
100g pitted dry black olives
6 x 150g boneless lamb leg steaks
2 tablespoons olive oil
1 raw beetroot
2 large carrots
½ cucumber
1 fennel bulb
12 radishes
1 celery stick
4 tablespoons double cream
1 teaspoon Dijon mustard
1 teaspoon balsamic vinegar
pinch of sugar
sea salt and freshly ground black pepper

Rhubarb, Raspberry & Amaretto Syllabub
400g rhubarb
200g raspberries, plus a few extra to decorate
250g caster sugar
1 lemon
500ml double cream
3 tablespoons Amaretto
4 amaretti biscuits

SUMMER HERB SOUP

You can use a selection of any of the soft summery herbs. Feel free to substitute tarragon, mint, chervil or dill for any of the other herbs included here.

Chop the leek, wash and drain well. Separate the leaves from the parsley and coriander stalks and roughly chop the stalks; set aside a small handful of the leaves for the garnish.

Melt the butter in a large pan, stir in the chopped leek and chopped herb stalks and cook over a low heat without colouring for about 15 minutes. Chop the potato and add to the pan with the stock. Bring to the boil and then simmer gently for a further 10 minutes or until the potato is tender. Add the chives and the parsley and coriander leaves and cook for a further 5 minutes.

Remove the soup from the heat and leave to cool slightly, and then blend until smooth. Finely chop the reserved herb leaves. Reheat the soup, season well and serve with a swirl of cream on top and a sprinkling of the reserved chopped herbs.

1 large leek
50g flat-leaf parsley
25g coriander
50g butter
1 large potato
1 litre chicken or
 vegetable stock
25g chives
100ml double cream
sea salt and freshly
 ground black pepper

LAMB PARCELS WITH BLACK OLIVE STUFFING & SUMMER SLAW

Preheat your oven to 220°C/gas mark 7.

Finely grate the zest from the lemon and bash in a pestle and mortar with the fennel seeds. Chop the anchovies and roughly chop the olives. Add to the lemon and fennel seed mixture and bash everything again to create a very rough paste. Season and mix again.

Place a lamb steak into a plastic bag or between 2 sheets of clingfilm and, using a rolling pin, gently bash out the meat, turning as you go, until it is about 8mm thick. Repeat with the remaining lamb steaks. Season the steaks well on each side and lay out on a board. Place a spoonful of the olive mixture into the middle of each steak, fold over and use a wooden cocktail stick or skewer to close.

Place the lamb parcels in a roasting tin, squeeze over the juice from the lemon and drizzle with the olive oil. Place in the oven and cook for about 10 minutes or until the lamb is tender but slightly pink in the centre. Remove, cover with foil to keep warm and leave to rest.

Meanwhile, make the slaw. Cut the beetroot, carrots and cucumber into very thin slices with a potato peeler or a mandolin (see page 28). Cut the fennel bulb in half, remove the core and slice very thinly. Thinly slice the radishes and cut the celery into very thin sticks. Place all the vegetables together in a large bowl.

To make the dressing for the slaw, mix the cream, mustard and vinegar in a bowl. Season with salt, pepper and a pinch of sugar, spoon over the vegetables and mix well together.

To serve, divide the slaw between 6 dinner plates and top with a lamb parcel.

1 lemon
1 teaspoon fennel seeds
3 tinned anchovy fillets
100g pitted dry
 black olives
6 x 150g boneless
 lamb leg steaks
2 tablespoons olive oil
1 raw beetroot
2 large carrots
½ cucumber
1 fennel bulb
12 radishes
1 celery stick
4 tablespoons double
 cream
1 teaspoon Dijon mustard
1 teaspoon balsamic
 vinegar
pinch of sugar
sea salt and freshly
 ground black pepper

RHUBARB, RASPBERRY & AMARETTO SYLLABUB

Rhubarb is actually a vegetable, and can be grown in the dark (forced rhubarb). This sort is usually available in early spring, but is less flavoursome than the field-grown summer variety.

Cut the rhubarb into 2cm pieces and place in a pan with the raspberries and 150g of the sugar. Cover and cook over a moderate heat, stirring occasionally, for 8–10 minutes or until tender.

Tip the rhubarb and raspberry mixture into a nylon sieve set over a bowl to catch the juices. Return the juices to the pan and simmer until reduced by half. Place the strained fruit in a bowl and stir in the thickened juices. Leave to cool.

Squeeze the juice from the lemon into a large bowl and add the double cream, the remaining sugar and the Amaretto. Whisk until soft peaks are formed. Gently marble the cooled fruit into the cream mixture and spoon into 6 dishes or glasses. Crumble the amaretti biscuits over the top and decorate with a few extra raspberries.

400g rhubarb
200g raspberries, plus
 a few extra to decorate
250g caster sugar
1 lemon
500ml double cream
3 tablespoons Amaretto
4 amaretti biscuits

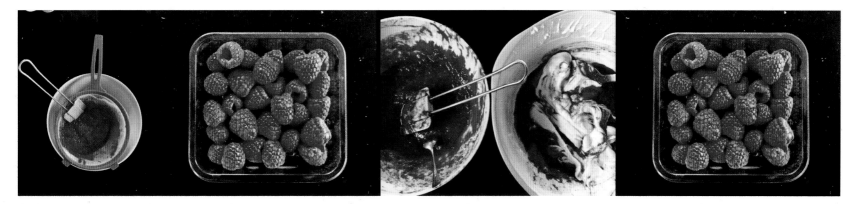

PEACH & PARMA HAM SALAD.
CHICKEN WITH GORGONZOLA & OVEN-BAKED CHORIZO & FENNEL RISOTTO.
BLUEBERRY PAIN PERDU.

60 min Preheat your oven to 190°C/gas mark 5. To make the starter, cut the peaches (or nectarines) in half, twist both halves, pull apart and remove the stones. Cut each half into 3 wedges and place in a bowl. Remove the leaves from the rosemary, chop roughly and add to the bowl with the peaches. Add the olive oil, season with salt and freshly ground black pepper and mix well together.

50 min Now for the main course. Finely chop the onion, garlic and celery. Cut the fennel bulbs in half, remove and discard the core and chop the rest into 1.5cm pieces. Cut the chorizo into 1.5cm pieces. Pour the stock into a pan and bring to a simmer. Meanwhile, heat 3 tablespoons of the olive oil in a large, flame-proof casserole over a low-to-moderate heat and add the onion, fennel, celery and garlic. Rip the bay leaves and add to the pan and cook together for 5–6 minutes without colouring until the onion is soft.

40 min Add the chorizo and cook for a further 5 minutes, stirring occasionally, then add the rice and stir-fry for a further minute to coat it in the oil and flavourings. Stir in the hot stock and season with pepper. Cover with a lid and place on the middle shelf of the oven for 25–30 minutes, or until the rice is just cooked and all the liquid has been absorbed. Finely grate the Parmesan and finely chop the parsley.

30 min For the main course, cut the Gorgonzola into 6 pieces. Lift the skin of each chicken breast with your fingers and pop a piece of cheese underneath. Press down to seal, and then place in a roasting tin. Squeeze over the lemon juice, add the lemon halves and drizzle with the remaining olive oil. Season well, add the thyme sprigs and toss everything together to coat. Place the tray on the top shelf of the oven and roast for 20–25 minutes, turning once or twice, or until tender and cooked through.

20 min To prepare the dessert, split the vanilla pod lengthways and place in a pan with the blueberries and 3 tablespoons of the sugar. Cover and cook over a low heat, stirring occasionally, for 5–6 minutes or until the blueberries start to collapse. Remove from the heat, hook out the vanilla pod and put both to one side.

Beat the whole egg, egg yolks, milk and remaining sugar in a bowl. Scrape the vanilla seeds from the pod into the bowl and whisk together. Pour into a dish wide enough to be able to dip your bread slices into.

10 min To finish the starter, heat a griddle pan over a moderate heat and add the peach wedges. Cook for 4–5 minutes, turning occasionally, until lightly seared on all sides. Tip back into the bowl. Mix together the honey and vinegar in a small bowl and pour over the peaches. Toss well to coat. Roughly chop the pistachios.

Once the risotto for the main course is cooked, season it to taste and stir in the soured cream or crème fraîche, two-thirds of the parsley and half of the grated Parmesan. Cover and leave to stand for 5 minutes and then taste again for seasoning, adding more if needed.

To serve the starter, divide the rocket between 6 flat bowls, add 3 peach wedges to each one and crumble the Roquefort (if using) over the top. Drape a slice of Parma ham over each plate and sprinkle with the chopped pistachios.

To serve the main course, spoon the risotto onto your dinner plates, sprinkle with the remaining parsley and top with a chicken breast. Accompany with the remaining Parmasan on the side.

To finish the dessert, melt a large knob of butter in a large frying pan over a low-to-moderate heat. Dip the bread one slice at a time into the egg and milk mixture, turning it so it is coated on both sides, and fry in the hot butter. Remove from the pan when it is golden and softly crisp on both sides and transfer to a dessert plate. Repeat with the rest of the bread, adding more butter as required.

To serve the dessert, top each slice of fried bread with a spoonful of warm blueberries and sprinkle lightly with sugar. Accompany with clotted cream, crème fraîche or vanilla ice cream.

Peach & Parma Ham Salad
3 ripe peaches (or nectarines)
2 sprigs of rosemary
2 tablespoons olive oil
1 tablespoon honey
1 tablespoon balsamic vinegar
25g shelled pistachios
100g rocket
150g Roquefort cheese (optional)
6 slices of Parma ham
sea salt and freshly ground black pepper

Chicken with Gorgonzola & Oven-baked Chorizo & Fennel Risotto
1 onion
2 garlic cloves
2 celery sticks
2 fennel bulbs
150g cooking chorizo
1.4 litres chicken or vegetable stock
6 tablespoons olive oil
6 fresh bay leaves
400g risotto rice (such as Carnaroli or Arborio)
100g Parmesan cheese
25g flat-leaf parsley
150g Gorgonzola cheese
6 x 200g chicken breasts, skin on (if possible, choose breasts with the little wing bone still attached as this keeps the meat moister)

1 lemon
10g sprigs of thyme
150ml soured cream or crème fraîche
sea salt and freshly ground black pepper

Blueberry Pain Perdu
1 vanilla pod
450g blueberries
4 tablespoons caster sugar, plus a little extra
 for sprinkling
1 egg and 2 egg yolks
100ml milk
85g butter
6 slices of white country bread
clotted cream, crème fraîche or good
 vanilla ice cream, to serve

PEACH & PARMA HAM SALAD

The chopped pistachios add a bit of crunch to this light salad.

Cut the peaches (or nectarines) in half, twist both halves and remove the stones. Cut each half into 3 wedges and place in a bowl. Remove the leaves from the rosemary, chop roughly and add to the bowl with the peaches. Add the olive oil, season with salt and freshly ground black pepper and mix well together.

Heat a griddle pan over a moderate heat and add the peach wedges. Cook for 4–5 minutes, turning occasionally, until lightly seared on all sides. Tip back into the bowl. Mix together the honey with the vinegar in a small bowl and pour over the peaches. Toss well to coat. Roughly chop the pistachios.

To serve, divide the rocket between 6 flat bowls, add 3 peach wedges to each and crumble the Roquefort (if using) over the top. Drape a slice of Parma ham over each plate and sprinkle with the chopped pistachios.

3 ripe peaches (or nectarines)
2 sprigs of rosemary
2 tablespoons olive oil
1 tablespoon honey
1 tablespoon balsamic vinegar
25g shelled pistachios
100g rocket
150g Roquefort cheese (optional)
6 slices of Parma ham
sea salt and freshly ground black pepper

CHICKEN WITH GORGONZOLA & OVEN-BAKED CHORIZO & FENNEL RISOTTO

Preheat your oven to 190°C/gas mark 5.

Finely chop the onion, garlic and celery. Cut the fennel bulbs in half, remove and discard the core and chop the rest into 1.5cm pieces. Cut the chorizo into 1.5cm pieces.

Pour the stock into a pan and bring to a simmer. Meanwhile, heat 3 tablespoons of the olive oil in a large, flame-proof casserole over a low-to-moderate heat and add the onion, fennel, celery and garlic. Rip the bay leaves and add to the pan and cook together for 5–6 minutes without colouring until the onion is soft. Add the chorizo and cook for a further 5 minutes, stirring occasionally, then add the rice and stir-fry it for a further minute to coat it in the oil and flavourings.

Stir in the hot stock and season with pepper. Cover with a lid and place in the centre of the oven for 25–30 minutes, or until the rice is just cooked and all the liquid has been absorbed. Finely grate the Parmesan and finely chop the parsley.

Cut the Gorgonzola into 6 equal-sized pieces. Lift the skin of each chicken breast with your fingers and pop a piece of cheese underneath. Press down to seal, and then place the chicken breasts in a roasting tin. Squeeze over the lemon juice, add the lemon halves to the tin and drizzle with the remaining olive oil. Season well, add the thyme sprigs and toss everything together to coat. Place on the top shelf of the oven and roast for 20–25 minutes, turning once or twice, or until tender and cooked through. Remove from the oven, cover and leave to rest.

Once the risotto is cooked, season it to taste and stir in the soured cream or crème fraîche, two-thirds of the parsley and half of the grated Parmesan. Cover and leave to stand for 5 minutes and then taste again, adding more seasoning if required.

To serve, spoon the risotto onto dinner plates, sprinkle with the remaining parsley and place a chicken breast on top. Accompany with the remaining Parmesan on the side.

1 onion
2 garlic cloves
2 celery sticks
2 fennel bulbs
150g cooking chorizo
1.4 litres chicken or vegetable stock
6 tablespoons olive oil
6 fresh bay leaves
400g risotto rice (such as Carnaroli or Arborio)
100g Parmesan cheese
25g flat-leaf parsley
150g Gorgonzola cheese
6 x 200g chicken breasts, skin on (if possible, choose breasts with the little wing bone still attached as this keeps the meat moister)
1 lemon
10g sprigs of thyme
150ml soured cream or crème fraîche
sea salt and freshly ground black pepper

BLUEBERRY PAIN PERDU

A sweetened version of eggy bread and a good way to use up a slightly stale loaf.

Split the vanilla pod lengthways and place in a pan with the blueberries and 3 tablespoons of the sugar. Cover and cook over a low heat, stirring occasionally, for 5–6 minutes or until the blueberries start to collapse. Remove from the heat, hook out the vanilla pod and put both to one side.

Beat the whole egg; egg yolks, milk and remaining sugar in a bowl. Scrape the vanilla seeds from the pod into the bowl and whisk together. Pour into a dish wide enough to be able to dip your bread slices into.

Melt a large knob of butter in a large frying pan over a low-to-moderate heat. Dip the bread one slice at a time into the egg and milk mixture, turning it so it is coated on both sides, and fry in the hot butter. Remove from the pan when it is golden and softly crisp on both sides and transfer to a dessert plate. Repeat with the rest of the bread, adding more butter as required.

To serve, top each slice of fried bread with a spoonful of warm blueberries and sprinkle lightly with sugar. Accompany with clotted cream, crème fraîche or vanilla ice cream.

1 vanilla pod
450g blueberries
4 tablespoons caster
 sugar, plus a little
 extra for sprinkling
1 egg and 2 egg yolks
100ml milk
85g butter
6 slices of white
 country bread
clotted cream, crème
 fraîche or vanilla
 ice cream, to serve

TOMATOES ON TOASTED BRIOCHE.
CRUNCHY MACKEREL & CREAMY CUCUMBER.
CHILLED MELON & RASPBERRY SOUP.

60 min Preheat your oven to 200°C/gas mark 6. Place 6 little cups or bowls in the freezer to chill for the dessert.

Slice the cucumber for the main course very thinly – a mandolin (see page 28) is great for this – and place in a large colander set over a bowl. Sprinkle liberally with salt, mix well and leave to stand for 30 minutes.

50 min To make the dessert, cut the melons in half across the middle and scoop out all of the seeds with a spoon. Scoop the flesh into a blender, add the raspberries (reserving 6 for the decoration) and the Grand Marnier (if using) and blitz until smooth. Strain through a fine sieve into a bowl, cover with clingfilm and refrigerate.

40 min Back to the main course. Melt the butter in a frying pan and remove from the heat. Tip the oats, sesame seeds and mustard seeds into a shallow dish, season well and toss together. Dip each mackerel fillet into the melted butter and then into the oat mixture, covering each side. Shake off any excess and arrange in a single layer on 2 baking trays. Set aside.

30 min To make the starter, cut a lid off the tomatoes about one-third of the way down. Using a teaspoon, scoop out the seeds into the bottom of an oven-proof dish. Crush the garlic and place in a small bowl. Stir in the olive oil and season well. Brush the tomatoes inside and out with the garlic oil and stand them upright in the oven-proof dish. Pop a basil leaf inside each one and put on the lids.

20 min Place the dish of tomatoes in the oven and bake for about 15 minutes, or until nearly tender. Remove from the oven, carefully take off the lids and drizzle 1 tablespoon of cream into each one. Return to the oven for 5 minutes.

10 min To finish the main course, rinse the cucumber well and pat dry with kitchen paper. Finely chop the dill. Squeeze the juice from the lemon into a medium-sized bowl. Add the cream, mustard, honey, dill and seasoning and mix well. Fold in the sliced cucumber, stirring to coat. Place the trays of mackerel in the oven and bake for 10–15 minutes or until the fish is just tender and the coating is lightly golden.

To serve the starter, toast the brioche (or bread) and serve with the warm tomatoes.

To serve the main course, place 2 fillets of mackerel on each plate and accompany with a spoonful of the cucumber on the side.

To serve the dessert, pour the soup into the chilled cups or bowls, drop a reserved raspberry into each one, add a swirl of cream and accompany with some biscuits on the side.

Tomatoes on Toasted Brioche
6 large ripe beef tomatoes
2 garlic cloves
2 tablespoons olive oil
6 large basil leaves
6 tablespoons cream
400g brioche (or crusty bread)
sea salt and freshly ground black pepper

Crunchy Mackerel & Creamy Cucumber
1 cucumber
100g butter
100g porridge oats
70g sesame seeds
3 tablespoons mustard seeds
12 x 100g mackerel fillets, skin on
1 small bunch of dill
1 lemon
3 tablespoons double cream
1 tablespoon wholegrain mustard
1 tablespoon honey
sea salt and freshly ground black pepper

Chilled Melon & Raspberry Soup
200g raspberries
2 ripe charentais or cantaloupe melons
1 tablespoon Grand Marnier (optional)
100ml double cream
fine biscuits, to serve

THANK YOU x

annie

Annika

Elderflaver Cocktails

I DON'T LIKE CRICKET BISC
300g PEANUTS - BLANC
200g CASTER SUGAR
2 TSP VANILLA
100g PITTED PRUNES
2 EGG WHITES
TSP BAKING POWDER
14 PIECES CRYSTILLISE
GINGER

15-08-09

Celia
Cna
Sam

Floss
Pink Gee
Caster

Watermelon Blackberry
& feta Salad

Hannah
Yaz
Congest

Baked whole Salmon
Danielle
Chalk

Watercress + toasted walnut
Pesto

Double Sided
Pint paper

Roast new pots
with bay
Runner beans

Tim

Petit pot au chocolat

W. up liquid Salmon 3 30 2 hrs

Trim runners

TOMATOES ON TOASTED BRIOCHE

Preheat your oven to 190°C/gas mark 5.

Cut a lid off the tomatoes about one-third of the way down. Using a teaspoon, scoop out the seeds into the bottom of an oven-proof dish. Crush the garlic and place in a small bowl. Stir in the olive oil and season well. Brush the tomatoes inside and out with the garlic oil and stand them upright in the oven-proof dish. Pop a basil leaf inside each one and put on the lids.

Place the dish in the oven and bake for about 15 minutes, or until nearly tender. Remove from the oven, carefully take off the lids and drizzle 1 tablespoon cream into each one. Return to the oven for 5 minutes.

Meanwhile, slice and toast the brioche (or bread). To serve, place a roasted tomato on each plate and accompany with the toasted brioche (or bread).

6 large ripe beef tomatoes
2 garlic cloves
2 tablespoons olive oil
6 large basil leaves
6 tablespoons cream
400g brioche
 (or crusty bread)
sea salt and freshly
 ground black pepper

CRUNCHY MACKEREL & CREAMY CUCUMBER

Slice the cucumber very thinly – a mandolin (see page 28) is great for this – and place the slices in a large colander set over a bowl. Sprinkle liberally with salt, mix well and leave to stand for 30 minutes. Preheat your oven to 200°C/gas mark 6.

Melt the butter in a frying pan and remove from the heat. Tip the oats, sesame seeds and mustard seeds into a shallow dish. Season well and toss together to combine.

Dip each mackerel fillet into the melted butter and then into the oat mixture, covering each side. Shake off any excess and arrange in a single layer on 2 baking trays. Place the trays in the oven and bake for 10–15 minutes or until the fish is just tender and the coating is lightly golden.

While the mackerel is in the oven, rinse the cucumber well and pat dry with kitchen paper. Finely chop the dill. Squeeze the juice from the lemon into a medium-sized bowl. Add the cream, mustard, honey, dill and seasoning and mix well. Fold in the sliced cucumber, stirring to coat.

Serve the mackerel with the creamy cucumber on the side.

1 cucumber
100g butter
100g porridge oats
70g sesame seeds
3 tablespoons mustard
 seeds
12 x 100g mackerel
 fillets, skin on
1 small bunch of dill
1 lemon
3 tablespoons double
 cream
1 tablespoon wholegrain
 mustard
1 tablespoon honey
sea salt and freshly
 ground black pepper

CHILLED MELON & RASPBERRY SOUP

Place 6 little cups or bowls in the freezer to chill for the soup. Reserve 6 of the raspberries for the decoration.

Cut the melons in half across the middle and scoop out all of the seeds with a little spoon. Scoop the flesh into a blender, add the raspberries and the Grand Marnier (if using) and blitz until smooth. Strain through a fine sieve into a clean bowl, cover with clingfilm and chill in the fridge until needed.

To serve, pour the soup into the chilled cups or bowls, drop a reserved raspberry into each one, add a swirl of cream and accompany with some biscuits on the side.

200g raspberries
2 ripe charentais or
 cantaloupe melons
1 tablespoon Grand
 Marnier (optional)
100ml double cream
fine biscuits, to serve

GRILLED AUBERGINE WITH GREEN OLIVE & WALNUT PASTE.
SARDINES & TOMATO BRUSCHETTA.
ROAST NECTARINE & BLUEBERRY MELBA.

60 min   Preheat the oven to 150°C/gas mark 2. Begin with the dessert. Cut the nectarines in half, remove the stones and place in a bowl with the icing sugar. Leave to stand for 15 minutes.

Meanwhile, get on with the main course. Cut the tomatoes in half lengthways, scoop out the seeds with a teaspoon so they resemble little boats and place in a large bowl. Crush the garlic and add to the bowl with the oregano and 5 tablespoons of the extra-virgin olive oil. Season and toss well together.

50 min   Arrange the tomatoes cut-side up on a baking tray, drizzle over any oil from the bowl and bake on the middle shelf of the oven for about 45 minutes, checking them every now and then. When they are ready, they will be slightly shrunken and still a brilliant red colour (if they are too dark, they will be bitter). Increase the oven temperature to 200°C/gas mark 6.

Back to the dessert. Tip the nectarine halves out onto a baking tray and turn them cut-side up. Roast on the top shelf of the oven for 25–30 minutes or until tender, sprinkling with the almonds for the last 5 minutes.

40 min   Place the blueberries in a small pan over a low heat with 1 tablespoon of the caster sugar. Cover and simmer for about 3–5 minutes until just soft. Stir in more caster sugar to taste. Leave to cool, and blend until smooth.

30 min   Now for the starter. Remove the stalks from the aubergines and, using a serrated bread knife, cut them lengthways into thin slices. Place in a bowl with half of the oil and coat thoroughly on all sides.

To make the olive and walnut paste, remove the leaves from the parsley and place them in the bowl of a food processor with the olives, walnuts, garlic and the remaining olive oil. Blitz until finely chopped, then scoop out into a bowl and stir in the vinegar and seasoning.

20 min   Brush the sardines with the chilli or olive oil, season and lay on a baking tray.

10 min   To cook the aubergines for the starter, heat a griddle pan until hot. Arrange the aubergine slices in a single layer – you will need to do this in batches – and cook for 1–2 minutes on each side or until tender. Keep them warm while you cook the rest.

Preheat the grill or barbecue for the sardines. Wash and dry the rocket. Whisk the balsamic vinegar in a large bowl with the remaining extra-virgin olive oil and season well. Set aside.

To serve the starter, arrange the aubergine onto 6 starter plates, spoon over a little of the olive paste and finish with a dollop of yogurt. Sprinkle with a pinch of paprika and serve the flatbread on the side.

To finish the main course, grill the sardines for about 3–4 minutes on each side. Meanwhile, toast the bread.

To serve the main course, lay a toasted slice of bread on each dinner plate. Arrange 4 tomato halves on top and drizzle with the cooking juices. Toss the rocket in the dressing and place a handful on each plate. Top with 2–3 sardines and serve immediately.

To serve the dessert, place 2 nectarine halves on each dessert dish, scoop a ball of ice cream on top and spoon over a little blueberry purée.

Grilled Aubergine with Green Olive & Walnut Paste
2 aubergines
150ml extra-virgin olive oil
25g flat-leaf parsley
100g pitted green olives
85g walnut pieces
1 large garlic clove
1 tablespoon red wine vinegar
sea salt and freshly ground black pepper
Greek yogurt, paprika and flatbread, to serve

Sardines & Tomato Bruschetta
12 large ripe plum tomatoes
2 garlic cloves
1 tablespoon dried oregano
8 tablespoons extra-virgin olive oil
12–18 x 150–175g sardines, gutted and scales removed
4 tablespoons chilli or olive oil
6 large slices of good-quality country bread or sourdough
1 tablespoon balsamic vinegar
85g rocket
sea salt and freshly ground black pepper

Roast Nectarine & Blueberry Melba
6 ripe nectarines
100g golden icing sugar
25g flaked almonds
250g blueberries
2 tablespoons golden caster sugar
500ml vanilla ice cream

GRILLED AUBERGINE WITH GREEN OLIVE & WALNUT PASTE

Make sure the aubergine is cooked through completely. There is nothing worse than undercooked aubergine with the texture of a dry sponge.

Remove the stalks from the aubergines and cut lengthways into thin slices, using a serrated bread knife. Place in a bowl and coat all over with half of the oil.

Remove the leaves from the parsley and place in the bowl of a food processor with the pitted olives, walnuts, garlic and the remaining olive oil. Blitz until finely chopped, and then scoop out into a bowl. Stir in the vinegar and season with salt and freshly ground black pepper.

Heat a griddle pan until hot. Place the aubergine slices on the griddle in a single layer – you will need to do this in batches – and cook for 1–2 minutes on each side or until tender. Keep them warm while you cook the rest.

To serve, arrange the aubergine onto 6 starter plates, spoon over a little of the olive paste and finish with a dollop of yogurt. Sprinkle with a pinch of paprika and serve the flatbread on the side.

2 aubergines
150ml extra-virgin
 olive oil
25g flat-leaf parsley
100g pitted green olives
85g walnut pieces
1 large garlic clove
1 tablespoon red
 wine vinegar
sea salt and freshly
 ground black pepper
Greek yogurt, paprika and
 flatbread, to serve

SARDINES & TOMATO BRUSCHETTA

If you can cook the sardines and toast the bread on a barbecue, all the better. You can always prepare the tomatoes a few hours beforehand.

Preheat your oven to 150°C/gas mark 2.

Cut the tomatoes in half – for plum tomatoes, cut lengthways; for round ones, cut around the middle. Using a teaspoon, scoop out the seeds so they resemble little boats.

Crush the garlic and combine in a large bowl with the oregano, 5 tablespoons of the extra-virgin olive oil and some salt and black pepper. Add the tomatoes and toss together to coat them completely, then tip out onto a baking tray and arrange so they are cut-side up. Bake on the middle shelf of the oven for about 45 minutes, checking them every now and then. When they are ready, they will be slightly shrunk and still a brilliant red colour. If they are too dark, they will be bitter.

Preheat the grill or barbecue.

Brush the sardines with the chilli or olive oil, season with salt and freshly ground black pepper and lay on a large baking tray. Grill the sardines for about 3–4 minutes on each side. Meanwhile, toast the bread.

To serve, lay a toasted slice of bread on each dinner plate. Arrange 4 tomato halves on top and drizzle over the cooking juices.

Whisk the balsamic vinegar in a large bowl with the remaining extra-virgin olive oil and season well. Add the rocket to the dressing in the bowl and toss until evenly coated. Place a handful of rocket on each plate and top with 2–3 sardines. Serve immediately.

12 large ripe
 plum tomatoes
2 garlic cloves
1 tablespoon
 dried oregano
8 tablespoons
 extra-virgin olive oil
12–18 x 150g–175g
 sardines, gutted and
 scales removed
4 tablespoons chilli
 or olive oil
6 large slices of
 good-quality country
 bread or sourdough
1 tablespoon
 balsamic vinegar
85g rocket
sea salt and freshly
 ground black pepper

ROAST NECTARINE & BLUEBERRY MELBA

Preheat your oven to 200°C/gas mark 6.

Cut the nectarines in half, twist both halves, pull apart and remove the stones. Place the nectarine halves in a bowl. Add the icing sugar, toss well together and leave to stand for 15 minutes.

Tip the nectarine halves out onto a baking tray and arrange them so they are all cut-side up. Roast in the oven for 20–25 minutes or until tender, sprinkling with the almonds for the last 5 minutes of cooking.

Place the blueberries in a small pan over a low heat with 1 tablespoon of the caster sugar. Cover and simmer for about 3–5 minutes until just soft. Stir in more caster sugar to taste. Leave to cool, and then blend until smooth.

To serve, place 2 nectarine halves on each dessert dish, scoop a ball of ice cream on top and spoon over a little of the blueberry purée.

6 ripe nectarines
100g golden icing sugar
25g flaked almonds
250g blueberries
2 tablespoons golden
  caster sugar
500ml vanilla ice cream

CRUNCHY FENNEL, CELERY & RADISH SALAD WITH RICOTTA & PARSLEY OIL.
GRILLED MISO TROUT WITH BAKED BABY CARROTS IN A BAG.
BAKED CHERRIES WITH BAY & FRESH GOAT'S CHEESE CREAM.

60 min   Preheat your oven to 200°C/gas mark 6. To make the marinade for the main course, squeeze the juice from the lime into a large bowl and add the mirin (or sake or dry sherry), soy sauce, miso and sugar. Whisk everything together to combine, and then put in the trout fillets and turn to coat. Set aside to marinate.

50 min   Spread the walnuts for the starter on a baking tray and cook for about 5–8 minutes or until lightly golden. Leave to cool, and then crumble into small pieces.

40 min   To make the parsley oil for the starter, remove the leaves from the parsley, discarding the stalks, and place in the herb chopper of a food processor. Reserve 2 tablespoons of the olive oil for the salad dressing and pour the rest into the food processor. Finely grate in the lemon zest and blitz together until smooth. Scrape into a bowl and season to taste.

30 min   Meanwhile, prepare the carrots for the main course. Peel and finely grate the ginger and finely shred the spring onions. No need to peel the baby carrots – just tumble them into a bowl with the grated ginger, shredded spring onions and salt and pepper. Take a large sheet of foil (or use individual foil bags) and tip the carrot and onion mixture into the centre. Dot evenly with the butter, pinch the corners of the foil together to seal and bake in the oven for about 30 minutes, or until the carrots are just tender.

20 min   Now for the dessert. Place the cherries in a large baking dish. Rip the bay leaves in two and add to the dish. Sprinkle with the sugar, cover and place in the oven for about 25–30 minutes or until the cherries are tender. Place the goat's cheese in a small bowl and beat in the soured cream until smooth.

10 min   To make the salad for the starter, use a mandolin (see page 28) or large knife to slice the fennel, celery and radishes very finely. Place together in a large bowl. For the dressing, squeeze the juice from half of the lemon into a small bowl, whisk in the 2 reserved tablespoons of olive oil and season to taste.

Remove the trout fillets from their marinade and arrange, skin-side down, on a large baking tray in a single layer.

To serve the starter, pour the dressing over the salad, toss well and divide between 6 serving plates. Crumble the ricotta over the top, drizzle with the parsley oil and scatter with the walnuts and black olives. Serve immediately with crusty bread.

To cook the trout for the main course, simply bake it in the oven for 3–4 minutes until tender. To serve, place 2 trout fillets on each dinner plate. Open out the foil-wrapped carrots at the table, tossing them together so they are nicely coated in the butter and juices.

To serve the dessert, divide the warm baked cherries between 6 dishes and place a spoonful of the goat's cheese cream on each one. Serve extra sugar on the side to dredge over if wished.

Crunchy Fennel, Celery & Radish Salad with Ricotta & Parsley Oil
50g walnut halves
25g flat-leaf parsley
100ml extra-virgin olive oil
1 lemon
2 fennel bulbs
3 celery sticks
18 radishes
1 lemon
250g ricotta
50g pitted dry black olives
sea salt and freshly ground black pepper
crusty bread, to serve

Grilled Miso Trout with Baked Baby Carrots in a Bag
½ lime
2 tablespoons mirin, sake or dry sherry
2 tablespoons soy sauce
2 tablespoons white, yellow or red miso paste
1 tablespoon brown sugar
12 x 100g trout fillets
4cm piece of fresh ginger
4 spring onions
500g baby carrots
50g butter
sea salt and freshly ground black pepper

Baked Cherries With Bay & Fresh Goat's Cheese Cream
750g fresh cherries
2 bay leaves, preferably fresh
3 tablespoons golden caster sugar, plus extra to serve
150g fresh mild goat's cheese
70g soured cream

CRUNCHY FENNEL, CELERY & RADISH SALAD WITH RICOTTA & PARSLEY OIL

If you have time, slice the fennel and radishes into a large bowl of iced water and leave for about an hour, as this will help to make them really crispy and crunchy.

Preheat your oven to 200°C/gas mark 6.

Place the walnuts on a baking tray and cook for about 5-8 minutes or until lightly golden. Leave to cool, then crumble into small pieces.

Using a mandolin (see page 28) or large knife, very finely slice the fennel, celery and radishes into a large bowl.

Finely grate the zest from the whole lemon and squeeze the juice from half of the lemon (use the other half for something else). Whisk the lemon juice and about 2 tablespoons of the olive oil to make a dressing and season. Set aside.

Remove the parsley leaves from its stalks and place the leaves in the bowl of a food processor or a spice grinder with the lemon zest and the remaining oil and whiz until smooth. Scrape into a bowl and season to taste.

Toss the dressing with the sliced vegetables and divide between 6 serving plates. Crumble over the ricotta, drizzle over the parsley oil and sprinkle with the walnuts and black olives. Serve immediately with crusty bread.

50g walnut halves
2 fennel bulbs
3 celery sticks
18 radishes
1 lemon
100ml extra-virgin
 olive oil
25g flat-leaf parsley
250g ricotta
50g pitted dry
 black olives
crusty bread, to serve
sea sea salt and freshly
 ground black pepper

GRILLED MISO TROUT WITH BAKED BABY CARROTS IN A BAG

Cooking vegetables in a bag means they gently steam in their own moisture and they smell amazing when you first open the bag. Try cooking other vegetables this way.

Preheat your oven to 200°C/gas mark 6.

Peel and finely grate the ginger and finely shred the spring onions. No need to peel the baby carrots — just tumble them together in a bowl with the grated ginger, shredded spring onions and salt and pepper.

To make the marinade for the fish, squeeze the juice from the lime into a large bowl and add the mirin (or sake or dry sherry), soy sauce, miso and sugar. Whisk together to combine, and then put in the trout fillets and turn to coat. Set aside to marinate for 30 minutes.

Take a large piece of tin foil (or use individual foil bags) and tip the carrots into the centre. Dot evenly with the butter, pinch the edges of the foil together to seal well and bake for about 30 minutes or until the carrots are just tender.

To cook the fish, lay the trout fillets, skin-side down, on a large baking tray in a single layer. Place in the oven and bake for 3–4 minutes until tender.

To serve, place 2 trout fillets on each dinner plate. Open out the foil-wrapped carrots at the table and quickly toss them in the buttery cooking juices, allowing everyone to help themselves.

4cm piece of fresh ginger
4 spring onions
500g baby carrots
50g butter
½ lime
2 tablespoons mirin, sake or dry sherry
2 tablespoons soy sauce
2 tablespoons white, yellow or red miso paste
1 tablespoon brown sugar
12 x 100g trout fillets
sea salt and freshly ground black pepper

BAKED CHERRIES WITH BAY & FRESH GOAT'S CHEESE CREAM

If you don't like goat's cheese, use mascarpone or a mild cream cheese instead.

Preheat your oven to 200°C/gas mark 6.

Place the cherries in a large baking dish. Rip the bay leaves in two and add to the dish. Sprinkle with the sugar, cover and place in the oven for about 25–30 minutes or until the cherries are tender.

Place the goat's cheese in a small bowl and beat in the soured cream until smooth. Divide the warm baked cherries between 6 dessert dishes and place a spoonful of the goat's cheese cream on each one. Serve extra sugar on the side to dredge over if wished.

750g fresh cherries
2 bay leaves, preferably fresh
3 tablespoons golden caster sugar, plus extra to serve
150g fresh mild goat's cheese
70g soured cream

WATERMELON, BLACKBERRY & FETA SALAD.
BAKED SALMON WITH ROCKET & PISTACHIO PESTO.
GRILLED PEACHES & CREAM.

60 min To make the pesto for the main course, finely grate the zest from the lemon and roughly chop the rocket leaves and garlic. Place together in the bowl of a food processor and add the pistachios, a good slug of the oil and a pinch of salt. Blitz until roughly chopped.

With the motor running, gradually pour in the remaining oil in a steady stream and blitz until amalgamated. Scrape into a bowl. Finely grate the cheese (if using) and stir into the pesto. Season with salt and black pepper.

50 min Preheat the grill to moderate. To make the dessert, cut the peaches in half, remove the stones and place the fruit cut-side up on a baking tray. Melt the butter in a pan and mix the cinnamon with the sugar in a bowl.

40 min Brush the peach halves with the melted butter and sprinkle with the cinnamon sugar. Place the tray of peaches under the grill – not too close or the sugar will burn – and grill for about 6–8 minutes, basting once or twice, until the peaches are tender and slightly caramelised.

30 min Preheat your oven to 200°C/gas mark 6. To prepare the starter, place 50g of the blackberries in a large serving bowl and squash well with a fork. Whisk in the vinegar and olive oil. Season to taste with salt, pepper and a pinch of sugar. Remove the rind from the watermelon and cut the flesh into 4cm pieces. Place in the bowl with the dressing, crumble in the feta and add the remaining blackberries. Wash and dry the lettuce leaves, rip into large pieces and add to the bowl. Set aside.

20 min Back to the main course. Bring a pan of lightly salted water to the boil and cook the new potatoes for 15–20 minutes or until just tender.

10 min To cook the salmon, season the fillets on both sides and lay them skin-side up in a single layer in a large baking dish. Dot with the butter, cover with foil and bake in the oven for about 10–15 minutes or until the fish is tender.

To serve the starter, season the salad and toss well together. Divide between 6 plates

To serve the main course, squeeze the lemon juice over the salmon fillets and transfer them to 6 dinner plates with the new potatoes. Top with a dollop of the pesto sauce and spoon over some of the buttery cooking juices.

To serve the dessert, place 2 peach halves in each dessert bowl and accompany with the single cream (or ice cream).

Watermelon, Blackberry & Feta Salad
250g blackberries
1 tablespoon raspberry vinegar
3 tablespoons extra-virgin olive oil
sea salt, freshly ground black pepper and sugar, to taste
1kg piece of watermelon
200g feta cheese
1 cos or romaine lettuce

Baked Salmon with Rocket & Pistachio Pesto
1 lemon
100g rocket
2 garlic cloves
50g shelled pistachios
125ml extra-virgin olive oil
50g Parmesan or Pecorino cheese (optional)
6 x 150g salmon fillets, skin on
50g butter
sea salt and freshly ground black pepper
new potatoes, to serve

Grilled Peaches & Cream
6 ripe peaches
50g butter
¼ teaspoon ground cinnamon
50g light brown sugar
single cream (or vanilla ice cream), to serve

WATERMELON, BLACKBERRY & FETA SALAD

So easy, yet so delicious. The blackberries add a tartness to the sweet watermelon and creamy feta.

Place 50g of the blackberries in a large serving bowl and squash well with a fork. Whisk in the vinegar and olive oil. Season to taste with salt, pepper and a pinch of sugar.

Remove the rind from the watermelon and cut the flesh into 4cm pieces. Place in the bowl with the dressing, crumble in the feta and add the remaining blackberries. Wash and dry the lettuce leaves and rip them in large pieces into the bowl.

Toss everything together, check the seasoning and serve immediately.

250g blackberries
1 tablespoon
 raspberry vinegar
3 tablespoons extra
 virgin olive oil
salt, freshly ground black
 pepper and sugar,
 to taste
1kg piece of watermelon
200g feta cheese
1 cos or romaine lettuce

BAKED SALMON WITH ROCKET & PISTACHIO PESTO

Preheat your oven to 200°C/gas mark 6.

To make the pesto, finely grate the zest from the lemon and roughly chop the rocket leaves and garlic. Place together in the bowl of a food processor and add the pistachios, a good slug of the oil and a pinch of salt. Blitz until roughly chopped.

With the motor running, gradually pour in the remaining oil in a steady stream and blitz until amalgamated. Scrape into a bowl. Finely grate the cheese (if using) and stir into the pesto. Season with salt and black pepper. Bring a pan of lightly salted water to the boil and cook the potatoes for 15–20 minutes or until just tender.

To cook the salmon, season the fillets on both sides and lay them skin-side up in a single layer in a large baking dish. Dot with the butter, cover with foil and bake in the oven for about 10–15 minutes or until the fish is tender.

To serve, squeeze the lemon juice over the salmon fillets and transfer them to 6 dinner plates with the new potatoes. Top with a dollop of the pesto sauce and spoon over some of the buttery cooking juices.

1 lemon
100g rocket
2 garlic cloves
50g shelled pistachios
125ml extra-virgin
 olive oil
50g Parmesan or
 Pecorino cheese
 (optional)
6 x 150g salmon
 fillets, skin on
50g butter
sea salt and freshly
 ground black pepper
new potatoes, to serve

GRILLED PEACHES & CREAM

Preheat the grill to medium. Cut the peaches in half, remove the stones and place the fruit cut-side up on a baking tray.

Melt the butter in a pan and mix the cinnamon with the sugar in a small bowl.

Brush the peach halves with the melted butter and sprinkle with the cinnamon sugar.

Place the tray of peaches under the grill — not too close or the sugar will burn — and grill for about 6–8 minutes, basting once or twice, or until the fruit is tender and slightly caramelised.

To serve, place 2 peach halves in each dessert bowl and accompany with single cream (or ice cream).

6 ripe peaches
50g butter
¼ teaspoon ground
 cinnamon
50g light brown sugar
single cream (or vanilla
 ice cream), to serve

TOMATO, MASCARPONE & ORANGE TART.
ROAST HADDOCK WITH SALMORIGLIO & WHITE BEAN HORSERADISH PURÉE.
FRUIT STUFFED WATERMELON.

60 min   Begin with the starter. Roll out the pastry thinly to a 33 x 22cm rectangle, cut into 6 11cm squares and transfer to a baking sheet. Using a small knife, score a border all the way round the inside of each pastry square, 1cm in from the edges, taking care not to cut all the way through. Chill in the fridge until needed.

50 min   Prepare the ingredients for the main course. Squeeze the juice from the lemons. Crush the garlic. Drain the beans, rinse well and drain again.

40 min   Preheat your oven to 200°C/gas mark 6. For the starter, finely grate the zest from the orange and crush the garlic. Combine in a small bowl with the mascarpone and season with salt, pepper and cayenne. Remove the pastry from the fridge and spread one-sixth of the mascarpone evenly over the centre of each pastry square inside the border. Top each one with 3 basil leaves.

30 min   Slice the tomatoes thinly and arrange so they are overlapping slightly on each pastry square. Sprinkle with salt and freshly ground black pepper and scatter each one with 4 olives. Finely grate the Parmesan and sprinkle evenly over the top. Bake in the oven for 20–25 minutes or until the pastry is golden and crisp.

20 min   Now for the dessert. Cut the watermelon in half and, using a teaspoon, scoop out the flesh in small pieces into a large bowl. Keep the hollowed-out skins to one side for later. Destone the cherries. Cut the peaches or nectarines in half, remove the stones, and then cut each half into 8 wedges. Dehull the strawberries. Combine all the fruit with the melon in the bowl, splash over the rose water (or orange flower water) and mix well together. Stand the 2 hollowed-out watermelon skins on a large serving platter and tumble the fruit over the top and around the sides. Place in the fridge until you are ready to serve.

10 min   Preheat the grill to high. To make the white bean purée for the main course, bring the stock (or water) to the boil and tip in the rinsed beans. Bring back to the boil to reheat the beans, stirring occasionally. Remove from the heat and mash with a potato masher (or blitz in a food processor). Stir in half of the crushed garlic, 6 tablespoons of the olive oil and 1–2 tablespoons of the lemon juice, to taste. Add the horseradish, and chop and stir in the celery leaves. Keep warm.

To make the salmoriglio, place the remaining crushed garlic in a bowl. Stir in the remaining lemon juice and 6 tablespoons of the remaining olive oil. Remove the leaves from the oregano and parsley and chop. Stir the herbs into the dressing and season to taste.

To serve the starter, place a handful of salad leaves on each plate, trickle with the balsamic vinegar and extra-virgin olive oil and top with a tomato tart.

To finish the main course, brush the haddock with the remaining oil and season with salt, pepper and a pinch of chilli flakes (if using). Place on a baking tray and set under the grill for about 5–6 minutes or until just tender.

To serve the main course, divide the white bean purée between each of 6 dinner plates. Top with a piece of haddock and drizzle with the salmoriglio.

To serve the dessert, place the platter of fruit-filled watermelon 'bowls' on the table, accompanied with Greek yogurt on the side.

<u>Tomato, Mascarpone & Orange Tart</u>
500g puff pastry
½ orange
1 garlic clove
125g mascarpone
salt, freshly ground black pepper and cayenne, to taste
18 large basil leaves
6 large ripe tomatoes
24 good-quality pitted black olives
50g Parmesan cheese
rocket, spinach and watercress salad, to serve
extra-virgin olive oil and balsamic vinegar, for drizzling

<u>Roast Haddock with Salmoriglio</u>
<u>& White Bean Horseradish Purée</u>
2 lemons
4 garlic cloves
3 x 400g tins butter beans (see page 8)
150ml vegetable or chicken stock (or water)
200ml extra-virgin olive oil
½–1 tablespoon grated horseradish or horseradish sauce
a handful of celery leaves from the heart of a head of celery
15g fresh oregano (or a pinch of dried oregano)
15g flat-leaf parsley
6 x 200g skinless haddock fillets (or pollack or other thick white sustainably sourced fish), skin on
pinch of crushed dried chilli flakes (optional)
sea salt and freshly ground black pepper

<u>Fruit Stuffed Watermelon</u>
1 watermelon
200g cherries
2 ripe peaches or nectarines
100g strawberries
100g blueberries or blackberries
100g raspberries
2 tablespoons rose water (or orange flower water)
Greek yogurt, to serve

TOMATO, MASCARPONE & ORANGE TART

Preheat your oven to 200°C/gas mark 6.

Roll out the pastry thinly to a 33 x 22cm rectangle, cut into 6 11cm squares and transfer to a baking sheet. Using a small knife, score a border all the way round the inside of each square of pastry 1cm in from the edges, taking care not to cut all the way through.

Finely grate the zest from the orange and crush the garlic. Combine in a small bowl with the mascarpone and season with salt, pepper and cayenne.

Spread one-sixth of the mascarpone evenly over the centre of each pastry square, inside the border, and top with 3 basil leaves.

Slice the tomatoes thinly and arrange so they are overlapping slightly on each pastry square. Sprinkle with salt and freshly ground black pepper and scatter each one with 4 olives. Finely grate the Parmesan and sprinkle evenly over the top. Bake in the oven for 20–25 minutes or until the pastry is golden and crisp.

To serve, place a handful of salad leaves on each plate, trickle with the balsamic vinegar and extra-virgin olive oil and top with a tomato tart.

500g puff pastry
½ orange
1 garlic clove
125g mascarpone
salt, freshly ground
 black pepper and
 cayenne, to taste
18 large basil leaves
6 large ripe tomatoes
24 good-quality
 pitted black olives
50g Parmesan cheese
rocket, spinach and
 watercress salad,
 to serve
extra-virgin olive oil and
 balsamic vinegar, for
 drizzling

ROAST HADDOCK WITH SALMORIGLIO & WHITE BEAN HORSERADISH PURÉE

Salmoriglio originates from southern Italy, and is a simple dressing for seafood or meat made mainly with olive oil and lemon juice.

Squeeze the juice from the lemons. Crush the garlic.

Drain the beans, rinse well and drain again. Bring the vegetable or chicken stock (or water) to the boil and tip in the beans. Bring back to the boil to reheat the beans, stirring occasionally. Remove from the heat and mash with a potato masher (or blitz in a food processor). Stir in half of the crushed garlic, 6 tablespoons of the olive oil and 1–2 tablespoons of the lemon juice, to taste. Add the horseradish and chop and stir in the celery leaves.

Preheat the grill to high. To make the salmoriglio, place the remaining crushed garlic in a bowl. Stir in the remaining lemon juice and 6 tablespoons of the remaining olive oil. Remove the leaves from the oregano and parsley and chop. Stir the herbs into the dressing and season to taste.

Brush the haddock fillets with the remaining oil and season with salt, pepper and a pinch of chilli flakes (if using). Place on a baking tray and set under the grill for about 5–6 minutes or until just tender.

To serve, divide the white bean purée between your dinner plates. Top with a piece of haddock and drizzle with the salmoriglio.

2 lemons
4 garlic cloves
3 x 400g tins butter beans
  (see page 8)
150ml vegetable or
  chicken stock (or water)
200ml extra-virgin
  olive oil
½–1 tablespoon
  grated horseradish or
  horseradish sauce
a handful of celery
  leaves from the heart of a
  head of celery
15g fresh oregano (or a
  pinch of dried oregano)
15g flat-leaf parsley
6 x 200g skinless haddock
  fillets (or pollack or other
  thick white sustainably
  sourced fish), skin on
pinch of crushed dried
  chilli flakes (optional)
sea salt and freshly
  ground black pepper

FRUIT STUFFED WATERMELON

Use lovely ripe fruit to go with the watermelon, then this is wonderful.

Cut the watermelon in half and, using a teaspoon, scoop out the flesh in small pieces into a large bowl. Keep the hollowed-out skins to one side to use as serving bowls. Destone the cherries. Cut the peaches or nectarines in half, remove the stones, and then cut each half into 8 wedges. Dehull the strawberries.

Combine all the fruit with the melon in the bowl, splash over the rose water (or orange flower water) and mix well together.

Stand the 2 hollowed-out watermelon skins on a large serving platter and tumble the fruit over the top and around the sides. Place in the fridge until you are ready to serve.

Serve the fruit-filled watermelon 'bowls' with Greek yogurt on the side.

1 watermelon
200g cherries
2 ripe peaches
 or nectarines
100g strawberries
100g blueberries
 or blackberries
100g raspberries
2 tablespoons rose water
 (or orange flower water)
Greek yogurt, to serve

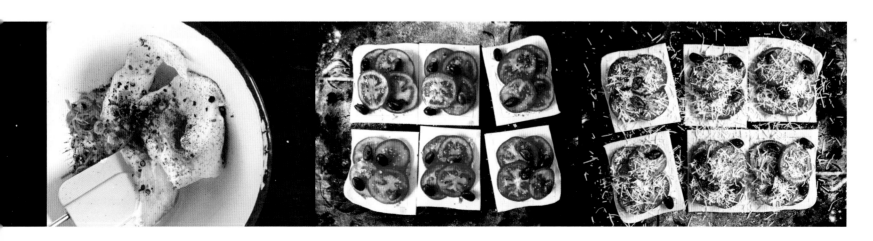

INDEX

Normally when food styling, I would be working with photographers, hiring cutlery and crockery, and cooking someone else's food. Not this time! I am proud to say I took the majority of the photos in this book in my studio where I live, with all my own things. I have voraciously collected the bits and bobs you see in this book since I was a child, and it was great to see them out, being used and being immortalised on the page.

Decorating your table doesn't have to be expensive. I have searched through dusty piles of stuff, hunted for cheap bits and pieces for my home table and kitchen at jumble sales, charity shops, vintage shops, markets and car boot sales. I like to mix and match old and new crockery, fabric, glasses and cutlery, and with a little imagination and for little expense, you can create a new look everytime. Throw a piece of fabric over a table, drape over some ivy cut from your back garden or scatter some flowers, drag out your Nan's old crockery, and mix it up with something new.